Praise for Jeffrey Toobin's

THE

OATH

"Not until scholars a generation hence gain access to the justices' papers are we likely to have a more useful, or more readable, picture of this oddly assorted group of judges at this moment in history."
—*The New York Times Book Review*

"A worthy successor to *The Nine*, *The Oath* is a work of probity, intelligence and exceptional reporting."
—*Richmond Times-Dispatch*

"Might . . . be viewed eventually as the best book about the court during the opening half-decade of John Roberts's reign as chief justice. . . . Toobin does his job well."
—*The Seattle Times*

"Court watchers, serious and occasional, will find Toobin's explanation of the issues at stake . . . before the Roberts court well worth their time."   —*St. Louis Post-Dispatch*

"Exceptionally readable. . . . Blends strong reporting with a sure historical grasp of the court."
—*The Columbus Dispatch*

"An artfully constructed chronicle. . . . *The Oath* delivers a bracing survey of the court's key decisions and divisions. . . . Toobin's sketches of the justices are fabulous." —*Bookforum*

Jeffrey Toobin

THE

OATH

Jeffrey Toobin is the bestselling author of *The Nine*, *Too Close to Call*, *A Vast Conspiracy*, and *The Run of His Life*. He is a staff writer at *The New Yorker* and the senior legal analyst at CNN. He lives with his family in New York.

ALSO BY JEFFREY TOOBIN

Opening Arguments: A Young Lawyer's First Case:
United States v. Oliver North

The Run of His Life: The People v. O. J. Simpson

A Vast Conspiracy: The Real Story of the Sex Scandal That
Nearly Brought Down a President

Too Close to Call: The Thirty-Six-Day Battle
to Decide the 2000 Election

The Nine: Inside the Secret World
of the Supreme Court

THE

OATH

THE

OATH

The Obama White House and the Supreme Court

Jeffrey Toobin

ANCHOR BOOKS
A Division of Random House, Inc.
New York

FIRST ANCHOR BOOKS EDITION, JUNE 2013

A portion of this work was previously published in
slightly different form in *The New Yorker*.

The Library of Congress has cataloged the Doubleday edition as follows:
Toobin, Jeffrey.
The oath : the Obama White House and the Supreme Court / Jeffrey Toobin.
p. cm.
Includes bibliographical references and index.
1. United States. Supreme Court—History—21st century.
2. United States—Politics and government—2009–
3. Constitutional history—United States.
4. Political questions and judicial power—United States—History—21st century.
5. Obama, Barack. 6. Roberts, John G., 1955– I. Title.
KF8742.T66 2012
347.73'26090512—dc23   2012029205

Anchor ISBN: 978-0-307-39071-4

Author photograph © 2007 Cable News Network. A Time Warner Company. All rights reserved.
Book design by Michael Collica

Printed in the United States of America
10 9 8 7 6 5 4 3

To McIntosh, of course

CONTENTS

THE OATHS

S o let me ask you this," Greg Craig said, "does anyone there think he's *not* the president?"

It was about 10:30 on the morning of January 21, 2009. Craig was settling into his first day of work as counsel to the president when he received an unexpected phone call.

David Barron was on the line. He, too, had just reported for duty, as the second-in-command in the Office of Legal Counsel, which served as the in-house legal team for the attorney general–designate, Eric Holder.

In the excitement and chaos of the previous day—when Barack Obama was sworn in as the forty-fourth president of the United States—neither Craig nor Barron had paid much attention to the peculiar way Chief Justice John G. Roberts Jr. had administered the oath of office. Early the next morning, Barron had read several newspaper articles about the botched oath and decided to look into the issue. He was concerned enough about what he found to place the call to Craig.

So was Obama really the president?

Barron's answer was, well, complicated.

The Constitution for the most part speaks in majestic generalities and employs the first person—"I" and "my"—in only a single provision. Article II, Section 1, states: "Before he enter on the Execution of his Office, he shall take the following Oath or Affirmation: 'I do solemnly swear (or affirm) that I will faithfully execute the Office of President of the United States, and will to the best of my Ability, preserve, protect and defend the Constitution of the United States.' "

Article I of the Constitution, which defines the powers of Congress, is more than twice as long as Article II, about the presidency. This difference reflected the framers' belief that the legislative branch of government would be the most powerful. (Article III, which creates the judicial branch, is just 376 words, half again as short as Article II.) Still, the inclusion of a formal oath in the constitutional text reflected the importance of the presidency—and, more to the point, the president. It is the only oath spelled out in the Constitution. In contrast, the vice presidential oath was established by act of Congress, and the current version has been in use only since 1884.

The model for the framers was England's Coronation Oath, which had been promulgated in 1689, but the differences between the two oaths were as significant as the similarities. The King had to swear before a bishop or archbishop in the Church of England; there was no such requirement in the United States, and George Washington began the tradition of judicial administration of the oath in 1789. New York chancellor Robert Livingston conducted the first inauguration. (At that point, of course, Washington had not had the chance to nominate anyone to the Supreme Court, and it was four years later that a justice, William Cushing, swore in Washington for his second term.) The ecumenical nature of the presidential oath is reflected also in the option of "swear (or affirm)." Some Christian sects, notably the Quakers, did not believe in the use of the word "swearing," so the Constitution made sure they were not excluded. (Only Franklin Pierce, in 1853, chose to affirm his presidential oath.)

Many of the traditions associated with the inauguration began with Washington, as the first president knew they would. "As the first of everything in *our situation* will serve to establish a precedent, it is devoutly wished on my part that these precedents may be fixed on true principles," Washington wrote to James Madison shortly after his inauguration. On the occasion, which took place April 30, 1789, on the steps of Federal Hall, in lower Manhattan, Washington took the oath from a judge, not a cleric; he wore civilian garb, not a military uniform; he placed his hand on a Bible as he recited the words; he gave a brief, inspirational speech immediately after the ceremony; he made sure that any citizen who so desired could attend and view the swearing in. Washington Irving, who was six years old in 1789 but apparently a spectator at the inauguration, recounted in the 1850s that the new president had concluded the oath by saying, "So help me God." No contemporary account mentioned Washington's use of that phrase, and it remains unclear whether he did. In any event, all modern presidents have chosen to follow the oath with those words.

Like many other aspects of American government, the administration of the presidential oath evolved in a haphazard manner. In 1797, Oliver Ellsworth became the first chief justice to administer the oath (to John Adams), and thus the tradition began of the nation's highest legal officer performing the honors. But sometimes he didn't. (John Tyler and Millard Fillmore were sworn in by lower court judges.) Assassinations led to improvisations. Following the murder of James A. Garfield, in 1881, Chester A. Arthur was sworn in by a judge of the New York Supreme Court; following William McKinley's death, in 1901, Theodore Roosevelt took the oath from a federal district court judge. Most famously, Sarah T. Hughes, a federal district judge in Texas, administered the oath to Lyndon B. Johnson, on Air Force One, on November 22, 1963. Sentiment sometimes played a part, too. Calvin Coolidge took the oath from a lowly notary public—John C. Coolidge, his father. In 1933, Franklin D. Roosevelt recited the full oath without interruption by Chief Justice Charles Evans Hughes.

Notwithstanding the constitutional text, the precise words of the oath varied over time. When Chief Justice William Howard Taft swore in Herbert Hoover in 1929, he said, "preserve, maintain, and defend" the Constitution. The error was largely ignored at the time, but a thirteen-year-old girl who had been listening on the radio wrote to the chief justice about it. Taft responded, and disclosed still another, earlier mistake. "When I was sworn in as President by Chief Justice Fuller, he made a similar slip," Taft wrote to the girl, Helen Terwilliger, "but in those days when there was no radio, it was observed only in the Senate chamber where I took the oath. . . . You are mistaken in your report of what I did say. What I said was 'preserve, maintain and protect.' . . . You may attribute the variation to the defect of an old man's memory." In 1945, Harlan Fiske Stone began the oath with "I, Harry Shipp Truman . . ." Truman, who had a middle initial but no middle name, responded, "I, Harry S Truman . . ." Twenty years later, Lyndon Johnson forgot to raise his right hand until halfway through the oath, and Chief Justice Earl Warren said "office of the Presidency," not "President."

On the morning of January 21, 2009, David Barron had only a brief chance to dip into this peculiar corner of American history. What mattered more to him than these historical curiosities was the law, which was . . . not entirely clear. A professor on leave from Harvard Law School (one of many in the new administration), Barron recognized quickly that there was no single authoritative source to instruct him about the legal significance of the oath. For starters, it wasn't even apparent whether the oath mattered at all. Under the Twentieth Amendment, George W. Bush's term ended at noon on January 20. The electoral college had met and certified Obama as the winner of the election. Thus, Obama may have become president the previous day at noon, even if he never took the oath. But the Constitution also said that "*before* he enter on the execution of his office, he *shall*" take the oath. The Constitution, of course, abounds in such ambiguities.

So, like any other good lawyer, Barron looked for precedents. There was no Supreme Court ruling on the subject, but the Office of Legal Counsel issues formal opinions on a variety of matters, and Barron found one from 1985, regarding presidential succession. The Twenty-fifth Amendment to the Constitution, which was ratified in 1967, lays out what happens when a president dies or becomes incapacitated. The OLC opinion noted that, although the Constitution, "which sets forth the Presidential oath, is not entirely clear on the effect of taking the oath, the weight of history and authority suggests that taking the oath is not a necessary step prior to the assumption of the office of President and is not an independent source of Presidential power. It is, nonetheless, an obligation imposed on the President by the Constitution, and should be one of the first acts performed by the new President." So taking the oath was recommended but not mandatory—probably.

For Barron and his colleagues at OLC, this was not just an abstract legal problem. There was a political dimension as well. Obama had made commitment to the rule of law a centerpiece of his campaign. How would it look if he skirted the rules on the oath? Perhaps more importantly, what would Obama's political adversaries do? Article II also states that "no Person except a natural born Citizen" is eligible to be president, and a persistent group of critics claimed that Obama was not, in fact, born in Hawaii in 1961. Was it wise to tempt another potential constitutional challenge to his qualification to serve as president?

Barron, too, saw the issue of the oath in the context of larger developments in constitutional law. Starting in the 1960s, liberals on the Supreme Court and elsewhere developed a theory built around the idea of "unenumerated rights." Even if a right was not specifically mentioned in the Constitution, the Court could draw on the implications of the explicit provisions of the Constitution, prior decisions, and the broader evolution of American society, to expand the liberties of Americans. Most famously (or notoriously) during this period, the Court recognized a constitutional right to privacy, which became the basis for protecting a woman's right to choose abortion.

In recent years, though, the doctrine of unenumerated rights had come under ferocious attack by conservatives. On the Supreme Court, Antonin Scalia and Clarence Thomas had led the charge for what became known as "textualism," which said that if the Constitution did not explicitly create a right, it did not exist. A close cousin to textualism was originalism, which asserted that the words of the Constitution must be interpreted as they were understood by the men who wrote and ratified it. Under either textualism or originalism, there was no such thing as a right to privacy and, of course, no constitutional right to abortion.

As Barron knew, textualism was ascendant, and that might have implications for the presidential oath. There might be judges out there who took a literal—a textual—approach to the oath of office. If Obama had not said the precise words mandated by Article II, perhaps—just perhaps—he was not actually the president. And on that ground, any formal action Obama took might be challenged in court. At a minimum, some federal district judge might be tempted to hold a hearing on the issue. Such a legal proceeding would be a distraction, to say the least. That, certainly, was not how Obama wanted to spend his first days in office.

All in all, Barron told Craig, it might be a good idea for Roberts and Obama to redo the oath and get it right.

Greg Craig listened in amazement as Barron spelled out his concerns. It was at that point that Craig realized that he was missing a key fact. At the moment Obama took the oath the previous day, Craig had been standing by the doorway to the Capitol, awaiting the new president, who would sign a ceremonial proclamation before heading inside to the luncheon. Craig had been sufficiently distracted that he barely heard the oath or Obama's inaugural address.

So almost twenty-four hours later, Craig had to ask himself: What exactly *did* Obama and Roberts say?

It's that time again!

In September 2008, well before Election Day, Cami Morrison sent that message to Vanessa Yarnall. Morrison was usually a staffer for the Senate sergeant at arms, but she had been detailed to the newly reconstituted Joint Congressional Inaugural Committee. Yarnall was the assistant to Jeffrey Minear, the counselor to the chief justice and his chief aide for all nonjudicial matters. Morrison and Yarnall had worked together on the presidential inauguration of 2005, and they were now starting to plan the events of January 20, 2009.

Yarnall knew that the late Chief Justice William H. Rehnquist had taken a methodical approach to the oath, and she started reassembling the paperwork he had last used. Rehnquist had sworn in five presidents, and he took an extra step to make sure that he and the president would be on the same page. Shortly before the inauguration, Rehnquist sent the White House counsel a card illustrating how he would divide up the words. In 2001, the card read:

PRESIDENT'S OATH

I, GEORGE WALKER BUSH, DO SOLEMNLY SWEAR//

THAT I WILL FAITHFULLY EXECUTE THE OFFICE OF
PRESIDENT OF THE UNITED STATES//

AND WILL TO THE BEST OF MY ABILITY//

PRESERVE, PROTECT AND DEFEND THE CONSTITUTION
OF THE UNITED STATES.//

SO HELP ME GOD.

On December 10, 2008, Yarnall sent Morrison a PDF of Rehnquist's oath card. She removed Bush's name and left a space for Obama's name. In her e-mail, Yarnall asked how Roberts should address the new president: With his middle name? Just middle initial? Just first and last? Yarnall and her boss, Minear, assumed that Morrison would forward the card to representatives of the president-elect. They were wrong. Morrison either never noticed the PDF, lost it, ignored it, or forgot about it. In any case, the oath card never reached anyone on Barack Obama's staff.

On December 15, Senator Dianne Feinstein, the chair of the Congressional Inaugural Committee, formally invited Roberts to administer the oath of office to Obama. The chief justice quickly accepted, and Feinstein's letter prompted him to sit down with Minear and discuss the ceremony for the first time. They went over Rehnquist's oath card with care. They added a comma after the word "ability." They discussed whether "So help you God" was a question or a statement. And since Yarnall's questions to Morrison had gone unanswered, they wondered what name Obama wanted to use. On December 17, Minear e-mailed Greg Craig to introduce himself and ask about Obama's name and "So help me God." Craig wrote back that the president-elect was on vacation, so it might take a few days for an answer.

On December 30, Michael Newdow filed a lawsuit in federal district court in Washington seeking to prevent Roberts from referring to "God" following the oath of office. In 2002, Newdow became famous when he won a ruling in the Ninth Circuit court of appeals that the Pledge of Allegiance in public schools should not include the phrase "under God." (The Supreme Court later overturned that decision on procedural grounds.) The Justice Department lawyers handling Newdow's latest case asked Minear to file an affidavit about how the chief justice would be administering the oath. But Minear had still not heard back from Craig. This time, Minear reached Craig by phone. Craig said that Obama wanted to include his middle name in the oath and that Roberts should say "So help you God" as a question. On January 8, 2009, Minear included Craig's responses in an affidavit in the Newdow lawsuit, which was quickly dismissed by a local federal judge.

Craig's answers allowed Minear to put Roberts's presidential oath card into final form. It now read:

PRESIDENT'S OATH

I, BARACK HUSSEIN OBAMA, DO SOLEMNLY SWEAR//

THAT I WILL FAITHFULLY EXECUTE THE OFFICE OF
PRESIDENT OF THE UNITED STATES,//

AND WILL TO THE BEST OF MY ABILITY,//

PRESERVE, PROTECT AND DEFEND THE CONSTITUTION
OF THE UNITED STATES.//

SO HELP YOU GOD?

Vanessa Yarnall e-mailed the revised version to Cami Morrison, who
again did not pass it along to the president-elect's team. Indeed, in the
days leading up to the inauguration, neither Obama himself, Craig, nor
anyone else associated with them knew that the card existed.

At this point, with the text in final form, John Roberts set about
memorizing the oath.

There never was a student like John Roberts at the La Lumiere School
in LaPorte, Indiana, a quiet town near Lake Michigan, on the outer
edges of the gravitational pull of Chicago. It was a Catholic school, but
it was independent of any order or diocese; the founders, all laymen,
built the institution around an ideal of academic excellence.

Roberts was not just the valedictorian of the class of 1973. He served
as captain of the football team, a varsity wrestler, member of both the
student council and the drama club. (He played Peppermint Patty in
You're a Good Man, Charlie Brown; the school was all boys in Roberts's
day.) He continued taking Latin, as a tutorial, after the school dropped
the language as a requirement. La Lumiere had a traditional curricu-
lum, but there was one slight novelty. Every year, the students were
expected to participate in what was known as a declamation contest,
where they would write and memorize their own speeches. In this Roberts excelled, too.

Over time, Roberts became famous for his superb memory. As a lawyer, both in the solicitor general's office and in private practice, he was known as perhaps the finest Supreme Court advocate of his generation. But it was not just his arguments that dazzled. Roberts's personality inspired confidence, especially because when he stepped to the podium to argue before the justices, Roberts brought nothing with him—no pad, no notes. He carried the facts and the law of each case in his head.

Roberts relied on his memory—and, as always, hard work—in preparing to administer the oath. He rehearsed many times. He recited the words so often at his home in suburban Maryland that he irritated his wife. "At this point the dog thinks it's the president," Jane Roberts told her husband.

On the late afternoon of January 13, 2009, Roberts went to the west front of the Capitol for a walk-through of the inauguration. A handful of congressional staffers showed him his assigned seat and told him when and where he would stand. Toward the end of the meeting, one of the aides offered a card to Roberts with the text of the oath. Did he want to rehearse?

"That's OK," Roberts said, declining the text, "I know the oath."

A week later, on the morning of the inauguration, the justices gathered at the Supreme Court for a small reception, before heading across First Street as a group to the Capitol. The chief justice is a largely invisible figure to most Americans, except for this single appearance every four years. Roberts seemed uncharacteristically subdued as he waited.

A throng of more than a million people filled the National Mall all the way to the Washington Monument. At the stroke of noon, Dianne Feinstein introduced Roberts and asked the audience to stand. (Feinstein called Roberts by his correct title, chief justice of the United States; four years earlier, Trent Lott, in the same role, managed two breaches of protocol in less than a minute. He incorrectly called Rehnquist the chief justice of the Supreme Court and then summoned him to the podium as "Justice Rehnquist." Rehnquist was a stickler for being called "Chief Justice.")

"That's for you," Obama whispered to his wife, Michelle, as she reached for the "Lincoln Bible," which had last been used when the sixteenth president placed his hand upon it in 1861.

"Are you prepared to take the oath, Senator?" Roberts said.

"I am," said Obama.

Roberts raised his right hand at a crisp right angle. Unlike Rehnquist, Roberts did not carry a copy of the oath in his left hand. The chief justice began, "I, Barack Hussein Obama, do so—"

Obama jumped in and began to recite, "I, Barack . . ."

Roberts and Obama clearly had different ideas about whether "do solemnly swear" would be included. Roberts's oath card included "do solemnly swear" in the first line—but Obama had never seen this text.

Recognizing that he had interrupted Roberts, Obama paused to let Roberts continue. Obama then recited correctly, "I, Barack Hussein Obama, do solemnly swear."

But Roberts—most uncharacteristically—became flustered when he thought that Obama had jumped the gun and interrupted him, and he said next, "That I will execute the office of President to the United States faithfully." "To" the United States? "Faithfully" after United States? Obama gave a half smile. He could tell it was wrong.

"That I will execute . . . " Obama said, but then he saw that Roberts was again trying to speak, endeavoring to salvage the situation on the fly.

"The off—" Roberts stumbled again. "Faithfully the office of President of the United States." This time he had left out "execute."

Obama was confused. He said, "the office of President of the United States faithfully"—incorrectly putting "faithfully" at the end of the sentence. The two men finally put that troublesome phrase behind them.

"And will to the best of my ability," Roberts said.

"And will to the best of my ability," Obama repeated.

"Preserve, protect and defend the Constitution of the United States," Roberts said quickly, trying to finish without further problems.

Obama repeated.

"So help you God?"

"So help me God."

"Congratulations, Mr. President," Roberts said, extending his hand. "All the best wishes."

Now what? Craig wondered.

Later on January 21—in a few minutes, in fact—Obama was to sign a series of executive orders and presidential memorandums relating to government ethics. He was going to freeze the salaries of White House staffers making more than $100,000 a year and establish new rules to limit lobbying by former government officials. But it was the events planned for January 22 that really worried Craig. Obama was scheduled to sign a lengthy executive order to begin the process of closing the detention facility at Guantánamo Bay. As a private lawyer, staffer to Senator Edward Kennedy, and Clinton-era State Department official, Craig had a long commitment to the cause of international human rights. Obama's passion for the subject drew Craig to support the young senator over Hillary Clinton in the primaries, even though Craig had known her for decades and served in her husband's administration. Many times during the campaign, Obama had pledged to close Guantánamo. The last thing Craig wanted to do was undermine Obama's authority to take this action.

Craig's deputy, Daniel Meltzer, another professor at Harvard Law School, had not yet arrived in Washington, so Craig called him in Cambridge for his advice. Given the political tensions surrounding everything in Washington, especially Guantánamo, it was possible that someone might demand a hearing on whether Obama was president and thus had the right to close Guantánamo. In the end, the new administration would probably win such a hearing, but legal proceedings had ways of taking on lives of their own. How would they "prove" Obama was president? Would they have to call witnesses? How long would this take? Would there be appeals? What would happen in the meantime?

Meltzer agreed that the safer course was to redo the oath. But that raised other questions. How? When? Where? Perhaps most importantly, by whom? They thought about asking a federal district judge to do it quickly and privately. Craig had been a law partner of Ellen Segal Huvelle, now a judge in Washington, and wondered if he should ask her to come to the White House. On further reflection, though, he and Meltzer decided that the better course was to be open about the whole process—and to ask the chief justice to do it again. (David Barron, at the Justice Department, had largely withdrawn from the discussion. Later he would reflect, with dark humor, that he had probably managed to annoy *both* the president and the chief justice on his very first day of work.)

Craig went downstairs in the West Wing to talk to David Axelrod, the president's top political adviser. Axelrod deferred to Craig's legal judgment about the necessity of the redo and agreed that the process should be open and include the chief justice, if possible. Still, they both wanted to downplay the event's significance. So Axelrod came up with a phrase to explain what they were doing: "out of an abundance of caution." Around lunchtime, Craig and Axelrod went up to the residence, where Obama was receiving visitors, to brief him and get his approval for the plan.

At 1:18 p.m., Obama entered Room 450, an auditorium in the Eisenhower Executive Office Building, which is part of the White House complex. When Obama and Vice President Joseph Biden walked into the room, the crowd of about thirty new appointees rose to their feet, which is customary when the president enters a room. At this point, though, Obama was startled by the gesture. "Please be seated," he said with a slightly embarrassed smile. "I'm still getting used to that whole thing. Please be seated."

Obama was supposed to sign the orders on government ethics, but he went to the lectern and introduced Biden: "Joe, do you want to administer the oath?"

Biden was surprised and puzzled by the request. "Am I doing this again?" he asked. He was then informed that he would be giving the oath to the senior staff. "For the senior staff, all right," Biden said. Never one to leave a silence unfilled, he then added, "My memory is not as good as Justice Roberts, Chief Justice Roberts."

There was no mistaking Biden's reference. The assembled staffers muttered a collective "woooo," followed by outright laughter. Biden smiled, and asked for the card with the oath.

Barack Obama had by this point constructed a public image of imperturbability, earning the well-deserved nickname of No Drama Obama. But Biden had irritated Obama. The president scowled, shook his head in clear disapproval, and then reached out toward Biden, almost pushing him away from the microphone. Obama knew—as Biden did not know—that the oath had been botched so badly that his staff was just then asking the chief justice to conduct a do-over. Obama wouldn't want anyone making fun of Roberts at this moment. Moreover, Obama had better manners than Biden. It was not the kind of joke the new president would ever make. (Biden later called Roberts to apologize.)

Greg Craig had made the awkward phone call to Minear, the aide to Chief Justice Roberts, who didn't hide his surprise. You want to do *what?* You want to do it *when?* Craig made clear that they would like the chief justice to come by the White House as soon as possible. Minear said he would have to check but quickly called back to say the chief justice would be pleased to stop by the White House on his way home from work.

Soon, in other words. Craig then called Robert Gibbs, the press secretary, to tell him that Roberts would be arriving shortly to readminister the oath.

What the fuck did you just say? Gibbs replied.

Craig repeated his news.

Gibbs was flabbergasted. When reporters had asked about the stumbles in the oath, he had directed his staff to check it out with the counsel's office. That particular game of telephone resulted in word getting back to Gibbs that the White House regarded the gaffes as no big deal. For the last twenty-four hours, Gibbs had been repeating that guidance to anyone who asked.

Now—Craig told him—they were about to redo the presidential oath for apparently the first time in American history. The press secretary was furious with Craig. Did you think that might be newsworthy? When did you think you might get around to telling me this?

Gibbs raced to the office of Rahm Emanuel, the chief of staff, and told him they needed to decide how to tell the press what was happening, and where. And they had to do it immediately.

Gibbs, Craig, Axelrod, and Emanuel made the decisions. The idea was not to keep the redo a secret, but not to call too much attention to it either. They agreed to conduct the ceremony in the Map Room, which is officially part of the White House residence, rather than in a working area, like the Oval Office. Presidents had long used the Map Room as a kind of hybrid, for occasions that they didn't want to recognize as presidential business but that weren't personal either. A decade earlier, for that reason, Bill Clinton gave his grand jury testimony to the Kenneth Starr investigation in the Map Room. Later, Obama would meet the Dalai Lama there, because an Oval Office meeting would have offended the Chinese government.

Precisely at 7:00, Craig met the chief justice's limousine. Roberts and Minear left the car, with Minear holding Roberts's robe. Craig offered profuse thanks, and Roberts in turn was equally gracious. "I always believe in belt and suspenders," Roberts said. "This is absolutely the right thing to do."

Gibbs had decided against television coverage of the event and instead invited only a print pool as witnesses. The pool consisted of representatives of the Associated Press, Reuters, and Bloomberg and a rotating newspaper reporter, who happened on this day to be Wes Allison of the *St. Petersburg Times*. Gibbs lent the event an air of mystery. He told the quartet of reporters to follow him from his office in the West Wing along the colonnade to the White House residence, but he wouldn't say why until they arrived in the Map Room.

There Gibbs paused and pulled out the statement that Craig and Axelrod had prepared. It said that the White House believed that the oath had been administered "effectively" the previous day, but "out of an abundance of caution," Roberts would be doing it again. Stunned, the reporters said nothing until Obama and Craig walked over to greet them. Smiling broadly, the president said, "Hey guys, we decided, you know, that it was so much fun that we'd do it again." Obama started quizzing the members of the pool about the inaugural balls. "How late did you stay up?" he asked. "Tell the truth." One reporter asked Obama if he had a good time. "I had a wonderful time with my wife," he said. "But she had to do it in high heels. That's something I could not imagine."

Wes Allison had had the presence of mind to turn on his Panasonic RR-US361 digital recorder, and his audio file remains the only full record of the proceedings.

Roberts put on his robe, and Gibbs and Pete Souza, the White House photographer (the only photographer present), steered Obama and the chief justice to a position in front of the fireplace. The Obamas had not had a chance to put their stamp on the residence, so the portrait above the mantel was more a placeholder than an object of any special significance to the first family. The subject was Benjamin Latrobe, the architect of the Capitol.

Still trying to keep the tone light, Obama said, "I don't have my Bible, but that's all right."

Obama then hesitated. Craig had brought along a copy of the oath, and he felt sure that this time Roberts would read it. Obama waited for the chief justice to pull out his own copy or take the one from Craig.

Roberts had thought about bringing the text with him. It would have been the cautious thing to do. But the chief justice was a proud man. He never publicly blamed anyone but himself for botching the initial ceremony. But he didn't want to admit defeat and read the oath.

Obama sensed this and said, "We're going to do it very slowly." Several onlookers glanced at one another with raised eyebrows. The new president was a polite man, but his remark to the chief justice had an . . . edge.

The second administration of the oath was completed without incident.

At that moment, standing before the fireplace, Barack Obama and John Roberts had a great deal in common. At the ages of forty-seven and fifty-three, respectively, they were probably the most accomplished members of their shared generation, and both were at the height of their powers. Even their adversaries would concede that each man possessed a powerful intellect and considerable charm. Some of the same influences and experiences shaped both the forty-fourth president and the seventeenth chief justice. Both were products of Chicago and its environs, and both were graduates of Harvard Law School. Both even served on the *Harvard Law Review*, the student-run scholarly magazine. (Obama was president his year; Roberts was managing editor, effectively second-in-command, during his.) Both were married, neither had had a previous marriage, and each man had two young children.

But the differences between Obama and Roberts were ultimately far more significant than the similarities. Roberts came from a stable, traditional, and prosperous home, where his father was an executive at a steel mill and his mother a homemaker. Obama's father, a Kenyan, abandoned his family when his son was a toddler and then saw the boy only one more time, when Obama was ten; Obama's mother, a lifelong free spirit and intellectual searcher who grew up in Kansas, gave birth to Obama in Hawaii, spent a few years with him in Indonesia, and then left him with her parents in a Honolulu high-rise. After going to college first in Los Angeles and then graduating from Columbia, in New York, Obama made his way to Chicago to become a community organizer.

Chicago left entirely different marks on the two men. Obama lived in the inner city, among the poor, desperate, and Democratic; Roberts grew up among Republican burghers who lived in large and sturdy homes well insulated from the winds off the lake. Even their Harvard experiences were different; the institution changed between the time Roberts, law school class of 1979, and Obama, class of 1991, studied there. The large gap between their times in law school was due to Obama's years as an inner-city activist; it is inconceivable to imagine Roberts spending any time in that field. His years in the private sector were spent representing corporations at the powerful law firm then known as Hogan & Hartson.

But the greatest, and certainly the most important, difference between the two concerned the work of the Supreme Court. Both men gave considerable thought to the Constitution, and they reached different conclusions about its current trajectory:

- One believed in change; the other in stability.
- One looked forward; the other harkened back.
- One was, in a real sense, a visionary; the other was, when it came to the law, a conservative.

And in this crucial realm, the roles of the two men were the opposite of what was widely believed. It was John Roberts who was determined to use his position as chief justice as an apostle of change. He was the one who wanted to usher in a new understanding of the Constitution, with dramatic implications for both the law and the larger society. And it was Barack Obama who was determined to hold on to an older version of the meaning of the Constitution. Obama was the fellow who was, in the words of a famous conservative, standing athwart history yelling "Stop!"

In the previous dozen years, the United States endured a terrorist attack, economic calamity, and several wars. But the Supreme Court's rulings may leave as important a legacy. The future of politics, business, public safety, individual freedoms—all hang in the balance before the justices. How will our elections be conducted? What is the place of race in American society? How much power may the federal government exercise? On those questions and many more, the Supreme Court will have greater sway than either the executive or the legislative branches of government.

Over those years, the Court has been transformed by the same devel-

opment that reconfigured American politics—the evolution of the
Republican Party. For two generations, since the liberal heyday of Chief
Justice Earl Warren, the Court was largely controlled by the moderate
wing of the Republican Party. During this period, first Lewis Powell
and then Sandra Day O'Connor self-consciously tethered the Court close
to the center of the political spectrum. Those justices, and indeed that
part of the Republican Party, are now gone. A court now dominated by
Roberts, Anthony M. Kennedy, Antonin Scalia, Clarence Thomas, and
Samuel A. Alito Jr. reflects the contemporary Republican Party.

Even in this heady company, Roberts towers above his colleagues,
conservative and liberal alike, in savvy, intelligence, and understanding of the place of the Supreme Court in American life. This was
especially evident in the stunning conclusion to the Court's 2011–12
term, when the chief justice joined with the Court's four liberals to
uphold the Affordable Care Act, the signal legislative achievement of
Barack Obama's presidency. Roberts's vote, at least in the short term,
was a shattering disappointment to conservatives, including his four
dissenting colleagues. In spite of that vote, Roberts still believes in
change—but not always, and not all at once. Roberts understands that
sometimes power must be tended as well as expended. The decision in
National Federation of Independent Business v. Sebelius may reward Roberts,
and the conservative cause, over time. As a man in robust middle age,
with life tenure, Roberts has the luxury of playing a long game, and
he is.

The conservative ascendency at the Court owes much to Republican
victories in presidential elections and to well-funded sponsors but also
to the power of ideas. The great conservative project of the previous
generation has been originalism—interpreting the Constitution supposedly as its framers understood it. The conservative bugaboo in this
process has been the "living Constitution"—the idea, supposedly liberal in origin, that the meaning of the Constitution changes with the
times. But in pressing originalism with such intensity and such success,
conservatives have proven, perhaps unintentionally, that the Constitution does indeed live—that it responds to and changes with the politics
of the day.

Obama and Roberts embody the larger conflict. They are both honorable and intelligent, but they see the Constitution in different ways.
The only certainty in the battle between them is the high stakes riding
on the outcome.

PART

ONE

THE POLITICIAN'S PATH

On February 14, 2008, a man named Steven Kazmierczak opened fire on the campus of Northern Illinois University, in DeKalb, Illinois. He killed five people, and injured twenty-one, before committing suicide. The following day, Barack Obama, the junior senator from the state and a candidate for president, was asked about the shooting at a news conference. In light of this tragedy, what did Obama think about the need for gun control, especially as it related to the Second Amendment?

The Second Amendment states: "A well regulated Militia, being necessary to the security of a free State, the right of the people to keep and bear Arms, shall not be infringed." There was and remains unanimous agreement that the text of the amendment is ungrammatical. For more than a century, there was also agreement on what the Second Amendment meant. According to this understanding, the Second Amendment related only to the rights of citizen militias and imposed no barrier to gun control; in other words, the amendment did not give private individuals a right to bear arms.

Obama had a different view.

"I believe that the Second Amendment means something. I do think it speaks to an individual right," Obama said at his news conference following the massacre. "There's been a long-standing argument among constitutional scholars about whether the Second Amendment referred simply to militias or whether it spoke to an individual right to possess arms. I think the latter is the better argument," he went on. "There is an individual right to bear arms, but it is subject to common-sense regulation just like most of our rights are subject to common-sense regulation. And so I think there's a lot of room before you start bumping up against a constitutional barrier."

Even a few years earlier, Obama's comments would have seemed bizarre. Since a Supreme Court case called *United States v. Miller*, in 1939, hundreds of courts had rejected the individual rights view of the Second Amendment. But then the National Rifle Association, the Republican Party, and their allies invested their time, money, and energy in creating a new understanding of the Second Amendment. Indeed, at the time of Obama's news conference about the massacre, the Supreme Court was preparing to decide *District of Columbia v. Heller*, a product of this long effort to create a new interpretation of the Second Amendment. The work of conservatives to change the accepted meaning of the framers' words was so successful that the recruits to the cause came to include the Chicago liberal who was a leading contender to be the Democratic nominee for president.

This, it turns out, was no surprise. Obama was an unusually well-credentialed lawyer. His life as a public figure began in 1990, when he was twenty-eight and won election as president of the *Harvard Law Review*, the first African American to hold that position. Obama practiced law for a dozen years and taught at the University of Chicago Law School for nearly as long. But by the time he ran for president, Obama was above all a politician, and a cautious one. Obama admired the heroes of the civil rights movement, including the lawyers, but he did not model his career on theirs. Obama did not believe the courts were the principal vehicle for social and political change. Elections, rather than lawsuits, were his battlefield of choice, and by 2008 he knew that the way to win the presidency was, in part, to embrace the individual rights theory of the Second Amendment.

Near the end of his memoir, *Dreams from My Father*, which he published when he was thirty-three, Obama reflected on his education at Harvard Law School. His tone was ambivalent. "The study of law can be disappointing at times, a matter of applying narrow rules and arcane procedure to an uncooperative reality; a sort of glorified accounting that serves to regulate the affairs of those who have power—and that all too often seeks to explain, to those who do not, the ultimate wisdom and justness of their condition." Then, in a gesture that was common in the book, and in Obama's character, he gave the other side of the story: "But that is not all the law is," he continued. "The law is also memory; the law also records a long-running conversation, a nation arguing with its conscience."

Obama's conversation with himself continued: "How far do our obligations reach? How do we transform mere power into justice, mere sentiment into love? The answers I find in law books don't always satisfy me—for every *Brown v. Board of Education* I find a score of cases where conscience is sacrificed to expedience or greed." As before, though, Obama followed that despairing remark with a hopeful one: "And yet, in the conversation itself, in the joining of voices, I find myself modestly encouraged, believing that so long as the questions are still being asked, what binds us together might somehow, ultimately, prevail."

Obama arrived at Harvard after spending three years as a community organizer in Chicago. There he had led a small group in a series of fights, usually with the city government, for better housing, for asbestos abatement, and for jobs on the South Side. Like many such endeavors to organize the poor, Obama's work was difficult and not especially successful; friends and colleagues found Obama more analytical than confrontational. In time, as his frustrations mounted, Obama began thinking about going to law school. Partly, Obama simply wanted to find a way to make a decent living, but the profession also seemed well suited to his particular kind of intelligence and ambitions. He was admitted to Harvard and began his studies in the fall of 1988.

Obama had just turned twenty-seven, which turned out to be a fact of some significance. Most of his fellow students were considerably younger, and Obama's maturity, both chronological and temperamental, set him apart. He approached law school, as he did much else, with a certain detachment, as both participant and observer. Law school, and Harvard in particular, would leave its mark on Obama, but his core remained unchanged.

There was much truth in the conventional view of a Harvard Law School degree as a passport to Wall Street law firms, but the school also produced eminent role models for an aspiring reformer like Obama. Louis Brandeis, class of 1877, practically invented Supreme Court litigation as a vehicle for social change and, in an article in the *Harvard Law Review*,

first identified a "right to privacy." Felix Frankfurter, class of 1906, provided much of the intellectual energy behind the New Deal, as well
as many protégés to Franklin Roosevelt, before following Brandeis on
to the Supreme Court. Archibald Cox, class of 1937, joined the faculty
and went on to serve as President Kennedy's solicitor general and then
Watergate special prosecutor. In subsequent decades, untold numbers of
Harvard Law graduates moved to Washington, and around the country,
to make their marks on the policies of the day.

And there was a time, too, when ideas, as well as people, also made
the trip from the Ivy League to Washington. In the Warren Court
years—the years of *Brown*—leading law schools provided much of the
intellectual firepower behind the Court's most liberal decisions. In
Goldberg v. Kelly, in 1970, the Court held for the first time that the
government must give an individual a hearing before cutting off his
welfare benefits. To do otherwise, Justice William J. Brennan Jr. said,
would violate the Fourteenth Amendment, by depriving the individual of "property" without due process of law. But were welfare benefits
"property"? In the key passage in the opinion, Brennan wrote, "It may
be realistic today to regard welfare entitlements as more like 'property'
than a 'gratuity.' Much of the existing wealth in this country takes the
form of rights that do not fall within traditional common-law concepts
of property." In support of this novel notion, Brennan cited the work
of Charles A. Reich, a professor at Yale Law School, and his articles
in the *Yale Law Journal*. At around the same time, Frank I. Michel-
man, a professor at Harvard (who was still teaching when Obama was
a student), suggested that the Fourteenth Amendment might require a
right to economic equality, not just freedom from discrimination. The
Supreme Court never went that far, but the idea was, at least for a
while, plausible. To write for a law review in those days could be seen
as an act of genuine political importance. Harvard's influence, though,
went in cycles, and there was a down period as the country and the
Supreme Court began to turn to the right in the 1970s—a period that
coincided with the tenure of John G. Roberts '79 on campus. Richard
Nixon famously referred to Harvard as the "Kremlin on the Charles,"
so faculty members were generally less welcomed in his administration.
Conservative Supreme Court justices needed no direction from liberal
academics. On the whole, in these days, the Harvard law faculty still
tilted left, but the school returned its focus to its mission as a professional school. As managing editor of the *Harvard Law Review*, Roberts

was known by his colleagues as a political conservative—a modest novelty among his fellow editors—but mostly as a skilled and demanding taskmaster.

Liberals may still have held sway in Cambridge, but conservatives were gaining in the rest of the world, and following his graduation, magna cum laude, Roberts began his Republican ascent. He clerked first in New York for Henry J. Friendly, a legendary judge of moderate Republican views on the Second Circuit, and then in 1980 for William Rehnquist, who was still an associate justice. From there, Roberts went to the Justice Department and Reagan White House. Clearly, then, the Kremlin in Cambridge could launch a brilliant conservative career as well as a liberal one.

Back at the law school, in the eighties, the politics took a peculiar turn. The faculty, and to a lesser extent the student body, became bitterly divided over a movement known as Critical Legal Studies. CLS was a hybrid of traditional Marxism and contemporary literary theory; its adherents purported to expose the contradictions and class biases inherent in all aspects of law. As far back as the 1920s, "legal realism"—which provided the intellectual basis for much of the New Deal—exposed the political nature of most legal rules. But the Crits, as they were known, practiced a kind of legal realism on steroids, taking an almost nihilistic pleasure in showing the meaninglessness of law. They portrayed law as first and foremost an instrument of oppression of the disenfranchised, and they did so in a manner that was both passionate and obscure, with articles full of citations to the work of "poststructuralists" like Jacques Derrida. Crits and conservatives on the faculty battled over tenure appointments, and the fights sometimes spilled into the classrooms, and even into courtrooms. The Kremlin on the Charles became known as Beirut on the Charles.

Roberts experienced a pre-CLS Harvard. Obama arrived just after its heyday. So it was notable that, while still in his first year, Obama sought out Laurence Tribe and went to work for him as a research assistant. The choice was a revealing one on the young student's part. Tribe was a liberal but no Crit—a description that also fit his prize student. Tribe had managed to avoid the Crits-versus-conservatives warfare on the faculty, largely because he was a leading modern exemplar of the Cambridge-to-Washington axis. After writing the best single-volume treatise on the Constitution, Tribe became an accomplished Supreme Court advocate and adviser to Democratic politicians. In 1987, Tribe gave damning testimony before the Senate Judiciary Committee against Reagan's nomination of Robert Bork to the Supreme Court. The stand made Tribe a Republican target and doomed his own chance of winning a nomination to the Court. Still, Tribe was more than an academic; he was a player on the larger stage, the real world.

Obama excelled in the classroom—he too would graduate magna cum laude—and he succeeded in the writing competition to join the staff of the *Harvard Law Review*. Students on law reviews edit articles that are submitted by law professors around the country; about forty out of five hundred students in a class make law review at Harvard. Every February, the staff of the law review holds an election to select the president, or editor in chief, of the magazine for the following year. Obama won with broad support. Conservative students, who were a growing presence at Harvard, turned out to be the key to Obama's victory. The Federalist Society—the national conservative legal organization—had been founded at Yale in 1982, but Harvard soon opened a chapter, and its members asserted themselves as a vocal minority on the staff of the *Review*. The conservatives recognized that Obama was not one of their own, but they felt he would give them a fair shake, especially about which articles to publish. In winning the confidence of conservatives, Obama's maturity proved a tremendous asset. In that tumultuous time on campus, Obama always seemed slightly removed from the battle lines, in his customary posture of both observer and participant. He had an innate grasp of the politician's gift for persuading others that you agree with them without ever making an explicit commitment. Obama's earnest style earned him some mockery from his friends. One of them told David Remnick that a group would go to the movies and tease Obama by imitating his solicitude: "Do you want salt on your popcorn? Do you even *want* popcorn?"

Suddenly, then, with his election as president of the *Review*, Barack Obama was a celebrity of sorts. The *New York Times* did a story about him. Turner Broadcasting asked Obama to record a "Black History Minute," and the young man, struggling with the teleprompter, gave a brief tribute to Charles Hamilton Houston, one of Thurgood Marshall's legal mentors. *Vanity Fair*, which does not generally track the leadership of scholarly publications, devoted a full page to Obama's election. *"The*

New York Times ran a 'First Black' headline, which probably won't be the last time that label is affixed to Barack Obama," Elise O'Shaughnessy wrote, before concluding that Obama "responds warily to the assumption that he himself will run for office. 'If I go into politics it should grow out of work I've done on the local level, not because I'm some media creation.' Though, as media creations go, he'd be a pretty good one." In addition, around this time, Jane Dystel, a literary agent in New York, approached Obama with the idea of his writing a book. Obama agreed, and signed a contract with a division of Simon & Schuster. (At that point, people embraced Obama without knowing much about him. One publisher thought he was raised in the Chicago ghetto; *Vanity Fair* said he grew up in Singapore, not Indonesia. No one seemed to know that his real home was Honolulu.)

It was all a rather extraordinary amount of attention to a mere law student, but during his debut as a public figure, Obama demonstrated precocious political skills. "The fact that I've been elected shows a lot of progress," he told Fox Butterfield, of the *Times*. "But it's important that stories like mine aren't used to say that everything is O.K. for blacks." Likewise, Obama was always careful to show respect for his forebearers in the civil rights movement, whose sacrifices, he said, made his own success possible. He told the *Boston Globe*, "To some extent, I'm a symbolic stand-in for a lot of the changes that have been made."

But for all that Obama showed respect for Marshall, Houston, and their peers, he also made clear in his own way what he expected of the contemporary legal system: not much. Those pioneers had used the courts to break down the legal barriers that oppressed African Americans. But by the time Obama was at Harvard, that work was mostly done. The task of legal progressives of Obama's vintage was to try to hang on to the gains that had been made in the courts—and that wasn't easy, or of particular interest to him. In 1991, Obama graduated from Harvard Law School into the world of the Rehnquist Court, where the social change on the agenda was (almost always) in the conservative direction. If the right was ascendant, the left was distracted—with the baroque inventions of Critical Legal Studies. For someone like Obama, who had spent years working on the real-world problems of poor people in Chicago, theories untethered to reality had no appeal.

Later, when Obama was a senator, he explained the nature of his disillusionment with the use of the courts for social change. It wasn't just that things looked bleak at the Rehnquist Court. "I wondered if, in our reliance on the courts to vindicate not only our rights but also our values, progressives had lost too much faith in democracy," he wrote in *The Audacity of Hope.* Yes, he pointed out that he believed in the right to privacy and celebrated the legacy of *Brown* in civil rights, but it wasn't up to lawyers to preserve those rights. "There was one way to ensure that judges on the bench reflected our values, and that was to win at the polls." Unlike his honored forebearers, Obama would devote his life to elections, not lawsuits.

Almost as soon as the president and the other new executives were elected to their positions on the masthead of the *Review,* most of them turned their attention to obtaining judicial clerkships. Many sought opportunities with judges on the circuit courts of appeals who were known as "feeders" to Supreme Court clerkships. After Obama won the presidency, Abner Mikva, a former congressman from Chicago, who then served as a judge on the D.C. Circuit, sought him out as a clerk. Mikva was a feeder, and virtually all presidents of the *Harvard Law Review* went on to clerk on the Supreme Court. But Obama turned Mikva down. It was further proof that his interests lay outside the legal system.

Obama's election as president of the *Review* drew particular attention in his adopted hometown of Chicago, and an article in the *Sun-Times* piqued the interest of a local lawyer named Judson Miner. Miner belonged to the small cadre of left-leaning Chicago lawyers who had devoted their careers to fighting the Daley machine as well as race discrimination in its many permutations in the city. At the time, Miner, who is white, had returned to his small law firm after a stint as the top lawyer on the staff of Harold Washington, who was the city's first black mayor before his sudden death in 1987. On a whim, Miner called the *Review,* to try to speak with Obama. The receptionist corrected Miner's pronunciation of the name and told him, "You're 643rd on the list." But Obama called Miner back that day. (Miner's daughter garbled the message. "Some guy with a funny name called," she told him.)

Obama had lived in the Chicago political world long enough to know of Miner, even if he did not yet know him personally. Obama told Miner he was coming to town shortly and he would be delighted to take up Miner's invitation to meet. Obama was returning on a recruiting trip paid for by Sidley & Austin, one of the pillars of the legal establishment in the city. (Obama had worked there the previous summer and hadn't cared for the big-firm environment. Still, the summer was not a total loss, because he met an associate at the firm named Michelle Robinson, and in time they started a romance.) At this point, Obama was looking for a job after graduation, and he wanted to talk to Miner about joining his firm, then known as Davis, Miner, Barnhill & Galland. Miner's firm did the kind of civil rights and political work that interested Obama, and it offered a sufficiently flexible and informal structure that might allow him to do other things as well. Obama approached the subject in his usual methodical fashion—there were about six or seven lunches with Miner, with each man interviewing the other, in a way—but Obama finally agreed to sign on following his graduation. He was one of about a dozen lawyers.

Obama was never a conventional associate. Almost immediately, he took a leave from the firm work to run Project Vote, a voter registration drive designed to build turnout for the 1992 elections. A little while later, Obama took time off to finish the book that became *Dreams from My Father*. (It was long overdue to the publisher.) Miner brought Obama along in some civil rights cases, like a suit against Illinois to compel the state to comply with the motor voter law. There were also routine commercial disputes and a few criminal matters. Soon enough, Obama had another claim on his time. At the law review, Obama had edited an article by Michael McConnell, a conservative professor at the University of Chicago Law School. (George W. Bush later appointed McConnell to the Tenth Circuit.) McConnell was so impressed with Obama's work on the piece, which concerned freedom of religion, that he suggested that the head of the appointments committee at the law school should take a look at Obama.

Obama told Douglas Baird, the chair of the committee, that he wasn't interested in a tenure-track job. But the University of Chicago was so eager to have Obama on campus that the law school offered him an office and a fellowship to work on his book. Two years later, in 1993, Obama started teaching law students. Because he was effectively an adjunct professor, he was given the title of lecturer, and he continued teaching a class every semester for about a decade. Obama was an elusive presence on the Hyde Park campus; he tended to teach his classes and leave. He was not expected to do scholarly work—writing law review articles and the like—and he didn't attend faculty meetings.

The University of Chicago long enjoyed a reputation for conservatism, especially in economics, and that was somewhat true at the law school as well. Richard Posner and Frank Easterbrook were two celebrated conservatives who were appointed to the federal bench by President Reagan and kept their ties to the law school. During Obama's time, there was a substantial core of liberals on the faculty too, notably Diane Wood and Elena Kagan. Obama's relations with all factions were the same: friendly but distant.

To the extent Obama had an academic specialty, it was voting rights—not surprising, given his interest in politics and his experience in the voter registration field. In the midnineties, Obama heard that a group of professors including Richard Pildes, then of the University of Michigan Law School, were preparing a casebook on what they called the law of democracy. Obama sought out Pildes, obtained a draft of the book, and used it to teach his class. The two men struck up a friendship based on their shared interest in what was then a fairly obscure field. (After *Bush v. Gore* in 2000, the law of elections drew more public and scholarly attention.)

The hot subject in voting rights at the Supreme Court, and in the academy, was racial gerrymandering. The Voting Rights Act of 1965, and its subsequent reauthorizations, forced states to draw their district lines so that African Americans would be positioned to win certain seats, both in Congress and in state legislatures. Most traditional civil rights groups, and black politicians, made a sacred cause of the creation of these so-called majority-minority districts. To them, this was the core purpose of the Voting Rights Act: to get more blacks elected to public office.

Obama was skeptical. After the census of 1990, Republicans, especially in the South, recognized that they could make the Voting Rights Act work for them, too. So GOP strategists joined with some black Democrats in creating overwhelmingly minority districts. As a result, black politicians won seats in several states where they had not won races since Reconstruction. At the same time these new districts drained Democratic votes from other districts—making them ripe targets for Republicans. A few black politicians gained sinecures, but the Democratic Party suffered. Indeed, the Republican takeover of the House of Representatives in 1994 came about in part because of losses by moderate Democrats in the South whose districts had been denuded of African American voters.

To Obama, the civil rights groups had it wrong on voting rights. Of course, Obama had no objections to blacks winning elections, but such victories alone were just symbols. He thought the point of politics was actually to accomplish something—to vindicate democratic (and Democratic) values by passing laws. If black politicians just hoarded Democratic voters to stay in office, they'd never get anything done once they were there. Without coalition building, Obama told Pildes, the progressive cause was doomed.

Five years after graduating from law school, in 1996, Obama began his political career by winning a seat in the state senate. Like most other Illinois legislators, Obama worked part-time for the state, and he kept up his association with Miner's firm and still taught a class every semester at the law school. At least initially, the Springfield post proved to be a disappointment to Obama. As a junior Democrat in a body run by Republicans, he had almost no power. He quickly started looking for an exit strategy. In 1999, Obama decided to challenge Bobby Rush, an incumbent congressman, in a Democratic primary. The Chicago district was exactly the kind of racial gerrymander that Obama abhorred—and Rush was the kind of candidate who tended to do well in that kind of district. A former Black Panther, Rush had authenticity in abundance but little in the way of accomplishments. Still, the Democratic establishment (including President Bill Clinton) backed the incumbent, and Obama was humiliated in the 2000 primary, losing 61 percent to 30 percent.

The defeat took Obama to a personal and professional crossroads. He thought seriously (with encouragement from his wife) about dropping out of politics altogether. A job as president of a local foundation beckoned. Instead, Obama decided to dedicate himself, for the first time, to his work as a legislator. Court-ordered social change still held little allure for him, as he made clear in a 2001 interview on local Chicago public radio. Many liberals tried for years to persuade the Supreme Court to step beyond desegregation orders and direct that public schools be funded equally. Obama explained why he believed that approach had failed, citing the 1973 case of *San Antonio Independent School District v. Rodriguez*. In *Rodriguez*, the Court found, by a 5–4 vote, that unequal funding of school districts in the same state did not amount to a violation of the equal protection clause of the Fourteenth Amendment. As Obama described the decision, the Court "basically slaps those kinds of claims down and says, 'You know what—we as a court have no power to examine issues of redistribution and wealth inequalities with respect to schools. That's not a race issue, that's a wealth issue, and something we can't get into.'" The Court said that it was up to legislatures, not courts, to make judgments about redistribution of wealth—which was fine with Obama. "Maybe I am showing my bias here as a legislator as well as a law professor," he went on, but "the institution just isn't structured that way."

This was an Obama credo of sorts. To him, the courts were (or should be) static in their protection of basic rights, but he was not going to push judges and justices to create new ones. In this way, Obama differed from both liberal heroes like Thurgood Marshall and conservative icons like Antonin Scalia; they believed that the courts could deliver social change. Obama did not, and this diffidence about the role of the courts shaped his professional life and, later, his presidency.

After Obama's defeat in the 2000 congressional race, his fortunes turned around. Just as he started paying more attention to the job in Springfield, the Democrats took control of the state senate in 2002, so he had the chance to accomplish something. He sponsored or cosponsored twenty-six successful bills in a row, including tax cuts for the lower middle class, health care for poor children, a ban on the diet supplement ephedra, and a careful compromise on racial profiling by the police. (The bill required police to record and report the race of every motorist who was stopped.) Obama decided to run for an open U.S. Senate seat in 2004. His good fortune multiplied. The candidacy of his leading opponent in the Democratic primary imploded in a sex scandal—and, incredibly, the candidacy of the Republican initially nominated to face him *also* ended in a sex scandal. He wound up facing only nominal opposition in the general election. Even though Obama was still just a state senator, he gave the keynote speech at the Democratic Convention in 2004—and it was a smash. His memoir was reissued and became a best seller.

By the time Obama arrived in Washington in 2005, he was a

national figure—but on his own terms. He was, of course, the only African American senator at that moment, but he went out of his way to define himself in other ways. He joined the Committee on Foreign Relations, not the Judiciary Committee, which is the principal guardian of the civil rights laws and a seat the only black senator might have been expected to take. Obama dabbled in legislating, but basically used his Senate office to prepare to run for president. He wrote a campaign-style manifesto, *The Audacity of Hope*, and turned a book tour into a testing-the-waters campaign. (The title of the book came from a sermon by his preacher in Chicago, Rev. Jeremiah Wright Jr.)

As Obama began playing to a statewide and then a national audience, he made some adjustments in his stands on the issues, notably gun control. When he was running for the state senate in Chicago, he took the conventional view of inner-city politicians that gun ownership should be sharply limited. In his first race for state senate he even said in a questionnaire that he supported "restrictions on the sale and possession of handguns." (Obama later said a staffer filled out the form.) Still, in the state legislature, Obama continued to vote in general support of restrictions on gun use and ownership.

But when he ran for the U.S. Senate in Illinois, a state with a thriving hunting culture, Obama began subtly turning away from his previous position. Like many Democrats nationwide in the post-Clinton era, Obama recognized that to push gun control was to court electoral disaster; the laws would never pass and the candidates who supported them would never win. Still, Obama had not at this point migrated entirely to the individual rights views of the Second Amendment. When Alan Keyes, the hapless Republican who wound up running against Obama in the 2004 Illinois Senate race, challenged Obama in a debate on his beliefs about the Second Amendment, Obama steered the conversation in a different direction. Obama said nothing about the Constitution but only that he believed in "common sense gun safety" measures like a ban on assault weapons.

But conservatives had succeeded on gun control and the Second Amendment in the new millennium the way liberals had won on school desegregation and equal protection in the 1960s. Through the use of politics, the courts, and the broader culture, each side in turn had changed the understanding of the Constitution. In both cases, the political victories were so overwhelming that opposition became futile.

By the 1970s, no serious politician advocated segregated schools; by 2008, no serious presidential candidate—at least one who hoped to win—advocated the traditional conception of the Second Amendment.

So, after Obama launched his presidential campaign in 2007, he began speaking out in support of an individual right under the Second Amendment. The mode of Obama's expression, which he repeated throughout the campaign, revealed the nature of the conservative ideological victory on this issue. As Obama put it in a debate with Hillary Clinton before the Pennsylvania primary, "As a general principle, I believe that the Constitution confers an individual right to bear arms. But just because you have an individual right does not mean that the state or local government can't constrain the exercise of that right, in the same way that we have a right to private property but local governments can establish zoning ordinances that determine how you can use it." It was, characteristically for Obama, a cautious position, but still an unmistakable endorsement of the individual rights theory. The future president picked his fights—and chose to avoid this one over the Constitution. It wouldn't be the last time, either.

"ON BEHALF OF THE STRONG IN OPPOSITION TO THE WEAK"

On gun control, Obama played to his instinct for compromise and conciliation. Politics often lends itself to these sorts of solutions. But sometimes a senator, like a justice, simply has to make a decision. On one of these occasions, during his brief career in the United States Senate, Obama had a real struggle: the nomination of John Roberts to be chief justice of the United States.

Obama and Roberts had met only once, in the fall of 2005. Roberts had already called on most of the senators when he finally made it to Suite 713 in the Hart Building, the remote lodging to which junior senators like Obama were assigned. Roberts was exceptionally good at these courtesy calls: knowledgeable but not arrogant, open but noncommittal. As far as Obama was concerned, the judge had a lot going for him. Obama valued credentials, and Roberts had the best of their shared generation, not least a Harvard Law degree. For his part, Roberts had the same instincts about Obama. Judicial candidates making the rounds of senators quickly suss out the gasbags from the players, and there was no doubt in Roberts's mind of the future president's intelligence.

In the end, Obama's vote on Roberts had little to do with the nominee's qualifications, or even Obama's feelings about him. The senator consulted some of his law professor friends, like Laurence Tribe, at Harvard, and they told him that Roberts was about as good as anyone could expect from the Bush administration. The judge was conservative, Tribe said, but perhaps he'd keep an open mind. But the advice that mattered most to Obama came from his own chief of staff, Pete Rouse, a Washington veteran. Rouse told Obama, in effect: *Cut the shit. You can't run for the Democratic nomination for president and also vote to confirm George Bush's nominee for chief justice. The Democrats who vote in primaries care too much about these issues—like abortion rights—for you to vote for a justice who might overturn* Roe v. Wade. Obama couldn't disagree.

So Obama voted no, one of only twenty-two negative votes. (Obama's future rival Hillary Clinton voted the same way.) Still, Obama's statement on the Senate floor reflected his ambivalence on the nomination. "There is absolutely no doubt in my mind Judge Roberts is qualified to sit on the highest court in the land," Obama said. "Moreover, he seems to have the comportment and the temperament that makes for a good judge. He is humble, he is personally decent, and he appears to be respectful of different points of view. It is absolutely clear to me that Judge Roberts truly loves the law." Exaggerating slightly, Obama said 95 percent of cases at the Supreme Court were easy; "a Scalia and a Ginsburg will arrive at the same place most of the time." (About a third of cases are unanimous each year.)

Obama went on: "What matters on the Supreme Court is those 5 percent of cases that are truly difficult. In those cases, adherence to precedent and rules of construction and interpretation will only get you through the 25th mile of the marathon. That last mile can only be determined on the basis of one's deepest values, one's core concerns, one's broader perspectives on how the world works, and the depth and breadth of one's empathy. . . . In those difficult cases, the critical ingredient is supplied by what is in the judge's heart.

"I talked to Judge Roberts about this. Judge Roberts confessed that, unlike maybe professional politicians, it is not easy for him to talk about his values and his deeper feelings. That is not how he is trained. He did say he doesn't like bullies and has always viewed the law as a way of evening out the playing field between the strong and the weak."

But that wasn't enough for Obama. "The problem I had is that when I examined Judge Roberts's record and history of public service, it is my personal estimation that he has far more often used his formidable skills on behalf of the strong in opposition to the weak. In his work in the White House and the Solicitor General's Office, he seemed to have consistently sided with those who were dismissive of efforts to eradicate the remnants of racial discrimination in our political process. In these same positions, he seemed dismissive of the concerns that it is harder to make it in this world and in this economy when you are a woman rather than a man."

Quickly, though, right after Obama voted no, he engaged in a characteristic gesture. The very next day, Obama posted a statement on DailyKos, the website that served as the unofficial home of the Democratic Party's Netroots, defending his colleagues who voted yes. The point Obama made was a familiar one for those who had followed his thinking about the courts. "There is one way, over the long haul, to guarantee the appointment of judges that are sensitive to issues of social justice, and that is to win the right to appoint them by recapturing the presidency and the Senate," Obama wrote. "And I don't believe we get there by vilifying good allies, with a lifetime record of battling for progressive causes, over one vote or position. I am convinced that, our mutual frustrations and strongly held beliefs notwithstanding, the strategy driving much of Democratic advocacy, and the tone of much of our rhetoric, is an impediment to creating a workable progressive majority in this country." As usual with Obama, it was about elections, not lawsuits.

Four months later, when Alito came up for a vote, that was an easier call for Obama, and for most other Democrats. Alito had little of Roberts's charm, and his record on the bench offered no promise of moderation. Like Roberts, Alito had been a young recruit to the Justice Department during the Reagan administration, first in the office of the solicitor general and then in the office of legal counsel. He was appointed United States attorney in his native New Jersey in 1987 and then three years later, at the age of forty, won appointment to the Third Circuit. There he never varied from the conservative line and made a particular name for himself as an opponent of abortion rights. Shortly after Alito joined the Third Circuit, he voted to uphold a Pennsylvania law that required wives to inform their husbands before they obtained an abortion. It was this provision in particular that offended O'Connor and prompted her vote to overturn the law in the famous *Planned Parenthood v. Casey* decision of 1992, the ruling that preserved the core of *Roe v. Wade*. For this reason, Alito was an especially fitting replacement for O'Connor—because he reflected how much the Republican Party had changed since her appointment. From the moment Bush named Alito, it was clear what kind of justice he would be. For this reason, Obama voted no, but Alito was confirmed by 58 to 42.

Obama's intelligence was tempered by a grace and serenity, but he was matched in these qualities by the new chief justice. From his earliest days, Roberts was an enormously successful student who excelled without calling a great deal of attention to himself. He had taken enough advanced placement tests at La Lumiere to skip his freshman year at Harvard, and it took him only three years to graduate summa cum laude. Three years later, in 1979, he earned his degree from Harvard Law. But Roberts's professional career was about ideology as much as brilliance and charm. At every step, Roberts's work mirrored, and hastened, the conservative movement in the law.

Roberts's two judicial clerkships traced the trajectory of the Republican Party at large. Henry Friendly was appointed to the Second Circuit by Dwight Eisenhower, in 1959. Friendly and his circle of lawyers were based in New York, and many received their start in law, and politics, when they worked for Thomas E. Dewey, the crusading local prosecutor and governor who nearly won the presidency in 1948. They were close to Wall Street and big business—Friendly had been general counsel to Pan American World Airways—and they took a progressive attitude toward the racial struggles that were convulsing the country. On the Supreme Court, this group was represented by John Marshall Harlan II, a frequent dissenter during the liberal heyday of the Warren Court. Friendly believed in respect for precedent, gradual change, and almost scientific expertise in the law. Friendly was as far from a Scalia-style conservative as he was different from a Brennan-style liberal. The politics of Friendly's law clerks ran the ideological gamut.

On the other hand, Rehnquist stood on the rightward fringe of the Court in 1980, when Roberts joined him. Rehnquist came of age politically as a westerner, an Arizonan, and he had little in common with the gradualism of northeastern Republicans like Friendly. Rehnquist was skeptical of government efforts to promote civil rights and downright hostile to the Court's effort to broaden individual rights. (In his second year on the Court, Rehnquist was one of only two dissenters in *Roe v. Wade*. Byron White, who was appointed by John F. Kennedy, was the other.) Rehnquist's ideology never changed, and it left a deep impression on Roberts.

Years later, Roberts gave a speech about Rehnquist that illustrated as much about Roberts as about his mentor. "When Justice Rehnquist came onto the Court, I think it's fair to say that the practice of constitutional law—how constitutional law was made—was more fluid and wide-ranging than it is today, more in the realm of political science," Roberts said. "Now, over Justice Rehnquist's time on the Court, the method of analysis and argument shifted to the more solid grounds of legal arguments—what are the texts of the statutes involved, what precedents control. Rehnquist, a student both of political science and the law, was significantly responsible for that seismic shift."

At the time Rehnquist joined the Court, its liberals had reigned for two decades. Through the Warren and even the Burger years the justices expanded civil rights protections for minorities, established new barriers between church and state, encouraged civil litigation to challenge business and government practices, and, of course, recognized a constitutional right to abortion for women. This "fluid and wide-ranging" jurisprudence, in Roberts's contemptuous phrase, had become the new status quo at the Supreme Court. In Roberts's telling, Rehnquist had been responsible for a "seismic shift" away from these liberal excesses, but that wasn't precisely accurate. Most of the Warren Court precedents were still on the books; there had been no seismic shift—yet. It was Roberts's mission to lead the counterrevolution that his mentor had begun.

In the middle of Roberts's clerkship, Ronald Reagan was elected president. "I was trying to decide what to do next," Roberts later recalled in a speech at the Reagan Library. "Then he spoke these words and, like so many of the president's words, I felt he was speaking directly to me. He said, 'I do not believe in a fate that will befall us no matter what we do; I do believe in a fate that will fall on us if we do nothing.' And that is what Ronald Reagan was and is and remains today to me: a call to action." Roberts put off more lucrative options and joined the new administration, first as an assistant to William French Smith, the attorney general, and then in the White House counsel's office. In his speech, Roberts recalled his first day of work at the White House. "Could I hold for the President? Well, yes, I could. This was an example of the President's famous charm, with all he had to do, calling a new staffer on his first day to wish him well. I did, I think, what most people do when they get a call from the President at their desk: I stood up. A few minutes went by, but of course that's understandable, he's the President, he's probably finishing up a call with Brezhnev or something. A few more minutes went by . . . I sat down. I figured that I'd stand up when the President came on the line . . . A few more minutes went by. Then I heard the muffled laughter outside my door . . . I put the phone down and went to the little anteroom. In there, of course, were my new colleagues in the White House Counsel's office, who had placed the phony call from the President. They had a betting pool how long I would stay on hold . . . Whoever had the 15- to 20-minute slot won that money."

Roberts was not a policy maker, of course, but his memos from that era reveal a self-assured and loyal member of the Reagan team. He referred in one memo to Smith to an article that mentioned the "so-called 'right to privacy,' arguing as we have that such an amorphous right is not to be found in the Constitution." For someone who was only twenty-seven when he joined the White House staff, Roberts wrote with unusual confidence. When a Democratic congressman proposed a conference on power sharing among the different branches of government and a report on the subject, Roberts dismissed the idea this way: "There already has, of course, been a 'Conference on Power Sharing.' It took place in Philadelphia's Constitution Hall in 1787, and someone should tell [Congressman] Levitas about it and the 'report' it issued." In the eighties, the Supreme Court was deciding as many as 150 cases a year, and the justices were laboring under the weight of the caseload. Warren Burger advocated a proposal to add a kind of super-appeals court above the circuit courts, to relieve the justices of some of their burdens. Roberts was not impressed with the idea, writing to his boss, the White House counsel: "While some of the tales of woe emanating from the Court are enough to bring tears to the eyes, it is true that only Supreme Court justices and schoolchildren are expected to and do take the entire summer off."

Roberts spent the last few years of the Reagan presidency beginning his career at Hogan & Hartson, but he returned to government at the start of the first Bush administration, when Kenneth Starr recruited him to be his deputy at the solicitor general's office. Starr had a genteel style as the government's principal advocate before the Supreme Court—he was nicknamed the Solicitous General—but the office took a series of strongly conservative stands on the merits. Again, Roberts was following administration policy, but he had no problem signing briefs that called for overruling *Roe v. Wade* and limiting traditional civil rights remedies. As was customary, Starr himself argued the most high-profile cases for the government in this period, but Roberts also became a regular presence before the justices. His earnest midwestern manner—matched, of course, by his keen intellect, sharp wit, and great memory—made him an immediate favorite of the justices. Roberts made such a powerful impression in the S.G.'s office that Bush nominated him for the D.C. Circuit in 1992, when he was only thirty-seven years old. The Democratic blockade of Roberts's nomination was a tribute of sorts as well. Both sides knew even then that he might well be destined for the Supreme Court. Roberts never received an up-or-down vote in the Senate, so he returned to private practice in 1993.

For much of the Court's history, cases were often argued by the lawyers who originally represented the clients in the lower courts. Lawyers in the solicitor general's office were almost the only Supreme Court specialists. But Roberts came of age at a time when Supreme Court advocacy became its own niche in the legal profession. Starting in the 1990s, a Supreme Court bar began to expand, and Roberts was the leading figure in his generation. In all, Roberts had thirty-nine arguments at the Court, and he won about twenty-five of them. (The number is not precise because some cases had mixed or inconclusive results.)

The professional background of a justice invariably shapes his or her approach to the job. Temperamentally, Rehnquist never left the Nixon Justice Department, where he was the assistant attorney general charged with building a tough-on-crime agenda; O'Connor, the former Arizona state senator, never stopped being a politician; Scalia and Stephen Breyer remained forever the law professors they once were. John Roberts was a litigator whose primary responsibility was to figure out ways to win. For Roberts, the law, ultimately, was all about winning.

The modern Republican Party put judicial issues near the top of its agenda. The priorities included the recognition of Second Amendment gun rights, the end of constitutional protection for the right to choose abortions, and the lowering of barriers between church and state. Democrats paid less attention to these issues, or the courts generally—as Obama himself demonstrated in his campaign.

Obama declared his candidacy for president on February 10, 2007, on the steps of the Old State Capitol, in Springfield, Illinois. The themes of his speech—hope, change, and an end to the war in Iraq—were central to his effort over the next twenty-one months. Through the many long days leading up to his victory in the Iowa caucuses, the four months of head-to-head combat with Hillary Clinton, and the general election campaign against John McCain, Obama limited his discussion of the Constitution to generalities. ("I believe in the Constitution, I've taught the Constitution, and I will obey the Constitution," he often said in his stump speeches.) Obama and Clinton differed on very little, including legal issues. Against McCain, Obama's message of change, which resonated even more strongly after the economic collapse, clearly seemed to be working. Obama's very existence, as the first African American to approach the presidency, said more about equality than any invocation of the Fourteenth Amendment. Still, it is at least worthy of note that Obama, who was, as he often mentioned, a law professor, managed to campaign for nearly two years without saying much of anything about the Supreme Court or the laws that it interpreted.

McCain took a different approach, at least once. Throughout his long political career, the Arizona senator had never shown a particular interest in legal issues; his signature causes were national security and campaign finance. But McCain felt obligated to express his fealty to the contemporary Republican vision about the Constitution. In a speech at Wake Forest University, in Winston-Salem, North Carolina, on May 6, 2008, he said, "The framers of our Constitution had a knack for coming right to the point, and it shows in the 35-word oath that ends with a pledge to preserve, protect, and defend the Constitution itself."

McCain had already clinched the Republican nomination, so he was in general election mode. He avoided direct mention of incendiary topics like abortion, and he spoke in a code familiar to those who follow constitutional law, leaving them in no doubt where he stood. He addressed what he called "the common and systematic abuse of our federal courts by the people we entrust with judicial power. For decades now, some federal judges have taken it upon themselves to pronounce and rule on matters that were never intended to be heard in courts or decided by judges." This, of course, was a view functionally identical to President Bush's often-expressed contempt for judges who "legislate from the bench." McCain then cited what he saw as an example of such abuse. "Sometimes the expressed will of the voters is disregarded by federal judges, as in a 2005 case concerning an aggravated murder in the state of Missouri," he said. "As you might recall, the case inspired a Supreme Court opinion that left posterity with a lengthy discourse on international law, the constitutions of other nations, the meaning of life, and 'evolving standards of decency.' These meditations were in the tradition of 'penumbras,' 'emanations,' and other airy constructs the Court has employed over the years as poor substitutes for clear and rigorous constitutional reasoning."

McCain did not reveal the subject matter of this supposed judicial outrage. The case was *Roper v. Simmons*, in which a seventeen-year-old boy was sentenced to death for murdering a woman after breaking into her home. Kennedy's 2005 opinion overturned the sentence and held that the Constitution forbade the death penalty for juvenile offenders. McCain's reference to the Court's "discourse" on the law of "other nations" referred to the justices' observation of the "stark reality that the United States is the only country in the world that continues to give official sanction to the juvenile death penalty." Likewise, Kennedy noted that the only other countries to execute juvenile offenders since 1990 were China, Congo, Iran, Nigeria, Pakistan, Saudi Arabia, and Yemen.

Nor were McCain's references to "penumbras" and "emanations" accidental. Those words came from Justice William O. Douglas's 1965 opinion for the Court in *Griswold v. Connecticut*, in which the justices recognized for the first time a constitutional right to privacy and ruled that a state could not deny married couples access to birth control. The "meaning of life" was a specific reference, too. It came from the Court's 1992 opinion in *Casey*, which reaffirmed the central holding of *Roe v. Wade* and forbade the states from banning abortion. In short, this one passage in McCain's speech amounted to a kind of dog whistle—a signal (to those who could hear it) that he would appoint justices who would eliminate the right to privacy, permit states to ban abortion, and allow the execution of teenagers.

Rather than challenge McCain or present an alternative vision for the courts, Obama chose to discuss only the subjects that had been working for him. When it came to the Constitution, it was clear that Obama's agenda was the opposite of change. In an interview with the *Detroit Free Press*, just one month before Election Day, he displayed characteristic caution. In the course of a single short answer, it was possible to watch Obama's mind in action. He was asked which justices would serve as models for his own Supreme Court appointments. "There were a lot of justices on the Warren Court who were heroes of mine, Warren himself, Brennan, [Thurgood] Marshall," Obama said, but then he appeared to realize that he might be endorsing an unduly liberal agenda, so he added: "But that doesn't necessarily mean that I think their judicial philosophy is appropriate for today."

Obama went on: "Generally, the court is institutionally conservative. And what I mean by that is, it's not that often that the court gets out way ahead of public opinion. The Warren Court was one of those moments when, because of the particular challenge of segregation, they needed to break out of conventional wisdom because the political process didn't give an avenue for minorities and African Americans to exercise their political power to solve their problems. So the court had to step in and break that logjam."

But times were different now, Obama said. "I'm not sure that you need that. In fact, I would be troubled if you had that same kind of activism in circumstances today. So when I think about the kinds of judges who are needed today, it goes back to the point I was making about common sense and pragmatism as opposed to ideology. I think that Justice Souter, who was a Republican appointee, Justice Breyer, a Democratic appointee, are very sensible judges." To some, this answer looked like political caution. Embracing Souter and Breyer, instead of Brennan and Marshall, was unlikely to cause offense or cost him votes. It is true that the answer was very, very careful—but it did accurately reflect Obama's temperament as well as his views about the Supreme Court. After Obama became president, some of his supporters urged him to nominate the kind of judges he "really" wanted—outspoken liberals. But that supposition misread the man. He "really" wanted judges like Souter and Breyer.

In that final month before Election Day, Obama had a clear lead in the polls and a final obstacle to overcome, the last of the three debates with McCain. Each campaign season, it was a tradition of sorts for the moderator to ask one question about abortion and Supreme Court appointments; on October 15, 2008, it fell to Bob Schieffer to raise the issue with the candidates.

McCain answered first, saying he would never impose a "litmus test" for his prospective appointments, but also making clear that he thought *Roe v. Wade* was "a bad decision."

Obama responded, "It is true that this is going to be, I think, one of the most consequential decisions of the next president. It is very likely that one of us will be making at least one and probably more than one appointments and Roe versus Wade probably hangs in the balance.

"Now I would not provide a litmus test, but I am somebody who believes that Roe versus Wade was rightly decided. I think that abortion is a very difficult issue, and it is a moral issue and one that I think good people on both sides can disagree on. But what ultimately I believe is that women in consultation with their families, their doctors, their religious advisers, are in the best position to make this decision. And I think that the Constitution has a right to privacy in it that shouldn't be subject to state referendum, any more than our First Amendment rights are subject to state referendum, any more than many of the other rights that we have should be subject to popular vote. So this is going to be an important issue. I will look for those judges who have an outstanding judicial record, who have the intellect, and who hopefully have a sense of what real-world folks are going through."

On November 4, 2008, Barack Obama was elected president, with 365 electoral votes. He received 69 million popular votes to McCain's 59 million, representing a margin of 53 percent to 46 percent. At the time of the election, the American economy was nearing free fall. The collapse of the bubble in housing prices had led to huge losses in financial firms that had sold securities based on mortgages. To prevent those firms from going out of business, Congress passed the Troubled Asset Relief Program (TARP), which Bush had signed on October 3, authorizing $700 billion in bailouts. The major banks survived, but business activity nearly ground to a halt. About 700,000 Americans per month were losing their jobs. Working from transition headquarters in a Chicago high-rise, Obama and his staffers spent most of their time figuring out how to address the crisis.

Still, the work of judicial selection, including for the Supreme Court, now moved from abstraction to reality. In August, after Obama had clinched the Democratic nomination, a lawyer in New York received a confidential assignment from the transition team, which was just then being formed. Preeta Bansal, who was then a partner at the law firm Skadden, Arps and formerly solicitor general of New York State, was asked to prepare a series of memorandums about how a President Obama might approach the federal judiciary. She projected the number of likely vacancies, examined the ethnic and professional backgrounds of current federal judges, and compiled the first list of possible nominees for the new president to consider. There were other issues, too. Should Obama announce his first nominations as a group, as Bush did, or one at a time? (Obama chose one at a time.) Should the new administration cooperate with the American Bar Association, which had traditionally rated nominees but which had been pushed out of the process by recent Republican administrations? (Obama's team decided to reestablish the connection, but only after securing a pledge from the ABA that the group would act quickly.)

As Obama himself now recognized, there was no longer time for abstract discussions—or even intentional evasions—on the subject of the Supreme Court. About a week after the election, while the group was still working in Chicago, Obama summoned Gregory Craig, the future White House counsel, and David Axelrod, his top political aide, to discuss judicial nominations for the first time.

"It looks like we might have a Supreme Court appointment soon, so we need to be ready," Obama told them. "I have a list."

THE ERA OF GOOD FEELINGS

The transition at the Supreme Court from William Rehnquist to John Roberts was not as dramatic as the one at the White House from George W. Bush to Barack Obama. In the stillness of the Court's marble halls, though, any change seemed dramatic. Everyone on the Court was fond of quoting a remark by Byron White, who had served for more than thirty years: "When you change one justice, you change the whole Court." As of early 2006, after no changes in membership for more than a decade, there were suddenly two new justices, including a new chief, in the space of four months.

To compound the sense of disorientation for the justices, the Supreme Court building was in the midst of a major renovation project. The building had opened in 1935, and there had never been a full update of its major systems. Rehnquist had begun studies for the project in the late nineties, and then, after September 11, 2001, the plans had to be reconfigured to accommodate the new emphasis on security. Ground was broken in 2003, and by the following year the justices were taking turns being thrown out of their offices, and into temporary quarters, for several months at a time.

When Roberts and Alito joined the Court, the remaining justices were all middle-aged or older. The youngest was Thomas, at fifty-seven, and Souter was next, at sixty-six. Scalia, Kennedy, Ginsburg, and Breyer were all in or soon to be in their seventies. Stevens was the oldest, at eighty-five. Like most other people in their cohort, the justices did not take easily to change—in colleagues or in lodgings. Under Rehnquist, they all won some cases and lost some, but they knew where they stood, with the chief and with each other. There are few more isolating jobs than justice of the Supreme Court. The telephones rarely ring in their chambers. Year after year, the justices have no one to talk to about the most important aspects of their work except one another and their law clerks. The stakes for any change were high.

Roberts understood this and asserted his authority with some finesse. During his confirmation hearing, Roberts said he hoped the Court could speak more often with a single voice—in unanimous opinions. In his first year, the whole Court pulled together in helping Roberts achieve this goal. During the Rehnquist years, the justices had reached unanimous rulings in about a third of all cases. During Roberts's first year, that percentage ticked up to about 45 percent.

Roberts provided a snapshot of his personality early in his first term, on October 31, 2005. *Central Virginia Community College v. Katz* concerned a fairly obscure issue in bankruptcy law. Toward the end of the argument, as Ginsburg was asking a question, what sounded like an explosion went off in the courtroom. The police officers reached for their sidearms.

"A lightbulb exploded," O'Connor said. "A lightbulb exploded."

As everyone resumed their focus, Roberts quipped, "It's a trick they play on new chief justices all the time." No one laughed harder than O'Connor.

There was really only one important case on the docket during Roberts's first full year—and the chief could not participate in it. It was the appeal of *Hamdan v. Rumsfeld*, the case that helped seal Roberts's nomination to the Court. (At the very moment that Bush was weighing whom to appoint, Roberts joined the decision in the D.C. Circuit in Bush's favor.) Because Roberts had already ruled on the case, he recused himself from playing a part in the Supreme Court's deliberations. Eight justices would render the next verdict on the Bush administration's treatment of the detainees at Guantánamo Bay.

The case illustrated how the politics of the country affected the justices—both in the cases before them and in the conclusions they reached. *Hamdan* itself had begun in the unlikeliest of ways. After 9/11, and the Bush administration's decision to open the facility at Guantánamo, the legal concerns of the detainees there were hardly a mainstream issue. The Pentagon assigned a handful of military lawyers to represent the prisoners, but these unlucky counselors had few resources and little support. Then in May 2003, Air Force Lt. Col. Will Gunn, the chief defense counsel for the tribunals, received an unsolicited e-mail from Neal Katyal, a thirty-three-year-old professor at Georgetown University Law Center and a former Breyer clerk. "I hope this e-mail reaches you, as I've tried to find your contact info from a variety of different sources," Katyal wrote. "I'm writing, in the event that you do lead the defense team at the military tribunals, to offer my help." Lacking any better offers, Gunn invited Katyal to work with Charlie Swift and Philip Sundel, the navy JAGs who would be handling the first cases.

It was a deeply unfashionable undertaking. Only a year and a half had passed since the terrorist attacks. The war in Iraq had just begun, and it enjoyed tremendous public support. Only the Center for Constitutional Rights, a stalwart of the left, had raised loud and consistent objections to the Bush administration's legal basis for the war on terror. The big law firms and major law schools were mostly silent. Even so, the first legal challenges to the detention policies began working their way through the courts. The administration had argued that the facility at Guantánamo, which was on Cuban soil, should be treated like a foreign battlefield; accordingly, the courts shouldn't be ordering American troops to help with the defense in such dangerous conditions.

The Guantánamo cases, known as *Hamdi* and *Padilla*, came before the Court for oral argument on April 28, 2004, and Ginsburg pressed the Bush lawyers about the logical extension of their arguments. If the Guantánamo detainees were outside the reach of the American legal system, she asked, were there any legal limits on how they could be treated? Could they be tortured? "Suppose the executive says, 'Mild torture, we think, will help get this information.' It's not a soldier who does something against the Code of Military Justice, but it's an executive command. Some systems do that to get information."

"Well," Paul Clement, the deputy solicitor general replied, "our executive doesn't."

That very night, CBS News's *60 Minutes II* broadcast the first photographs of the treatment of Iraqi prisoners at Abu Ghraib. The photographs, which showed extensive abuse by American soldiers, created a national scandal. By that point, too, a year after the invasion, the war had settled into a bloody stalemate. In all, the political tide was turning against the war, and in June 2004 the justices issued their first rulings against the Bush policies. Stevens, in his opinion for the Court, made short work of the argument that Guantánamo was like a battlefield. The American military "exercises exclusive jurisdiction and control" over the base, he wrote; Donald Rumsfeld, the secretary of defense, sent these dangerous prisoners to such a remote location precisely because it was so secure from outside interference. O'Connor, a reliable vector for public opinion, was even more contemptuous of the Bush administration's position: "We have long since made clear that a state of war is not a blank check for the President when it comes to the rights of the Nation's citizens."

By the time Katyal argued the *Hamdan* case before the eight sitting justices on March 28, 2006, the Iraq War had deteriorated further and the political climate surrounding the issue of Guantánamo had been transformed. In *Hamdi*, the Court had rejected the notion that the detainees were not entitled to any due process at all. In response to that initial defeat at the Court, the Bush administration had set up a system of military commissions that gave the detainees the right to a kind of truncated trial. The *Hamdan* case was a challenge to the adequacy of these hearings.

The case served also as a useful introduction to the Roberts Supreme Court. Scalia, Thomas, and Alito were sure votes to uphold the president's policy and Roberts's ruling in the D.C. Circuit. Stevens, Souter, Ginsburg, and Breyer, on the other hand, would definitely vote to strike down the new rules. In this case—and so many that followed—the verdict would be rendered by Anthony Kennedy.

Kennedy was weeks away from turning seventy years old. He was Ronald Reagan's third choice to fill the seat vacated by Lewis Powell in 1987. (Bork had been voted down by the Senate, 58 to 42, and Douglas Ginsburg, a judge on the D.C. Circuit, had withdrawn following news reports that he had smoked marijuana as a young law professor at Harvard.) Since his appointment, Kennedy's hair had receded and whitened, but in all other respects he had thrived on the Court. Age had not withered his sinewy six-foot frame. When Kennedy began to speak, he often hesitated, almost stuttered, in what appeared to be an attempt to show humility, but he invariably found the right cruising speed, especially in front of an audience. He spoke (as he wrote) in grand and vague phrases—about "the poetry of the law," "the defense of liberty," and "dignity," his favorite word. To anyone who asked, Kennedy insisted that he did not enjoy his role as the crucial vote on the Court. Few believed him.

All the justices (except Souter and, in recent years, Stevens) traveled the world. It was one of the perks of a job that paid considerably less than their law clerks made as soon as they entered private practice. (The chief justice makes $223,500, the associate justices $213,900.) They all received multiple invitations to attend conferences or do some light teaching all over the world. Thomas enjoyed the New York University villa in Italy. Scalia and Ginsburg traded reviews of opera festivals in Europe. Breyer visited his wife's family in England and friends in France. (He speaks fluent French.) Roberts himself was teaching in London when Bush nominated him for the Court.

Few justices reveled in the international scene as much as Kennedy. There was some irony in this distinction because Kennedy appeared to be, at the time of his appointment, the most provincial of men. He grew up in Sacramento and still lived in the house where he was raised. He had gone to Stanford, then to Harvard Law School, but soon returned to his hometown to take over his father's firm and teach part-time at the local law school, McGeorge.

In fact, during all those years, Kennedy nursed a considerable wanderlust. When he was still a teenager, his uncle, an oil driller, hired him to work on rigs in Louisiana and Canada. While he was in college, he studied for several months at the London School of Economics. (Later, he would recall with affection how much the range of student views differed from those at home. "You had to sit in the room according to your place on the ideological spectrum, and, to give you an idea of what it was like, the Communists—the Communists!—were in the middle!") His father's law practice focused heavily on lobbying California state government, especially for the liquor industry. But when young Tony joined the family firm he took it in a more cosmopolitan direction; for instance, he helped create the legal basis for American companies to open factories, known as maquiladoras, in Mexico. In the small world of Sacramento, Tony Kennedy was also a presence in Republican politics and an ally of Edwin Meese, who became a top aide to Governor Ronald Reagan.

Kennedy's scholarly bent, and Republican connections, led Gerald Ford to appoint him to the Ninth Circuit in 1975. (Kennedy was only thirty-nine.) He kept his chambers in Sacramento and could have contented himself, as many circuit judges do, with a life of reading briefs and writing opinions. He wouldn't have had to travel farther than the Ninth Circuit's headquarters in San Francisco. But Kennedy took an assignment from Chief Justice Warren Burger to supervise the territorial courts in the South Pacific, which meant that the young judge had to travel to Guam, Palau, Saipan, American Samoa, Australia, New Zealand, and Japan. Despite his heavy schedule, Kennedy kept teaching at McGeorge, which had set up a summer program in Salzburg, Austria. Starting in 1990, Kennedy would spend about a month there every summer.

These years were a crucial time in the history of international judiciary. The fall of Communism in the Soviet Union and Eastern Europe set off a flurry of constitution writing and the appointment of judges to enforce the laws. American Supreme Court justices were coveted participants in the process, and no one relished the opportunities more than Kennedy. (O'Connor did a lot of work in this area, too.) Salzburg in particular became a critical crossroads in this process, with much of the action taking place at the Schloss Leopoldskron, a former palace that was used as a set in several scenes of *The Sound of Music*. The schloss was the headquarters of the Salzburg Seminar, a venerable international exchange program.

Kennedy spent his summers in the company of judges from around the world, who came to tap his expertise and enthusiasm. But the influence went two ways. Kennedy was and remained a conservative on most subjects, but the issues on which he moved left invariably coincided with the views of the foreign judges he met. In Europe and most of the civilized world, for example, the death penalty is viewed with revulsion. (Even to be considered for membership in the European Union, a country must abolish the death penalty.) Gay rights and even same-sex marriage have made progress faster in Europe than in the United States. By the time he reached the Supreme Court, Kennedy was well to the left of his near contemporary Scalia on the death penalty and gay rights.

Foreign judges also embraced international institutions and international law with far greater enthusiasm than their American counterparts. As McCain noted in his Wake Forest speech, Kennedy earned the enmity of American conservatives by citing the laws of other nations in his opinion in *Roper v. Simmons*, which struck down the death penalty for juveniles. By 2005, the international judicial elites viewed George

W. Bush with special disdain, abhorring the Texas swagger that produced, among other things, the Iraq War. As Kennedy knew better than most, judges around the world held a special reverence for the Geneva Conventions, which attempt to regulate the treatment of prisoners in wartime. And the Geneva Conventions were at the heart of *Hamdan v. Rumsfeld*.

In Hamdan's case before the Supreme Court, a key issue was whether the American government was required to treat the detainees in accord with the Geneva Conventions. Paul Clement, who had been promoted to solicitor general, said in the oral argument, "I don't think he's protected by the Geneva Conventions, but that's largely because he chose not to comply with the basic laws of war." In public and private, the Bush administration had described the detainees not as soldiers but as terrorists.

Souter pressed Clement on the conventions. "Well, do you agree that it applies as part of the law of war?" he asked.

"Well, I don't think, consistent with the position of the executive, that the Geneva Convention applies in this particular conflict," Clement answered.

"But that, I guess, is the problem that I'm having," Souter replied.

Making his first argument before the justices in *Hamdan*, Neal Katyal insisted the government had to prove that its procedures complied with the Geneva Conventions. He clearly impressed Kennedy, who played his words back to Clement, saying, "He says there is a structural invalidity to the military commission. . . . And the historic office of habeas"—a legal action asking to free a wrongfully imprisoned individual—"is to test whether or not you are being tried by a lawful tribunal. And he says, under the Geneva Convention, as you know, that it isn't."

"Well, and we disagree with those claims," Clement replied.

A 4–4 vote would have affirmed Roberts's judgment on the D.C. Circuit, but Kennedy voted with the liberals, and the military commissions were struck down. Stevens wrote the opinion for the Court and, with characteristic directness, stated that the United States must comply with the Geneva Conventions and, accordingly, the law "requires that Hamdan be tried by a regularly constituted court affording all the judicial guarantees which are recognized as indispensable by civilized peoples." Kennedy wrote a concurring opinion that was, in his fashion, more expansive: "Respect for laws derived from the customary operation of the Executive and Legislative Branches gives some assurance of stability in time of crisis. The Constitution is best preserved by reliance on standards tested over time and insulated from the pressures of the moment." Either way, the point was the same—another clear rebuke to the Bush administration's methods of conducting war on terror.

With the exception of *Hamdan*, Roberts's first year was generally a quiet one. As a rule, most of the eighty or so cases a year heard by the Supreme Court attract little attention from the general public. They involve the interpretation of federal statutes, the criminal sentencing practices of the federal courts, or disagreements between circuit courts on any number of issues. There are always several tax cases, a few bankruptcy matters, and a case or two involving the unique legal status of Native Americans. Among law clerks (and occasionally among justices), these low-profile controversies are known, uncharitably, as "dogs."

Sometimes, though, there are cases that are so powerfully obscure, so utterly insignificant while at the same time so maddeningly complex, that the justices (and certainly their clerks) stare at the briefs and wonder—what were we thinking? Why? *Why?* Holding the briefs at some distance, like a mysterious discovery from the back of the refrigerator, the denizens of One First Street, steeling themselves against boredom and fatigue, begin reading.

One such dog—a veritable Great Dane—hit the Court's docket toward the end of Roberts's first year. Each petitioner for certiorari to the Court includes a section called Questions Presented, which the lawyers use to define the issues in a way that will entice the justices to accept the case for review. In this one, the questions were:

1. What is the scope of the probate exception to federal jurisdiction?
2. Did Congress intend the probate exception to apply where a federal court is not asked to probate a will, administer an estate, or otherwise assume control of property in the custody of a state probate court?

The *what* exception? The stupefying dullness of these questions, and of the case as a whole, was apparent to all, and the matter of *Marshall v. Marshall* would have passed into obscurity but for one thing. The legal name of the plaintiff may have been Vickie Lynn Marshall, but she was better known by her stage name—Anna Nicole Smith.

It later became a kind of sport among the law clerks to speculate whether any of their bosses had heard of Anna Nicole before the briefs in the case first crossed their desks. The consensus (for all nine) was no. Her renown, such as it was, appeared so far on the cheesy end of the celebrity spectrum that it was indeed possible that her name did not ring a bell. Breyer cheerfully acknowledged to his clerks that he had never heard of her, but he also enjoyed a good laugh more than most of his colleagues, so he started referring to her, and her case, as "the stripper."

This was not precisely accurate. Her name at birth was Vickie Lynn Hogan, and she was the second child born to her sixteen-year-old mother. At the age of nineteen, with a child of her own, she became an exotic dancer (not a stripper, exactly) in one of Houston's lesser clubs. To add to her appeal, according to a biographer, she had several rounds of plastic surgery "to create her infamous 42DD bra size, the product finally of two implants on each side and a total of three pints of fluid." She also began using the name Anna Nicole Smith.

One day a man in a wheelchair named J. Howard Marshall II stopped in to watch her at a place called Gigi's. Many years earlier, Marshall had been a professor at Yale Law School, where he had cowritten scholarly articles with his faculty colleague William O. Douglas. Marshall left academia for the oil business and became an early investor in the company later known as Koch Industries (which would later have its own place in Supreme Court history). At the time he was wheeled into Gigi's, Marshall was worth as much as $1.6 billion.

The first time they met, Marshall and Anna Nicole spent the night together, and they married two years later, on June 27, 1994. Marshall was eighty-nine, and Anna Nicole twenty-six. He died thirteen months later, on August 4, 1995. In the meantime, Anna Nicole had become famous as a model and an actress of sorts as well as the subject of an early reality television series.

Marshall did not mention Anna Nicole in his will, and he left virtually his entire fortune to his son E. Pierce Marshall. (Another son,

J. Howard Marshall III, was also excluded from the will.) A protracted legal struggle over the estate ensued in courts all over the United States. Notwithstanding the omission in the will, one court awarded Anna Nicole $474 million, which another knocked down to $88 million, which still another reduced to zero. Five years after Marshall's death, a federal court in California and a state court in Texas both asserted jurisdiction over the will, and it was this dispute that eventually wound up before the justices. When they heard arguments in this arcane matter of federal jurisdiction, the courtroom was nearly as crowded as it had been for *Bush v. Gore*.

Responding to the buzz in the audience, the two justices most inclined to show off, Scalia and Breyer, dominated the argument with questions. Breyer may not have heard of Anna Nicole at the start of the case, but he had clearly studied the material about her. "The fact that three pages of the living trust, according to the judge, were created after the event of that trust and slipped in without his knowledge," he said to Pierce's lawyer, "I mean, it's quite a story."

Anna Nicole herself wore a subdued black suit for the occasion, and, according to her spokesman, she wept during the argument because she was overwhelmed by loving memories of her late husband. As it happened, the Court ruled unanimously in Anna Nicole's favor and returned the case to federal court in California. Roberts assigned the case to Ginsburg, the Court's leading expert on federal procedure.

The postscript to *Marshall v. Marshall* was melancholy, even tragic. About a month after the Court's decision, Pierce Marshall died suddenly, at the age of sixty-seven. Three months later, Anna Nicole's twenty-year-old son died of a drug overdose. Five months after that, Anna Nicole herself died of an accidental drug overdose in a hotel room in Hollywood, Florida. Anna Nicole's estate continued the litigation against Pierce's estate (over the proceeds of J. Howard II's estate). In an extremely rare development, the Supreme Court agreed to hear the case a second time, in 2010, to consider an issue relating to bankruptcy law. The case was by then known as *Stern v. Marshall*, as the lead plaintiff was Howard Stern, Anna Nicole's paramour. (He was not the radio shock jock, though they were often confused.) Without Anna Nicole's presence, the second oral argument drew little notice. The Court ruled 5–4 against her estate, but the litigation continues in 2012.

More than his colleagues, Roberts brought a literary flair to opinion writing. Inevitably, then, given the circumstances, Roberts began his opinion for the Court in the second Anna Nicole case with a quotation from *Bleak House*, by Charles Dickens. "This 'suit has, in course of time, become so complicated, that . . . no two . . . lawyers can talk about it for five minutes, without coming to a total disagreement as to all the premises. Innumerable children have been born into the cause: innumerable young people have married into it'; and, sadly, the original parties 'have died out of it.' "

THE LEGACY OF APPENDIX E

As the Court convened on the first Monday in October 2006, the beginning of the second full year of the Roberts Court, Ruth Bader Ginsburg had more on her mind than the new lineup of cases. Someone in her family had cancer. Again. The disease haunted her life.

Ruth Bader was born in 1933. Her father was a furrier and her mother cared for Ruth and Marilyn, her older sister, in their Brooklyn home. Few people were buying furs at the height of the Depression, so the family struggled. When Ruth was a toddler, Marilyn was stricken with meningitis and died. Ruth was raised as an adored only child, escorted by her mother to cello lessons and the local public library, which was located above a Chinese restaurant. When Ruth was thirteen, her mother was diagnosed with cervical cancer. Throughout Ruth's high school years—when she was a cheerleader, editor of the school paper at James Madison High School, and the designated "rabbi" at her summer camp—Celia Bader endured the agonies of cancer treatment in the 1940s. She died the day before Ruth's graduation. After the funeral, the Bader house filled with mourners, but only the men were allowed to participate in the minyan, the quorum for the official prayers. The teenaged Ruth took note.

Ruth went to Cornell, where on a blind date she met Martin Ginsburg, who was a year older and also from Brooklyn, though he was raised in more prosperous circumstances, on Long Island. Ethnicity notwithstanding, they were almost comically mismatched. Ruth was shy, bookish, and reserved; Marty was ebullient, outgoing, and amusing. Each one remained that way for a remarkable half-century-plus of marriage. Their personalities could scarcely have differed more, but as a partnership based on love and respect, their union served as a happy model for all who knew them.

They married just after she graduated, in 1954. Ruth followed Marty to Oklahoma, where he was completing his service in the army. This corner of the military had entered a postwar lull, and Marty found a good deal of time on his hands. He took the opportunity to read Escoffier and turned into an accomplished chef, which his wife, emphatically, was not. Their daughter Jane was born in 1955, and the family moved to Cambridge, where Marty was a year ahead of Ruth at Harvard Law School. She was one of nine women in a class of more than five hundred. (Ruth again noted the rules limiting female freedom, often without rhyme or reason. For example, at Cornell, women were required to live in the dorms; at Harvard, they were forbidden from living in the dorms.)

While they were law students, Marty was stricken with testicular cancer, then as now a devastating disease. Through two surgeries and extensive treatments, Ruth cared for Marty, took class notes for him (as well as herself), typed his papers, made law review, and tended to their young daughter. It is said that these years made Justice Ginsburg somewhat intolerant of her law clerks' complaints of overwork. Marty survived, of course, and the couple had a son a few years later.

The Ginsburgs moved to New York, where Marty practiced tax law at a big firm and Ruth spent her final year of law school at Columbia. She then began a career in teaching law, first at Rutgers, in New Jersey. In her early years as a professor, she specialized in federal civil procedure, a subject she continued to find fascinating throughout her long career. (Rehnquist shared this unusual fondness, and it contributed to the warm relationship between the two.) In the fall of 1970, though, Ruth was thinking about doing some work for the budding women's movement. One evening, as the couple was working in their adjoining home offices, Marty handed Ruth a few pages from a recent tax court decision. "Read this," he said.

"I don't read tax cases," she told him.

"Read this one," he said.

In the five minutes it took to read the brief opinion, Ruth Ginsburg realized that a new chapter in her career was about to begin.

Charles E. Moritz lived in Denver and worked as a book editor. In 1958, Moritz, who never married, brought his elderly mother to live with him, hiring a part-time caregiver a few years later. Under the tax law at that time, a single woman who paid for the care of a dependent could take a deduction; a single man who made the same expenditure could not. Representing himself before the tax court, Moritz wrote in a one-page brief, "If I were a dutiful daughter instead of a dutiful son, I would have received that deduction. That makes no sense." (Both Ginsburgs later described Moritz's homemade brief as one of the finest they'd ever seen.)

After reading the case, Ruth said to Marty, "Let's take it." The husband and wife represented Moritz pro bono and won their appeal in the Tenth Circuit, in Denver. The Court found that Moritz was entitled to receive the same deduction as a woman would have received. (It came to about $600.) As it happened, though, by the time the case was decided, Congress had prospectively changed the law to eliminate that particular sex-based differential; the legal issue now appeared to be moot. But Erwin Griswold, the solicitor general under Presidents Johnson and Nixon (and the former dean of Harvard Law School), thought the Moritz decision was so significant, and so wrong, that he asked the Supreme Court to reverse the Tenth Circuit decision. Griswold told the Court that it was important to preserve the principle of treating men and women differently under the law. Take the case, the solicitor general urged, because the Tenth Circuit's decision "casts a cloud of unconstitutionality upon the many federal statutes listed in Appendix E."

What was Appendix E? Griswold had prevailed upon the Department of Defense to use one of its first computers to scour federal laws and regulations to find all rules "containing differentiations based upon sex-related criteria." There were hundreds of them, and it would not have been possible for a mere law professor, in those days before simple computer databases, to track them down. The Supreme Court declined to hear the appeal, but Appendix E gave Ginsburg a road map for the next decade of her life—she wanted to undo as many of that long list of laws as possible. She later said Appendix E was a "treasure trove." Moritz turned out to be the only case where Marty joined Ruth on a brief. He went back to tax law, and she became a founding director of the Women's Rights Project for the American Civil Liberties Union, as well as the first tenured woman professor at Columbia Law School.

When Ginsburg first contemplated bringing women's rights cases to the Supreme Court, her prospects did not look promising. The Court had a long history of sanctioning discrimination against women. In 1873, the Court ruled that states had the right to bar women from the practice of law. As one justice explained, "The paramount destiny and mission of women are to fulfill the noble and benign offices of wife and mother. This is the law of the Creator." In 1961, the Court unanimously upheld a Florida law that made jury duty mandatory for men but voluntary for women. Despite some changes in recent years, Justice John Marshall Harlan II observed, "woman is still regarded as the center of home and family life." The question for Ginsburg was how to change this mind-set—in a Court made up of men.

But the Moritz case had given her a useful insight about how to persuade judges to strike down laws that differentiated between the sexes. She brought cases on behalf of *male* plaintiffs, not just women. Ginsburg's larger goal, of course, was to see that men and women were treated equally under the law, but she recognized that male judges might well have an easier time ruling for their fellow men than for women. Many of the laws that ostensibly favored women were based on outmoded stereotypes about how families and society were organized. She looked for cases that displayed such archaic biases.

In the first case Ginsburg argued before the Supreme Court, Sharron Frontiero, a lieutenant in the air force, applied for housing and medical benefits for her husband, whom she claimed as a dependent. Under the law, male officers could automatically claim their wives as dependents, but women had to prove that their husbands were dependent on them. In 1973, the Supreme Court in *Frontiero v. Richardson* ruled 8–1 in Ginsburg's favor. As Brennan wrote in the lead opinion, "There can be no doubt that our Nation has had a long and unfortunate history of sex discrimination. Traditionally, such discrimination was rationalized by an attitude of 'romantic paternalism' which, in practical effect, put women not on a pedestal, but in a cage."

Two years later, in *Weinberger v. Wiesenfeld*, Ginsburg successfully argued in the Supreme Court against a provision in the Social Security Act that denied to widowed fathers benefits afforded to widowed mothers. "Obviously, the notion that men are more likely than women to be the primary supporters of their spouses and children is not entirely without empirical support," Brennan wrote again for a unanimous result. "But such a gender-based generalization cannot suffice to justify the denigration of the efforts of women who do work and whose earnings contribute significantly to their families' support."

Ultimately, Ginsburg won five of the six cases she argued before the Supreme Court and became known as the Thurgood Marshall of the feminist movement. In light of Ginsburg's eminence, it was no surprise that Jimmy Carter named her to the D.C. Circuit in 1980, and Clinton nominated her for the Supreme Court in 1993.

There were other, less happy parallels between the careers of Marshall and Ginsburg. Marshall became famous in the 1950s when he led the legal effort to end segregation; his greatest success came in 1954, when he won the epic case of *Brown v. Board of Education*, which ended the doctrine of "separate but equal" in public education. President Johnson named Marshall to the Court in 1967, just before Richard Nixon's four appointments ended the era of liberal hegemony. Consequently, Marshall spent most of his twenty-four years as a justice trying to hang on to the gains of the Warren Court years. It was neither easy nor enjoyable. He was not always successful, and his persistent health problems compounded his unease on the bench. That he was replaced by Clarence Thomas—whose politics Marshall abhorred—capped the disappointments of his tenure.

Ginsburg joined the Court after Rehnquist became chief justice. Though Rehnquist never succeeded in achieving his greatest judicial goals—overturning *Roe v. Wade* and ending race-conscious affirmative action—he won a great many more cases than he lost, and Ginsburg, like Marshall, often found herself in dissent. She did have occasional triumphs, none sweeter than the VMI case. The Virginia Military Institute, which was funded by taxpayers, admitted only men as cadets. In a 7–1 decision in 1996, the Court struck down the single-sex policy at VMI as a violation of the equal protection clause. Ginsburg's opinion gave her the rare pleasure of surveying the history of sex discrimination law at the Court and citing several cases that she herself had argued. "'Inherent differences' between men and women, we have come to appreciate, remain cause for celebration, but not for denigration of the members of either sex or for artificial constraints on an individual's opportunity," she wrote. "But such classifications may not be used, as they once were, to create or perpetuate the legal, social, and economic inferiority of women." (Rehnquist, knowing how much the issue meant to Ginsburg, assigned the opinion to her. Scalia dissented. Thomas recused himself from the case because his son was a cadet at VMI.)

Triumphs like the VMI case were few. Ginsburg, like Marshall, suffered serious health problems. Over the years, many had been fooled by Ginsburg's fragile appearance. She barely topped five feet and weighed less than a hundred pounds, but she was as tough, in her way, as an NFL linebacker. (In this area and others, Marty was a diligent steward of his wife's good name. He once surprised a reporter with the question, "How many push-ups can you do?" When the reporter stumbled for a response, Marty Ginsburg said, "My wife can do twenty-five—and you wrote that she was 'frail.'")

In 1999, Justice Ginsburg was diagnosed with colon cancer. Over the next several months, she went through radiation and chemotherapy but never missed a day on the bench. During this period she received enormous support from O'Connor, who had been treated for breast cancer in 1988. The shy Ginsburg and charismatic O'Connor appeared to have little in common, including their judicial philosophies, but the first and second women on the Court shared a warm friendship. In 2005, O'Connor's departure from the Court hit Ginsburg hard, especially since Alito ended up as her replacement. As Ginsburg often said, it had never occurred to her that she would ever be the only woman on the Court.

When Ginsburg took her seat in October 2006, she was already melancholy. There was worse news. Marty had cancer again. And for the first time in the Roberts era, the most incendiary topic of all had returned to its docket—abortion.

The Court's 1973 decision in *Roe v. Wade* was rooted in a ruling that came eight years earlier. The result in *Griswold v. Connecticut* was not especially controversial, but the reasoning behind it was and remains a flashpoint of constitutional debate. (*Griswold* the case should not be confused with Erwin Griswold, the onetime solicitor general and dean of Harvard Law School.)

Even in the midsixties, Connecticut rarely enforced its legal ban on the sale or use of birth control, which stated, "Any person who uses any drug, medicinal article or instrument for the purpose of preventing conception shall be fined not less than fifty dollars or imprisoned not less than sixty days nor more than one year." Still, the executive director of the Planned Parenthood League of the state, seeking to create a test case, arranged to be arrested for violating this law by giving birth control advice to married couples. In 1965, the Supreme Court overturned the conviction by a vote of 7–2. The justices produced six different opinions, but Justice William O. Douglas spoke for the majority.

"This law operates directly on an intimate relation of husband and wife and their physician's role in one aspect of that relation," Douglas wrote. There was clearly something wrong with the Connecticut law, but what? In his characteristically terse style, Douglas appeared to be searching for a rationale. The law was not a violation of due process of law or freedom of speech, he said, though clearly the values underlying those provisions were implicated. He also believed the case was not really about freedom of association either, though that too was involved. Rather, Douglas concluded, it wasn't a single provision of the Constitution that was violated by this law. Instead, he wrote, in one of the most famous (and infamous) passages in Supreme Court history: "Specific guarantees in the Bill of Rights have penumbras, formed by emanations from those guarantees that help give them life and substance. Various guarantees create zones of privacy." The Connecticut law interfered with this zone of privacy and thus had to be struck down. (McCain mocked this passage in his campaign speech about the courts.)

Roe relied on Douglas's *Griswold* opinion to establish a woman's right to choose abortion. In *Roe*, Justice Harry Blackmun wrote for the Court, "The Constitution does not explicitly mention any right of privacy. In a line of decisions, however, going back perhaps as far as [1891], the Court has recognized that a right of personal privacy, or a guarantee of certain areas or zones of privacy, does exist under the Constitution." This right of privacy, Blackmun went on, "is broad enough to encompass a woman's decision whether or not to terminate her pregnancy."

In Blackmun's opinion, though, the abortion decision was as much about the physician as about the woman. "The attending physician, in consultation with his patient, is free to determine, without regulation by the State, that, in his medical judgment, the patient's pregnancy should be terminated," he wrote. "The abortion decision in all its aspects is inherently, and primarily, a medical decision, and basic responsibility for it must rest with the physician." (Blackmun had once been general counsel to the Mayo Clinic, and he maintained a reverence for doctors throughout his tenure on the Court.)

Liberals have long regarded the right to privacy, and Blackmun's opinion, as a touchstone of American liberty—a vindication of what Justice Louis Brandeis called "the right to be let alone—the most comprehensive of rights and the right most valued by civilized men." Conservatives have always reviled *Roe* as the ultimate power grab by a liberal judiciary. As Robert Bork summed up the conservative critique of *Roe*, the right to privacy "does not come out of the Constitution but is forced into it. . . . This is not legal reasoning but fiat."

Ginsburg favored abortion rights, but she departed from the liberal orthodoxy in her distaste for the privacy rationale undergirding *Roe v. Wade*. She believed abortion rights were about equality, not privacy. Ginsburg regarded the denial of abortion rights to women as just another form of the broader denial of equal rights. As she said in 1984, the right to abortion places in the balance "a woman's autonomous charge of her full life's course—her ability to stand in relation to man, society, and the state as an independent, self-sustaining, equal citizen." Ginsburg also resented Blackmun's patronizing emphasis on the rights of doctors, rather than of women. As she put it in an interview later, "It's the woman in consultation with her doctor. So the view you get is the tall doctor and the little woman who needs him."

Against this backdrop Ginsburg—and the Court—weighed the abortion case of 2006.

The specific issue was not a new one. Indeed, the Court had considered a nearly identical case just a few years earlier.

In the modern post-*Roe* era, the anti-abortion movement focused its efforts on limiting what it called "partial birth" abortion. The medical details were complex, but the movement had seized on a procedure, which usually took place late in a pregnancy, that many ordinary people regarded as gruesome. These kinds of abortions were rare and often undertaken because the woman's health or life was in danger. But there was no denying the shock value of the details.

Still, in the 2000 case of *Stenberg v. Carhart*, the Supreme Court struck down a Nebraska "partial birth" abortion law by a vote of 5–4. As ever, O'Connor provided the swing vote, concluding that the law was unconstitutional because it failed to include an exception allowing the procedure to be used to protect the health of the mother. Breyer wrote the opinion for the Court in 2000, the highest-profile majority opinion of his career.

But when George W. Bush took office the next year, along with a Republican Congress, one of his first priorities was to sign the Partial-Birth Abortion Ban Act, which was almost identical to the Nebraska law that the Court had just struck down. It was immediately challenged in Court in a case called *Gonzales v. Carhart.* (The 2000 and 2006 cases had the same plaintiff, LeRoy H. Carhart, who was one of the few doctors willing to admit publicly that he performed the partial-birth procedures. George Tiller, another doctor who performed such abortions, was murdered by an anti-abortion terrorist in 2009.)

There was, of course, one critical change in the Court between 2000 and 2006: Alito had replaced O'Connor. In this case, as in many others, the switch made all the difference and the Court now voted 5–4 to uphold the federal law. (Alito said nothing during the oral argument, but it wasn't hard to guess how he would vote; his wife and family doctor, who were in the audience, scowled and shook their heads as the lawyer for Planned Parenthood argued her case.) Roberts assigned the opinion in *Gonzales v. Carhart* to Kennedy.

Kennedy had a complex history in abortion cases. Reagan nominated Kennedy in 1987, following the Senate's rejection of Robert Bork. There had been no doubt that Bork would have joined the anti-*Roe* forces, but Kennedy's history and his confirmation testimony were opaque about abortion. In 1992, Kennedy joined with O'Connor and Souter in the *Casey* decision to preserve what they called the "essential holding" of *Roe v. Wade.* (Their unsigned collaborative opinion was joined by Blackmun and Stevens to give them a majority.) In subsequent years, though, Kennedy had been moving to the anti-abortion side of the Court, voting to uphold various restrictions on the practice. In 2000, Kennedy dissented vigorously in the first *Carhart* case. Now, six years later, Roberts gave Kennedy the chance to turn that dissent into a majority opinion, which was released in April 2007.

Kennedy made the most of the opportunity. He discussed the abortion procedures in great and gory detail. ("Rotating the fetus as it is being pulled decreases the odds of dismemberment. . . . The doctor opened up the scissors, stuck a high-powered suction tube into the opening, and sucked the baby's brains out.") He said almost nothing about the kind of medical conditions that would prompt a woman to subject herself to such procedures. Overall, Kennedy's rhetoric was straight out of the anti-abortion movement. He referred to the fetus as a "baby" and a "child." The obstetricians and gynecologists who performed the procedures were "abortion doctors." The state "has respect for human life at all stages in the pregnancy" and a "legitimate and substantial interest in preserving and promoting fetal life." Kennedy's opinion was a vivid demonstration of the significance of Alito's appointment—and of the dedication of the conservatives on the Court to change. The addition of one new justice posed a clear threat to *Roe*, *Casey*, and abortion rights generally.

Ginsburg had little patience for Kennedy in the best of circumstances. The Californian's airy and vague rhetoric about dignity and the like offended the practical New Yorker. (Ginsburg agreed with Kennedy on the merits of cases more often than she did with Rehnquist, but she had a temperamental affinity for the late chief's plainspoken, forthright opinions.) There was one passage in Kennedy's *Carhart* opinion that offended Ginsburg as much as anything she had seen during her tenure on the Court. Kennedy wrote:

Respect for human life finds an ultimate expression in the bond of love the mother has for her child. The Act recognizes this reality as well. Whether to have an abortion requires a difficult and painful moral decision. While we find no reliable data to measure the phenomenon, it seems unexceptionable to conclude some women come to regret their choice to abort the infant life they once created and sustained. Severe depression and loss of esteem can follow.

Ginsburg had devoted her life to fighting this kind of patronizing reasoning. Appendix E consisted almost entirely of rules written by men who thought they knew what was best for women. Kennedy's opinion belonged to that lamentable tradition.

Ginsburg prided herself on her professional tone; no Scalia-style hysterics for her. Her model and partner in this decorous approach was David Souter, who also resisted the use of invective in even the most controversial cases. But in *Carhart*, Ginsburg did not, or could not, restrain herself. In her dissent, she wrote that Kennedy's opinion rested on "ancient notions about women's place in the family and under the Constitution—ideas that have long since been discredited."

Ginsburg also took the opportunity in her *Carhart* dissent to clear up some of her lingering dissatisfactions with *Roe* itself. Her long-standing preference was for equality rather than privacy as the governing rationale. Challenges to abortion laws, she wrote, "do not seek to vindicate some generalized notion of privacy; rather, they center on a woman's autonomy to determine her life's course, and thus to enjoy equal citizenship stature." Harry Blackmun notwithstanding, abortion rights belonged to women, not their doctors. Later cases, she noted, "described more precisely than did *Roe* v. *Wade* the impact of abortion restrictions on women's liberty. *Roe*'s focus was in considerable measure on 'vindicat[ing] the right of the physician to administer medical treatment according to his professional judgment.'" Finally, she took on Kennedy's claim that, in her words, "having an abortion is any more dangerous to a woman's long-term mental health than delivering and parenting a child that she did not intend to have." Kennedy's assertion was based on junk science, she said, proving her point with a four-hundred-word footnote summarizing the actual scholarly research about women who had had abortions. Ginsburg was appalled by the Court's decision—and she wanted everyone to know it.

In their first decade or so, Supreme Court justices usually announced their rulings in the manner of their British forebearers, with each justice presenting his view of each case. In this area as in so many others of the Court's history, Chief Justice John Marshall, who presided from 1801 to 1835, created a new and enduring tradition. Under Marshall, the Court began to render opinions that represented the collective judgment of the Court. In his day, Marshall wrote most of the opinions himself, but there were occasions when one or more of his colleagues disagreed with him. These disputes, rare though they were, gave rise to the tradition of dissenting opinions.

Outsiders (and sometimes the justices themselves) often asked about dissents: why bother? There was no higher court to persuade. What was the point of writing down the losing side of an argument? The most famous answer to this question came from Chief Justice Charles Evans Hughes, who wrote, "A dissent in a Court of last resort is an appeal . . . to the intelligence of a future day, when a later decision may possibly correct the error into which the dissenting judge believes the court to have been betrayed." Dissenting opinions also offered reasons to the public, who, in a democracy, were the ultimate judges of the political branches of government. Many justices cared deeply about how their work was perceived beyond the walls of the Supreme Court building, and dissenting opinions shaped perceptions of the winners and the losers almost as much as the words of the majority.

It was true, too, that some of the most famous dissenting opinions were ultimately vindicated, either by the course of events or by future justices. Dissenting in the infamous Dred Scott case of 1857, Benjamin Curtis anticipated the Civil War; the first Justice John Marshall Harlan, dissenting in *Plessy v. Ferguson* in 1896, presaged the ruling in *Brown v. Board of Education* fifty-eight years later; Louis Brandeis and Oliver Wendell Holmes protested the Court's restrictions on free speech in the repressive period after World War I. Later the Court explicitly embraced their understanding of the First Amendment. These were exceptions. Most dissents remained just that.

But the justices kept writing them, and sometimes did more to call attention to the minority view. When the justices finally moved from their cramped quarters in the Capitol to their commodious new building across First Street, in 1935, their new courtroom looked more like a theater. Some justices began playing to the audiences and, on major occasions, read their dissenting opinions out loud. Intentionally or not, justices sometimes also ad-libbed additions to their formal opinions. When, for instance, James McReynolds announced his dissent from the Court's approval of FDR's decision to take the government off the gold standard in 1935, he reportedly uttered a line not found in his written opinion: "The Constitution, as we have known it, is gone."

Justices recognized that reading a dissent from the bench represented their most visible and intense form of protest, and they exercised the privilege sparingly. There were rarely more than a half-dozen dissents read aloud over the course of a year; in some years, like 1984, there were none. William Brennan and William Rehnquist, through their long careers on the bench, each read dissents from the bench exactly once. (Brennan read his dissent in the *Bakke* affirmative action case of 1978, and Rehnquist read in the *Casey* abortion case of 1992.)

Still, Ginsburg had no doubt she wanted to register a vocal protest against Kennedy's opinion in *Gonzales v. Carhart*. Decades after she'd moved away, Ginsburg's voice still carried hints of Brooklyn as she began: "Four members of this Court, Justices Stevens, Souter, Breyer and I strongly dissent from today's opinion."

Ginsburg made clear that she thought the decision in *Carhart* came about only because of the changing composition of the Court. "Although today's opinion does not go so far as to discard *Roe* or *Casey*, the Court, differently composed than it was when we last considered a restrictive abortion regulation, is hardly faithful to Casey's invocation of the rule of law and the principles of stare decisis"—the rule of precedent. The message was plain. Abortion rights were under siege. "In candor," Ginsburg said, "the Partial-Birth Abortion Ban Act and the Court's defense of it cannot be understood as anything other than an effort to chip away at a right declared again and again by this court and with increasing comprehension of its centrality to women's lives. A decision of the character the Court makes today should not have staying power."

A few weeks later, Ginsburg would be reading another dissent from the bench.

THE BALLAD OF LILLY LEDBETTER

J ohn Roberts, no less than Ginsburg, was shaped by the cases he argued before the Court. *Lujan v. National Wildlife Federation*, which Roberts argued during his tenure as George H. W. Bush's deputy solicitor general, seems to have had special resonance for him. An environmental group had challenged the Reagan administration's effort to assign as much as 180 million acres of federal land for mining. Roberts did not defend the Interior Department's designation of the land on the merits but rather asserted that the plaintiffs had no right to bring the case in the first place. The issue involved the doctrine known as standing—one of many subjects before the Supreme Court that appear to be just procedural in nature but are in fact freighted with political significance.

In his argument before the Court on April 16, 1990, Roberts said that the mere allegation that a member of the National Wildlife Federation used land "in the vicinity" of the affected acres did not give the group the right to bring the case. "That sort of interest was insufficient to confer standing, because it was in no way distinct from the interest any citizen could claim, coming in the courthouse and saying, 'I'm interested in this subject,'" Roberts told the justices. By a vote of 5–4, the Justices agreed and threw out the case.

Roberts's argument in *Lujan* represented a template for how to defend environmental, civil rights, and other "public interest"–type lawsuits. The goal, to the extent possible, was to avoid a judgment on the merits but rather to employ a variety of procedural doctrines to persuade courts to dismiss these cases. There are any number of procedural doctrines that can be used for this purpose. Other examples include ripeness (is it too early for a court to decide the case?), mootness (is it too late for a court to decide?), venue (is this court the right one?), and the "political question" doctrine (is the subject matter appropriate for a court to decide at all?). Everyone agrees that these doctrines are necessary, at some level; the courts cannot be allowed to weigh in on controversies simply because judges feel like deciding the merits. But the ideological divisions on these issues are clear. Liberals want flexible rules that allow courts to reach a lot of decisions on the merits, and conservatives want strict rules to prevent cases from being heard.

Roberts came of age as a lawyer when controversies about procedural doctrines were hot topics. The liberal activism of the Warren Court was based, to a great extent, on flexible rules of procedure. Warren and his colleagues wanted to push the law into new fields and to create new rights. The justices began to allow plaintiffs to bring new kinds of cases. While Roberts was at Harvard, a professor there, Abram Chayes, wrote a famous law review article celebrating this trend. "In our received tradition," Chayes wrote, "the lawsuit is a vehicle for settling disputes between private parties about private rights." But that was changing, Chayes said, and for the better. Contemporary lawsuits, especially class actions, amounted to "public law litigation," which required courts to consider the needs and views of a wide variety of people, who may or may not be actual parties to the case. "School desegregation, employment discrimination, and prisoners' or inmates' rights cases come readily to mind as avatars of this new form of litigation," Chayes wrote. (The Boston school busing crisis was ongoing.) In these cases, Chayes wrote, "the party structure is sprawling and amorphous, subject to change over the course of the litigation. The traditional adversary relationship is suffused and intermixed with negotiating and mediating processes at every point." He went on, "Most important, the trial judge has increasingly become the creator and manager of complex forms of ongoing relief, which have widespread effects on persons not before the court."

Like many other conservatives of his generation, Roberts built his career fighting the ideas extolled in Chayes's piece. In the vision of Roberts, Alito, and others, courts should play a narrower role than the one Chayes envisioned. They should interpret rules strictly, construe laws narrowly, and decide only what they must. Indeed, in the one famous line from Roberts's brief tenure on the D.C. Circuit, he had described "the cardinal principle of judicial restraint—if it is not necessary to decide more, it is necessary not to decide more." George W. Bush put the same point another way, in describing the kind of judges he wanted to appoint to the Supreme Court. "Every judge I appoint," Bush said, "will be a person who clearly understands the role of a judge is to interpret the law, not to legislate from the bench." Procedural doctrines were the principal tool to keep plaintiffs from persuading judges to legislate.

The political lineup in these procedural disputes, and in civil litigation generally, was clear. "Trial lawyers," as they are known, are actually plaintiffs' lawyers, who tend to represent individuals and skew overwhelmingly Democratic. The "defense bar" represents corporations, often insurance companies, and are usually Republicans.

When Roberts was a private lawyer at the firm then known as Hogan & Hartson, he was part of the defense bar. The cases he argued before the Supreme Court were typically for corporations against individuals, and they often involved the procedural doctrines. For example, shortly before Roberts became a judge, he successfully argued in the Supreme Court that a woman who suffered from carpal tunnel syndrome could not win a recovery from her employer, Toyota, under the Americans with Disabilities Act. A strict reading of the statute—always the preference of defendants in civil rights cases—meant the plaintiff had no right to make her case. Likewise, Roberts won a Supreme Court ruling that the family of a woman who died in a fire could not use the Alabama wrongful-death statute to sue the city of Tarrant, Alabama. The family of Alberta Jefferson, an African American woman, sued the city, claiming that the fire department failed to save her because of "the selective denial of fire protection to disfavored minorities."

In one of his early decisions as chief justice, Roberts had a chance to put his expertise in standing doctrine to work—to characteristic ends. In *DaimlerChrysler v. Cuno*, a group of taxpayers in Toledo, Ohio, went to court to challenge local tax breaks that were given to the carmaker to expand its operations in the city; the Supreme Court held that the plaintiffs lacked standing and dismissed the case. In a broadly worded opinion that relied in part on the *Lujan* case (offering Roberts the same kind of satisfaction that Ginsburg received from citing the cases she had litigated), Roberts suggested that most state and local government activities were off limits to challenges from taxpayers. "Affording state taxpayers standing to press such challenges simply because their tax burden gives them an interest in the state treasury," Roberts wrote, "would interpose the federal courts as virtually continuing monitors of the wisdom and soundness of state fiscal administration, contrary to the more modest role Article III envisions for federal courts." As usual under Roberts, the citizen plaintiffs were out of luck.

The justices built their judicial philosophies on the foundation of their prior lives. From differing perspectives, Ginsburg and Thomas had long experience with (and strong feelings about) civil rights; Roberts had neither. Breyer had given years of thought to the role of the administrative state; Roberts had not. Scalia endorsed an overarching theory of the Constitution; Roberts did not. Kennedy viewed the Supreme Court in the context of an international community of judges; Roberts saw no such thing. But the chief justice had spent decades thinking about how to throw plaintiffs in civil cases out of court—the faster, the better. Civil procedure, so dreary even to most lawyers, was for Roberts the surest route to victory for his political side. One of Roberts's fellow conservatives on the D.C. Circuit used to offer his law clerks a small cash bonus if they could find a procedural issue in any case that would allow the court to dismiss the action. Roberts provided no such cash incentives, but he shared the impulse.

The real-world implications of these procedural roadblocks were clear. With so many barriers at every stage of the process, plaintiffs' lawyers hesitated before filing new cases, or did not bring them at all. The costs and risks were too high. (Legislative efforts at tort reform, like limits on punitive damages, compounded the difficulties for plaintiffs.) If claims could never get to trial because of procedural barriers, there would be fewer cases brought in the first place. This was especially true in civil rights cases—in "public law" cases, in Chayes's phrase—because these ambitious undertakings had the greatest procedural vulnerabilities. The defense bar understood these economic realities and, with a sympathetic judiciary, pushed to capitalize on its advantages. As a lawyer and judge, Roberts was more skilled at this kind of work than anyone.

All of which helps explain the fate of Lilly Ledbetter.

The Goodyear Tire & Rubber Company was founded around the turn of the last century, in Akron, Ohio, which soon became known as Tire City. The firm vaulted to prosperity during World War I and the postwar boom, and in time its leaders began looking for new locations to open their vast tire-making factories. In 1929, Goodyear established a base in Gadsden, Alabama. By 1954, it was the largest tire-making facility in the United States. In the seventies, Goodyear prospered, even in the face of the energy crisis, by making steel-belted radial tires, which offered greater stability and traction than traditional models. Still, it was a polluting, competitive business, increasingly susceptible to lower-priced imports from abroad. For employees, even more than for the company, manufacturing tires was a tough, dirty way to make a living.

In 1979, a forty-year-old woman named Lilly Ledbetter went to work at the Gadsden plant. She already had fifteen years of experience at other factories, and Goodyear hired her as a production supervisor. In 1985, she scored the second highest of forty-five applicants to become an area manager. But Goodyear in Gadsden was never an easy place for a woman to work. One male boss pressured her for sex. When she refused, Ledbetter said, he lowered his evaluations of her work. When she confronted him about the poor evaluations, he told her that it was "a lot easier to downgrade you. You're just a little female and these big old guys, I mean, they're going to beat up on me and push me around and cuss me." According to Ledbetter, that boss "continued to ask me out, go out with him. And I finally told him no. And then from that standpoint, my evaluations, the audits got worse." Nevertheless, Ledbetter, who was one of the very few female area managers at the plant, did receive a top performance award in 1996. She planned to retire the next year.

Shortly before Ledbetter was planning to leave the company, someone anonymously slipped a note inside her mailbox at Goodyear. The message informed her that she was making $3,727 per month while men who were doing the same job were paid between $4,286 and $5,236 per month. The same kind of differences had persisted for years. Ledbetter hired a lawyer, and as she was required to do under the Title VII anti-discrimination law, she took her complaint to the Equal Employment Opportunity Commission. (In her last months at the company, after she had filed her formal protest with the government, she was transferred to a new job that required her to carry tires around the plant. Ledbetter was just short of sixty years old at the time. She asserted that the transfer was retribution.)

Ledbetter put her case before a federal jury in Alabama, which awarded her $3.3 million. The judge reduced the award to $300,000, but Goodyear still appealed the case to the Eleventh Circuit, which overturned the judgment altogether. The company's claim was straightforward. Goodyear asserted that an employee alleging disparate pay must file an EEOC charge within 180 days of the pay decision giving rise to the disparity. Under that theory, Ledbetter could try to prove only that her 1997 pay adjustment (the last one she had received) was discriminatory. She had no recourse for the earlier years because she had missed the 180-day deadline.

In other words, according to Goodyear, virtually all of Ledbetter's claims were barred by the statute of limitations. Like ripeness, mootness, and all the other procedural doctrines, statutes of limitations were another roadblock to successful civil rights claims in federal court. The argument was like the ones Roberts made in private practice. Even if Ledbetter had suffered discrimination (which Goodyear did not concede), she was barred from bringing her case because she had waited too long to charge the company.

The Ledbetter case reflected the practical impediments to plaintiffs in civil rights cases. She initiated the case in 1998, and the Supreme Court decided it nine years later. As with most plaintiffs, her lawyers worked for a contingency fee, which meant they earned nothing on the case for nearly a decade (or, as it turned out, ever). Not many lawyers are willing to take such risks. Indeed, Ledbetter's case only reached the Supreme Court because after her loss in the Eleventh Circuit, her original lawyers brought the case to the Supreme Court Litigation Clinic at Stanford Law School. There, the teachers and students agreed to represent Ledbetter for free.

"Mr. Chief Justice, and may it please the Court," Kevin Russell, the lawyer with the Stanford clinic began his argument on November 27, 2006. "A jury found that at the time petitioner filed for a charge of discrimination with the EEOC, respondent was paying her less for each week's work than it paid similarly situated male employees and that it did so because of her sex." The question for the Court was whether all of the paychecks that reflected the discrimination were violations of Title VII, or just the last one.

Ginsburg, the only woman on the Court at the time, ranked around the middle of the Court in terms of how often she asked questions: behind Scalia, Roberts, and Breyer, but ahead of Alito and, of course, Thomas. (Thomas asked his last question in oral argument during the previous term, on February 22, 2006; he has not asked one since.) The diminutive Ginsburg never looked smaller than she did on the bench; her head came nowhere close to the top of her leather chair. But in this case, like almost no other, Ginsburg dominated the argument. Her questions—they were more like speeches—left no doubt about where she stood. Shortly after Russell began, Ginsburg said, "Mr. Russell, I thought that your argument was that 'yes, you know that you haven't got the promotion, you know you haven't got the transfer,' but the spread in the pay is an incremental thing. You may think the first year you didn't get a raise, 'well, so be it.' But you have, you have no reason to think that there is going to be this inequality." Quite so, said Russell.

Roberts took the lead in defending Goodyear, relying on the venerable argumentative tactic of the slippery slope. Under the plaintiff's theory, Roberts charged, companies could be liable for acts that were committed many years ago. "I suppose all they'd have to do is allege that sometime over the past. I mean, it doesn't have to be 15 years," he said. "It could be 40 years, right . . . that there was a discriminatory act, in one of the semi-annual pay reviews I was denied this, a raise that I should have gotten."

Wrong, replied Ginsburg, who was two seats to Roberts's left. If the case were based on a single disputed small raise many years ago, there would be no point to bringing a case. "If she's going to bring a case [alleging] I got a 2 percent raise, he got a 3 percent raise, her chances are very slim," she said. But Kennedy—the key vote—weighed in on Goodyear's side, by raising the possibility that a company may have been sold between the time of the alleged discrimination and the commencement of the lawsuit.

In this case, Goodyear had an important advantage. The Bush administration, through the solicitor general, entered the proceedings and urged the justices to rule for Goodyear. Irving Gornstein, the assistant to the SG, told the justices, "Employees who allow the 180-day period to pass may not years later and even at the end of their careers challenge their current paychecks on the grounds that they are the result of a number of discrete individually discriminatory pay decisions that occurred long ago." The Court agreed, by the customary 5–4 split (the same as in *Gonzales v. Carhart*, the abortion case that was pending at the time). Roberts assigned the opinion to Alito.

Alito had been a judge on the Third Circuit for fifteen years when Bush nominated him to the Supreme Court. That meant that he had served as an appeals court judge for longer than any of the other justices; at the time of his promotion, Alito had already written hundreds of opinions. So it was not surprising that Alito brought an established style that reflected his long experience. Circuit court opinions tend to be drier, less rhetorical than Supreme Court opinions, and this approach suited Alito's careful, even phlegmatic temperament. In rejecting Ledbetter's claim on statute of limitations grounds, Alito hewed closely to the facts and his view of the precedents. "She argues simply that Goodyear's conduct during the charging period gave present effect to discriminatory conduct outside of that period," he wrote. "But current effects alone cannot breathe life into prior, uncharged discrimination. . . . Ledbetter should have filed an EEOC charge within 180 days after each allegedly discriminatory pay decision was made and communicated to her. She did not do so."

Alito was short on sympathy for Ledbetter but long on the risks cases like hers posed for corporate defendants. "Statutes of limitations serve a policy of repose," he wrote. "They represent a pervasive legislative judgment that it is unjust to fail to put the adversary on notice to defend within a specified period of time and that the right to be free of stale claims in time comes to prevail over the right to prosecute them." (A graceful stylist like Roberts would never have written such a clunky sentence.) The EEOC filing deadline, Alito went on, "protects employers from the burden of defending claims arising from employment decisions that are long past."

As the senior associate justice in the minority, Stevens was responsible for choosing which justice should write the primary dissent. For workload purposes, Stevens (and Roberts) liked to spread these assignments around, and Ginsburg already had the major dissent in *Gonazales v. Carhart* on her plate. But since Ginsburg felt strongly about this case too, Stevens gave it to her as well.

Sex discrimination cases, like civil rights cases generally, had changed since Ginsburg was a litigator in the seventies. The Court in recent years had focused on affirmative action programs, testing whether racial or gender preferences violated the rights of the majority. But *Ledbetter* was not a case about special privileges. It was a case, simply, about equality, very much like the kind that Ginsburg herself had brought to the Court three decades earlier. Alito's bloodless opinion, with its tender regard for the Goodyears of the world and none at all for the Ledbetters, inspired Ginsburg to unleash a powerful and thorough dissent. (At 6,200 words, it was nearly as long as Alito's opinion for the Court.)

As someone who had actually litigated sex discrimination cases, Ginsburg had some idea of how they unfolded in the real world. "The Court's insistence on immediate contest overlooks common characteristics of pay discrimination," she wrote. "Pay disparities often occur, as they did in Ledbetter's case, in small increments; cause to suspect that discrimination is at work develops only over time. Comparative pay information, moreover, is often hidden from the employee's view. Employers may keep under wraps the pay differentials maintained among supervisors, no less the reasons for those differentials. Small initial discrepancies may not be seen as meat for a federal case, particularly when the employee, trying to succeed in a nontraditional environment, is averse to making waves."

This was obvious, of course, since it's clear that employers that discriminate rarely make public announcements to that effect. Ginsburg also made short work of the slippery slope argument, noting she was only proposing to allow suits by plaintiffs who did not know they had been discriminated against until much later. For those plaintiffs who knew about pay differentials and simply waited to sue, Ginsburg noted, "No sensible judge would tolerate such inexcusable neglect."

Ginsburg's words were endorsed only by the three other losing justices in the case. And *Ledbetter* (both the case and the person) was still fairly obscure; the news media rarely pays attention to cases about procedural doctrines like statutes of limitations. But Ginsburg had a plan to turn Lilly Ledbetter, and her own dissenting opinion, into something more than just another quickly forgotten loss for the liberal quartet.

In this Ginsburg had an edge. Notwithstanding the arcane details of federal procedure at issue in the case, Ginsburg knew that Ledbetter's predicament was easy to understand. Ledbetter had been a clear victim of discrimination and, perversely, the longer Goodyear violated her rights to equal pay, the weaker her case became. People outside the Court, and especially across First Street, at the Capitol, would respond to her story.

Ginsburg's idea for her dissent was also rooted in an important difference between the *Carhart* and *Ledbetter* cases. *Carhart* was a decision based on the Constitution. The only people who could change or over-rule it were the justices themselves. Accordingly, as Chief Justice Hughes put it, Ginsburg's only recourse in her dissenting opinion in *Carhart* was to appeal "to the intelligence of a future day." *Ledbetter* was different. It was not based on any constitutional provision. Rather, the issue in *Ledbetter* was the interpretation of an act of Congress—specifically, the statute of limitations provision of Title VII of the Civil Rights Act of 1964. Only the Court could interpret the Constitution—but Congress can always change a law.

On May 29, 2007, Ginsburg waited, sunken in her big chair, as Alito read his summary of the majority opinion. In her fourteen years on the Court at that point, Ginsburg had gone as long as four years between reading dissents from the bench. Now, only about a month after *Carhart*, she was reading another. That alone would have generated a good deal of attention.

In dissents from the bench, the tradition was for the justice to give, in essence, a shortened version of the published opinion. But that was not what Ginsburg did. Rather, she described the Ledbetter case in plain English, not the legalese of her dissent. "In our view, the court does not comprehend or is indifferent to the insidious way in which women can be victims of pay discrimination," she said. "Today's decision counsels, sue early on when it is uncertain whether discrimination accounts for the pay disparity you are beginning to experience. Indeed, initially you may not know that men are receiving more for substantially similar work. Of course, you are likely to lose a less-than-fully baked case."

But Ginsburg was just warming up. (Overall, she spoke twice as long as Alito.) She then gave a detailed summary of Ledbetter's long career at Goodyear and the acknowledged differences in her pay and that of comparably situated men; she went on to explain how those differences expanded and multiplied over the years. "As the court reads Title VII, each and every pay decision Ledbetter did not properly challenge, wiped the slate clean," Ginsburg said. "Never mind the cumulative effect of a series of decisions that together, set her pay well below that of every male Area Manager." All through these years, Ginsburg pointed out, Ledbetter had no idea that she was making less than her male peers.

At last Ginsburg came to the climax—and the point—of her long speech. "This is not the first time this court has ordered a cramped

interpretation of Title VII, incompatible with the statute's broad reme-
dial purpose," she said. Ginsburg was referring to a series of cases in the
late 1980s when the Court made winning discrimination cases much
harder. "In 1991," Ginsburg went on, "Congress passed a Civil Rights
Act that effectively overruled several of this court's similarly restrictive
decisions including one on which the court relies today." In other words,
in the 1991 act Congress repaired the damage the Court did in a series
of wrongheaded decisions.

"Today, the ball again lies in Congress' court," Ginsburg concluded.
"As in 1991, the legislature has cause to note and to correct this court's
parsimonious reading of Title VII."

Rarely in the history of the Court had a justice, speaking from the
bench no less, called so directly on another branch of government to
nullify a decision by her colleagues. And rarely had a justice's words
in dissent created so powerful and immediate an impact. Ginsburg's
words were intended to, and did, draw the notice of the Democratic legislators who had just won control of both houses of Congress. In addition, the Democratic candidates for president—among them, at that
point, Hillary Clinton, Barack Obama, and Joseph Biden—quickly
took up Ginsburg's challenge. Thanks to Ginsburg, a legislative overruling of *Ledbetter v. Goodyear Tire & Rubber Co.* became a central plank
of the Democratic Party.

Very suddenly, in her seventieth year, Lilly Ledbetter was a famous
woman.

6

THE WAR AGAINST PRECEDENT

With her dissent in *Ledbetter*, Ginsburg executed a nimble feat of jujitsu, turning a setback into a possible long-term victory. But in that second year of the Roberts Court, there was no mistaking the full picture of what was happening. The era of good feelings among the justices lasted precisely twelve months. Unanimous opinions in year two plummeted from 45 percent to 25 percent. More importantly, in contested cases the conservatives were winning, almost all the time. A full third of the cases were decided by a margin of 5–4, the highest percentage in more than a decade. The liberal quartet of Stevens, Souter, Ginsburg, and Breyer was able to assemble a majority in only a quarter of them.

The conservative victories ranged over the Court's docket, but some of the most important came in areas that especially mattered to the chief justice. In a famous decision from 1968, Chief Justice Warren held that taxpayers had the right to sue the government to block expenditures that might violate the First Amendment's prohibition on establishment of a state religion—that is, to maintain the barrier between church and state. Warren's theory in *Flast v. Cohen* was that if taxpayers did not have standing to bring these suits, there would be no effective way for the courts to examine possible constitutional violations. Conservatives like Roberts had targeted the *Flast* case for decades, part of their larger effort to rein in standing doctrine. In *Hein v. Freedom from Religion Foundation*, the five conservatives chipped away at the *Flast* precedent, holding that taxpayers lacked standing to challenge any action by the executive branch on church-state grounds.

In a case with the evocative title of *National Association of Home Build-*

ers v. Defenders of Wildlife, the Court shut the courthouse door to plaintiffs in a different way. The majority held that an environmental group
could not stop the Environmental Protection Agency from returning
jurisdiction over water pollution permits to states.

In death penalty cases, where Kennedy often joined the liberals, he
voted with the other side to uphold two planned executions. One case
involved jury selection in death penalty cases, and the other weighed
whether the defendant was entitled to a hearing on the issue of ineffec-
tive assistance of counsel.

Even one vaguely comic case from Alaska turned into a political standoff. On January 24, 2002, the Olympic Torch Relay passed
through Juneau on its way to the Winter Games in Salt Lake City. The
principal of a local high school allowed students and staff to skip class
and watch from the sidewalk as the runners passed by. Joseph Frederick,
an eighteen-year-old senior, stood across the street from the school with
a group of friends, with a fourteen-foot banner that said, BONG HiTS
4 JESUS. The principal told the group to take it down, and all except
Frederick agreed. The principal forcibly took the sign from Frederick
and later suspended him for ten days.

The issue in the case was whether the First Amendment protected
Frederick's display. At the time, Deborah Morse, the principal, said she
removed the sign because she thought it encouraged drug use. In fact, it
remains unclear to this day what, if anything, the sign meant. Frederick
always denied that he was talking about drugs; indeed, he maintained
that the whole thing was a joke and "that the words were just nonsense meant to attract television cameras." Still, in Morse v. Frederick, the
Court agreed to weigh the limits of students' First Amendment rights.

The subject had a rich history. In 1969, at the height of the Vietnam
War, the Court ruled that three students in Iowa could not be sent
home from their local schools for wearing black armbands to protest
the war. In Tinker v. Des Moines Independent Community School District, the
most famous opinion Abe Fortas wrote during his brief tenure on the
Court, he said, "It can hardly be argued that either students or teachers
shed their constitutional rights to freedom of speech or expression at
the schoolhouse gate." In the years since, though, conservative justices
had cut back on the freedoms granted to students, which they did in
Morse v. Frederick as well.

The dueling opinions, by Roberts for the majority and Stevens for the
dissenters, took issue over the less-than-momentous question of what

Frederick's slogan meant. "The message on Frederick's banner is cryptic," Roberts wrote. "It is no doubt offensive to some, perhaps amusing to others. To still others, it probably means nothing at all." Roberts and the four others were willing to trust the principal's conclusion that the banner encouraged drug use. On the other hand, Stevens took Frederick at his word: the banner was gibberish and he only wanted to get on television. The question was whether, in a matter involving freedom of speech, the principal or the student should receive the benefit of the doubt. Roberts won by backing the school authorities. (Thomas wrote a separate concurring opinion, arguing that *Tinker* should be overturned because students should have no free speech rights *at all* under the First Amendment.)

Morse v. Frederick could be dismissed as a silly aberration, but the overall tenor that year was unmistakable, and deadly serious. There was no doubt which one of the liberals was most traumatized by the Court's sharp turn to the right. It was Stephen Breyer.

Breyer was always very clear about his happiest professional memory. He had grown up in San Francisco, gone to Stanford and Harvard Law School, clerked for Justice Arthur Goldberg, and then returned to Harvard in the late sixties to teach. Less than a decade later, though, Breyer surprised his colleagues in Cambridge by returning to Washington. It was common for Harvard law professors to work in the executive branch—much later, Obama would practically deplete the faculty—but Breyer went to work in Congress. He became chief counsel to the Senate Judiciary Committee, which was then chaired by Edward M. Kennedy.

Almost every morning, Breyer had breakfast with the top lawyer for Strom Thurmond, who was then the senior Republican on the committee. Together, cordially, the two staffers mapped out plans for the committee. Of course Kennedy and Thurmond were ideological adversaries, but they directed their representatives to find areas of common ground. Indeed, it turned out to be a remarkably successful legislative partnership, producing landmark laws that deregulated the trucking, airline, and natural gas industries. Breyer loved that time in his life.

His tenure on the Judiciary Committee staff also yielded a very tangible benefit. In 1980, when Breyer was just forty-two, President Jimmy Carter nominated him to the First Circuit. Breyer was so popular among the senators on the committee, the Republicans as well as the Democrats, that he was confirmed *after* Carter had lost the presidential election to Ronald Reagan. Later, when the political environment on judicial nominations turned poisonous, this kind of bipartisanship on a circuit court nomination became inconceivable. But this period—this golden age, as Breyer recalled it—became the model that he hoped to replicate on the Supreme Court.

Breyer never lost respect for the legislators he came to know during his days on Capitol Hill. He believed in the Congress, and in government generally. To him, compromise was a virtue, not a vice. The point was to give everyone a say and reach a result that . . . *worked.* Breyer loved that word (and its cognates) and used it incessantly. "Our constitutional history," Breyer wrote in his book *Active Liberty*, published in 2005, "has been a quest for workable government, workable democratic government, workable democratic government protective of individual personal liberty." Five years later, Breyer wrote another book, which he called *Making Our Democracy Work*.

After Clinton appointed Breyer to the Court in 1994, Breyer dissented in most of the major cases up to and including *Bush v. Gore*, in 2000. But then Breyer had had his own brief period as a force in the majority, thanks largely to O'Connor. During George W. Bush's first term as president, as O'Connor grew more and more alienated from the Republican in the White House, Breyer and O'Connor became a formidable team. They also shared a genuine fondness for each other, for they had similar practical, problem-solving temperaments. They traveled the world, giving speeches and advice to judges and legislators. (After the 9/11 attacks, they were stranded in India together.)

The highpoint of Breyer's influence can be marked with precision. At the end of the term in June 2005, the Court decided two cases about public displays of the Ten Commandments, both by votes of 5–4. The Court rejected a decision by local authorities to post the Commandments in Kentucky courthouses but at the same time allowed the Commandments to remain in a public park, near the state capitol, in Austin, Texas. Four justices thought both displays should remain; four others thought both should be taken down.

Only Breyer was in the majority in both cases. He endured some mockery for his seemingly inconsistent positions, but his reasoning made sense. The Kentucky Commandments, which everyone in the courthouse could see, were clearly intended as a provocation, and the display had been controversial from the moment it was posted. In Texas, on the other hand, the monument with the Commandments drew no notice at all for forty years. (The plaintiff in the case was a homeless man who sometimes lived in the park.) Breyer thought the difference in public reactions to the displays was critical. The Texas display "has stood apparently uncontested for nearly two generations. That experience helps us understand that as a practical matter of *degree* this display is unlikely to prove divisive," Breyer wrote. But he added, referring to the Kentucky display, that "in a Nation of so many different religious and comparable nonreligious fundamental beliefs, a more contemporary state effort to focus attention upon a religious text is certainly likely to prove divisive in a way that this long-standing, pre-existing monument has not." It was, to use Breyer's favorite word, a workable compromise.

In any case, Breyer's moment was brief. The decisions in the Kentucky and Texas cases were announced on June 27, 2005. Four days later, O'Connor announced her departure from the Court.

When Breyer was appointed, he was often described, with good reason, as a technocrat. He taught antitrust and administrative law at Harvard, and he was more deeply steeped in those arcane specialties than in the constitutional law at the center of the Court's work. Once Breyer settled into his new position, however, he tried to come to terms with the Constitution and the place of the Court in the broader history of the country.

It is easy, if unwise, to romanticize the history of the Supreme Court. During John Marshall's tenure as chief justice, from 1801 to 1835, the Court built a noble template for American democracy. Marshall himself, more than any framer of the Constitution or even any president, defined the terms of separation of powers, the breadth of federal power, the relationship between the national government and the states, and the place of the Supreme Court in the government of the young nation. Thanks to Marshall, the Court made a glorious debut.

For the next twelve decades, however, the Supreme Court was for the most part a malign force in American life. The landmarks of this era, which still constitutes more than half the history of the Court, were nearly all negative. In 1857, to the eternal shame of the institution, the Court held in *Dred Scott v. Sanford* that African Americans were property and that they could never possess the rights that belonged to human beings. This decision hastened the Civil War and was technically overruled by the passage of the Thirteenth, Fourteenth, and Fifteenth Amendments. The Court then proceeded to give those amendments such cramped and narrow meanings that the justices allowed African Americans to endure perpetual discrimination, and much violence, for a great many more years. In *Plessy v. Ferguson*, from 1896, the Court gave its formal imprimatur to American apartheid by approving Louisiana's system of separate railcars for blacks and whites. In 1905, the Court decided *Lochner v. New York*, rejecting a state law that limited the number of hours bakers could work. This dismal decision set off several more decades when the Court dedicated itself to obstructing legislative initiatives that might protect the nation's less powerful citizens.

Earl Warren's tenure as chief justice ushered the United States into the modern era of race relations and, in some deeper sense, saved the Supreme Court as an institution. Warren recognized that a court that had the legend EQUAL JUSTICE UNDER LAW carved into its façade could no longer tolerate state-sponsored segregation. In just his second year as chief justice, on May 17, 1954, Warren steered his colleagues to a unanimous decision in *Brown v. Board of Education*. Warren himself wrote the opinion in simple, direct prose. "We conclude that, in the field of public education, the doctrine of 'separate but equal' has no place," he wrote, formally overruling *Plessy v. Ferguson*.

The case, and the Warren Court's decisions on race, became Breyer's special interest. On the fiftieth anniversary of *Brown*, Breyer volunteered to be the Court's emissary to the official celebration, in Topeka, Kansas, where the case began. "As a member of the Supreme Court, I am here today to represent that Court, not nine individual Justices, but the institution itself—an institution as old as the Republic, charged with the responsibility of interpreting the Constitution of the United States," Breyer told the crowd, including President Bush. "May 17, 1954, was a great day—many would say the greatest day—in the history of that institution," he continued. "Before May 17, 1954, the Court read the Constitution's words 'equal protection of the laws,' as if they protected only the members of the majority race. After May 17, 1954, it read those words as the post–Civil War Framers meant them, as offering the same protection to citizens of every race." (Not everyone on the Court was so moved by the anniversary; William Rehnquist also gave a speech on May 17, 2004, and he didn't even mention *Brown*.)

Brown also had a special resonance for Breyer because of his own experiences in the public schools. Breyer grew up in San Francisco in what he regarded as a unique and glorious moment in the city's history. The post–World War II boom there created an equality of opportunity that was rare, if not unprecedented, in American history. Steve and his younger brother, Chuck, graduated from Lowell High School, the jewel of the San Francisco system, a selective academy that served generations of strivers. Breyer's father spent decades as a lawyer for the San Francisco school board, helping to manage the influx of immigrants from around the world. (Breyer still wears the wristwatch that his father received upon his retirement. The inscription reads, "Irving G. Breyer, Legal Advisor, San Francisco Unified School District, 1933–1973, from his friends.") Lowell led to good things for Chuck, too. In 1997, Clinton appointed Charles Breyer to the federal district court in San Francisco.

No Breyer speech (and he gave many) was complete without the story of *Cooper v. Aaron*, the famous case that directed the public schools of Little Rock, Arkansas, to cease obstructing the rule of law and integrate forthwith. (The opinion remains the only one in the Court's history to which all nine justices affixed their names as coauthors.) Describing the aftermath of *Cooper v. Aaron*, Breyer said that Warren's words in *Brown* "forced the Nation to ask themselves whether it believed in a rule of law—a rule of law that the Nation's history had sometimes denied, a rule of law that President Dwight D. Eisenhower enforced in 1957 when he sent federal paratroopers to Arkansas to take those black schoolchildren by the hand and walk them safely through that white schoolhouse door. We now accept that rule of law as part of our heritage, thanks to *Brown* and to its aftermath. But too often we take that rule of law for granted."

That was the final question for the Court in Roberts's second year: Was *Brown* now taken for granted?

Seattle and Louisville, on opposite ends of the country, different in spirit, history, and orientation, confronted a similar problem. In both cities, kids generally went to public schools near where they lived, and neighborhoods tended to be highly segregated by race. The school boards in both cities wanted to nudge enrollment in a more integrated direction. In Seattle, where citywide enrollment was about 41 percent white and 59 percent nonwhite, students were allowed to choose their high schools. For the more popular schools, the city had a tiebreaker formula. The first tiebreaker was whether a sibling already attended the school. The second was race; if the school's racial makeup was more than ten percentage points different from that of the city as a whole, race would determine whether a particular student was admitted. Kentucky's Jefferson County, which included Louisville, had a roughly similar plan. Proximity of the student's home to the school was the first tiebreaker; race was the second. Very few students, probably less than five hundred in each city, were affected by the second part of the formula.

So if the two cases only affected a handful of students, why did they matter so much? There was the simple historical resonance of public school integration at the Court. More importantly, the Seattle and Louisville lawsuits represented the first time the Roberts Court addressed the legacy of *Brown*. Was *Brown* essentially a libertarian decision, which simply forbade all recognition of race by the government? Or did *Brown* mandate, or allow, government to take steps to foster integration? When can the government consider your race in assigning you to a school—or hiring you for a job, or assigning you to a congressional district? Can government consider race at all?

In the most important opinion of her career, O'Connor had answered a version of these questions in 2003. In *Grutter v. Bollinger*, she spoke for a narrow majority of the Court in approving the admissions policy of the University of Michigan Law School. Under that policy, the law school considered race as one of many factors, including grades and test scores, in deciding whom to admit. O'Connor approved the practice for the same reason that her mentor, Lewis Powell, approved of affirmative action in graduate school admissions in the *Bakke* case of 1978. O'Connor ruled in *Grutter* that "student body diversity is a compelling state interest that can justify the use of race in university admissions." But her decision came with a warning and, even more unusual in a Supreme Court decision, a time limit. "It has been 25 years since Justice Powell first approved the use of race to further an interest in student body diversity in the context of public higher education," O'Connor wrote, referring to *Bakke*. "Since that time, the number of minority applicants with high grades and test scores has indeed increased. We expect that 25 years from now, the use of racial preferences will no longer be necessary to further the interest approved today." In the Seattle and Louisville cases, just four years after *Grutter*, the question was whether O'Connor's words remained the law.

In the lead case, which was known as *Parents Involved in Community Schools v. Seattle School District No. 1*, Roberts took the opportunity to display what had been, at that point, something of a secret weapon in his arsenal. The quality of writing in Supreme Court opinions generally ranges from serviceable to opaque, and the justices' attempts at eloquence often fall flat. For his part, Breyer wrote in a kind of prose PowerPoint, with paragraphs that began *First, Second, Third.* Souter's style was so gnarled that the justice himself made fun of it. Receiving an eloquent draft from a law clerk, Souter would say, "Time for me to put some lead in . . ." In his earlier years, Stevens tended toward a midwestern directness—he did all his own drafting for a long time—but eventually he too migrated toward the mean. Scalia put a gift for invective on display in dissents but wrote with less verve, and interest, for the Court. Kennedy had a weakness for bloviation.

Chief Justice Roberts, it soon became evident, was a brilliant writer—clear, epigrammatic, eloquent without being verbose. The peroration of his decision in *Parents Involved* made his case with characteristic force. "For schools that never segregated on the basis of race, such as Seattle, or that have removed the vestiges of past segregation, such as Jefferson County, the way to achieve a system of determining admission to the public schools on a nonracial basis is to stop assigning students on a racial basis," he wrote. "The way to stop discrimination on the basis of race is to stop discriminating on the basis of race."

The way to stop discrimination on the basis of race is to stop discriminating on the basis of race. Who could disagree with that?

The four dissenters did not just disagree—they were enraged. Stevens assigned the main dissenting opinion to Breyer, but he could not resist adding a short, incredulous dissent of his own, not least because the legacy of *Brown* was at stake. "There is a cruel irony in The Chief Justice's reliance on our decision in *Brown* v. *Board of Education*," Stevens wrote. "The first sentence in the concluding paragraph of his opinion states: 'Before *Brown*, schoolchildren were told where they could and could not go to school based on the color of their skin.' This sentence reminds me of Anatole France's observation: 'The majestic equality of the law, forbids rich and poor alike to sleep under bridges, to beg in the streets, and to steal their bread.' The Chief Justice fails to note that it was only black schoolchildren who were so ordered; indeed, the history books do not tell stories of white children struggling to attend black schools. In this and other ways, The Chief Justice rewrites the history of one of this Court's most important decisions."

Stevens had turned eighty-seven shortly before the Court's decision in *Parents Involved.* Stevens knew that, at his age, his time as a force on the Court was shrinking fast. More than in his earlier days, Stevens did not mince words. The conservative torrent of Roberts's second year moved him to something close to outrage.

"The Court has changed significantly," Stevens wrote in his *Parents Involved* dissent. It was once "more faithful to *Brown* and more respectful of our precedent than it is today. It is my firm conviction that no Member of the Court that I joined in 1975 would have agreed with today's decision."

The last day of a term always arrived laden with drama. Almost invariably, it was when the Court's most important and controversial decisions of the year were announced or when the justices revealed their plans to retire. As a rule, it was also a time when the justices were both tired and sick of one another. Everyone needed a haircut and a vacation.

Plainly, on June 28, 2007, Breyer was distraught. This kind of career— writing dissent after dissent—was not how he envisioned his life as a justice. Breyer clerked for the liberal Arthur Goldberg in 1964–65, near the liberal apogee of the Warren Court. Breyer was not naïve. He didn't think everyone would agree with him all the time. But Breyer did at least think the atmosphere at the Court might resemble the collegiality he found at the Judiciary Committee thirty years earlier. In the heyday of the O'Connor-Breyer Court, he read less than one dissent a year from the bench. But on this final day of the 2006–07 term alone, he read two protests in 5–4 cases.

The first, called *Leegin Creative Leather Products,* involved antitrust law. Since a 1911 case called *Dr. Miles,* the Court had held that a manufacturer who required retailers to sell a product for a minimum price was always guilty of an antitrust violation. With the urging of the Bush administration, Kennedy's opinion for the Court overruled that ninety-six-year-old precedent and said that such violations should now be determined on a case-by-case basis. (The political divisions in antitrust cases are clear. Democrats favor strict enforcement, while Republicans defer to the market.)

As the second-most-junior justice, Breyer had the seat to the chief justice's extreme right, which happened to be only about a dozen feet from the benches reserved for journalists. As he read his first dissent of the day—a short one—Breyer turned toward the reporters to make sure they were paying attention. He knew that antitrust cases rarely attracted much public notice, but he used the case to highlight a broader issue about the Roberts Court.

"I just want to emphasize one point here, and it is stare decisis," Breyer said. "The legal rule that forbids vertical price fixing—it comes from the case called *Dr. Miles*—is nearly 100 years old. It's well known to those in the law and in business. This court and lower courts have followed it consistently for decades." Breyer used the term "stare decisis"—the rule of precedent—three more times in his brief statement. His message was clear: the Roberts Court was on the warpath against the Court's own history.

Then, finally, came the last case of the year, *Parents Involved*. Roberts began by giving his summary of the case, and it was plain that one more precedent was now endangered—O'Connor's opinion in *Grutter*. O'Connor had written broadly about the value of diversity in education, but Roberts said that the Court now viewed *Grutter* as relating only to "diversity in higher education." Since *Parents Involved* concerned only high schools, Roberts said, the reasoning in *Grutter* was irrelevant. This was what the Supreme Court did when it was preparing to jettison a precedent: first limit it, then overrule it.

Breyer followed, reading from a dissent that he noted was more than twice as long as any he had written. School boards, like the one to which his father had devoted his life, had done their best in Seattle and Louisville. "They began with racially segregated schools," Breyer said. "They sought remedies. They tried forced busing. They feared or experienced white flight. They faced concerns about de facto re-segregation, and they ended up with plans that end forced busing, that rely heavily upon student choice. In both cities all the students choose. The majority, indeed almost all of them, received their first-choice school." And to Breyer, there was nothing wrong, indeed everything right, with what the school boards had done.

To Breyer, the efforts of these cities honored *Brown* rather than defied it. "*Brown* held out a promise, it was a promise embodied in three

Amendments designed to make citizens of former slaves," he said. "It was the promise of true racial equality, not as a matter of fine words on paper, but as a matter of everyday life of the Nation's citizens and schools. It was about the nature of democracy that must work for all Americans." Democracy that *worked*—this was always Breyer's goal.

But Breyer's dissent was not just about *Parents Involved*, or *Brown*, or even civil rights. It was about what had happened to the Court in this one short year—on abortion, and women's rights, and civil procedure, and freedom of speech, and antitrust, and the death penalty, and on and on. Breyer departed from the text of his dissenting opinion to offer an introduction to the real Roberts Court.

"It is not often in the law," he said, "that so few have so quickly changed so much."

PART
TWO

7

THE HUNTER

As the Roberts era began, Antonin Scalia's spirits were low. Notwithstanding his halfhearted denials, he had hoped to be named chief justice. His old friend Dick Cheney, with whom he served in the Ford administration, raised the possibility of the promotion for Scalia, but the idea never went anywhere with President Bush. Much as Scalia was a hero to conservatives, he was also nearly seventy years old. The opportunity to control the Court for a generation was far more important to Bush, and even to most fellow believers, than rewarding Scalia for a job well done.

In truth, Scalia had mixed feelings about being on the Court at all. He often said that he would have left the Court years earlier if he could have found another place where people would pay as much attention to his ideas. But there was no such place. In routine cases, Scalia barely went through the motions. For these, his clerks learned to operate with minimal guidance from their boss. Scalia's belligerence at oral arguments, particularly in minor cases, was a way for him to keep paying attention—and getting attention. Scalia craved the spotlight. When O'Connor left the Court, Scalia often took over her custom of asking the first question during oral arguments. When another justice made a joke, Scalia invariably tried to top it.

On the cases that mattered most to him, though, Scalia hated to lose, and for most of his career on the Court, he lost more of these than he won. In 1992, Scalia thought he was within reach of overturning the hated *Roe v. Wade*. But then O'Connor, Kennedy, and Souter betrayed him in *Casey*. Scalia's dissent was splenetic. ("The Imperial Judiciary lives," he sneered.) Scalia was even more apoplectic in 2003, when the

Court ruled in *Lawrence v. Texas* that gay people could no longer be prosecuted for having consensual sex. ("Today's opinion is the product of a Court, which is the product of a law-profession culture, that has largely signed on to the so-called homosexual agenda, by which I mean the agenda promoted by some homosexual activists directed at eliminating the moral opprobrium that has traditionally attached to homosexual conduct," he wrote.) Scalia's gift for invective made his dissents far more memorable than his majority opinions, but still, he grew weary of writing them.

It was no coincidence that cases involving the culture war moved Scalia the most. He regularly spoke to Catholic groups, and over the last decade he often gave them the same speech in slightly different forms. It was a sarcastic look at how he thought true believers were viewed by secular elites. "We must pray for courage to endure the scorn of the sophisticated world," he would say. "Surely those who adhere to all or most of these traditional Christian beliefs are to be regarded as simple-minded. Devout Christians are destined to be regarded as fools in modern society." His remarks would often close, "If I have brought any message today, it is this: Have the courage to have your wisdom regarded as stupidity. Be fools for Christ. And have the courage to suffer the contempt of the sophisticated world." Biblical literalism was never far from constitutional literalism, or, as Scalia called it, textualism.

There was some irony in Scalia's sense of victimhood, because his own career had been one of perpetual ascent. He was born in Trenton and raised in Elmhurst, Queens, where his father commuted to a job as a professor of Romance languages at Brooklyn College. (He translated works of Italian literature.) His mother taught elementary school. Nino, their only child, excelled academically. He made law review at Harvard. While a law student, he met his future wife, Maureen, who was a Radcliffe undergraduate. They have nine children. One is a priest.

After a brief stop at a Cleveland law firm, Scalia became a professor at the nation's top law schools. (He taught at Chicago, Stanford, Georgetown, and Virginia.) Like Breyer, Scalia was principally interested in administrative law, but Scalia generally took stronger antiregulatory positions than Breyer did. His views drew the attention of the conservatives ascendant in Washington, and he served in the Justice Department under President Ford. Reagan put him on the D.C. Circuit in 1982, when he was just forty-six, and on the Supreme Court four years later. Scalia's Italian roots and Catholicism, far from being disabilities, were the deciding factors in his getting the nomination over Robert Bork.

Scalia had, in some ways, the best of both worlds, even if he didn't see it that way. He was by far the favorite justice of the cultural warriors—the religious groups, the Federalist Society—and he reflected and encouraged their sneers at "the sophisticated world" and the "law-profession culture." At the same time, he earned the admiration of that world, too. Even if his former colleagues in the legal academy didn't share Scalia's judicial philosophy, they recognized his achievement in placing a fully formed ideology at the center of American constitutional law. The magnitude of Scalia's accomplishment should not be understated. In the modern era of the Court, only Scalia, Oliver Wendell Holmes, and perhaps William Brennan introduced their own judicial philosophies into the life and work of the Court.

This was apparent in 2006, after Scalia saw the chief's chair slip away from him forever. Over two days in November, Harvard Law School held a celebration of Scalia's twentieth anniversary on the Supreme Court. The event was the brainchild of the dean of Scalia's alma mater, Elena Kagan. Kagan was a veteran of the Clinton administration, a failed nominee to the D.C. Circuit herself. Everyone in Cambridge knew she didn't share Scalia's politics or his judicial philosophy, but that made it all the sweeter for Scalia when Kagan and her colleagues paid such fulsome tribute to him. "His views on textualism and originalism, his views on the role of judges in our society, on the practice of judging, have really transformed the terms of legal debate in this country," Kagan said in her speech. "He is the justice who has had the most important impact over the years on how we think and talk about law."

Given his background, Scalia's embrace of such culture war touchstones as opposition to abortion and gay rights was unsurprising. He also had a long history with guns, which was not exactly what one might expect of a native New Yorker.

As a teenager, Scalia commuted from Queens to Manhattan to attend Xavier High School, an all-male Jesuit institution on Sixteenth Street. Even for its time—Scalia was class of 1953—Xavier was an unusual place because every student was required to participate in junior ROTC. After school, young Antonin participated in drills at an armory, and he took his rifle, a .22 carbine, with him on the subway—a novelty, to be sure, and not then a violation of law. For many years, the exigencies of adult life took Scalia far away from the world of guns, but eventually he returned.

In 1991, Scalia replaced Byron White as the justice responsible for the Fifth Circuit, which includes several southern states. Scalia started making regular trips to the region, and friends down there began inviting him along on hunting expeditions. Scalia fell hard for the sport, especially the pursuit of birds like turkeys. Briefly, though, Scalia became the most famous duck hunter in the country. In January 2004, he invited Dick Cheney to join him on a duck-hunting trip in Louisiana. As it happened, a legal challenge to the secrecy of the vice president's energy task force was pending before the justices, and Scalia faced robust criticism for socializing with a litigant. In a characteristically combative riposte, Scalia filed a twenty-one-page memorandum justifying his trip. "The Vice President and I were never in the same blind, and never discussed the case," he wrote. "Washington officials know the rules, and know that discussing with judges pending cases—their own or anyone else's—is forbidden." In any event, more than his colleagues, Scalia had a personal interest in the constitutional status of firearms— a subject the Court had not addressed in many years.

In its first two hundred years, the Supreme Court discussed the Second Amendment in any depth on only one occasion. The case arose on April 18, 1938, when state troopers arrested a small-time hood named Jack Miller and an accomplice in Siloam Springs, Arkansas. Miller was a suspect in the killing of a court reporter (of all people) in a bar fight, and he had turned state's evidence after a string of bank robberies. At the time of his arrest, there were two unregistered sawed-off shotguns in the car, and Miller was charged with violating the National Firearms Act, which had been passed in 1934 in response to the St. Valentine's Day massacre and other notorious crimes of the era. A federal district judge in Arkansas threw the case out on the ground that the law violated Miller's rights under the Second Amendment.

In 1939, the Supreme Court unanimously reversed the district judge and held that the firearms act complied with the Second Amendment. To achieve that result, Justice James McReynolds had to excavate a part of American history that was obscure even then. In the days before the American Revolution, there was no standing army in the colonies. Instead, when there was need for collective military action—usually against Indians—the colonists formed militias. The militias relied on the guns and gunpowder of private citizens, which were sometimes stockpiled together for later use. During the period immediately before and during the Revolution, the British took to seizing the guns of the colonists, who were understandably outraged.

When it came time to write a Constitution, the framers took care to preserve the independence of these local militias from interference by the central government. There are several references to militias in the Constitution, though the Second Amendment is today by far the best known. Article I states that Congress has the power:

> To provide for calling forth the Militia to execute the Laws of the Union, suppress Insurrections and repel Invasions; [and]
>
> To provide for organizing, arming, and disciplining, the Militia, and for governing such Part of them as may be employed in the Service of the United States.

Article II says the president is commander in chief of the army, navy and "Militia of the several States, when called into the actual Service of the United States." In other words, when the Constitution was being framed, the militias were a vibrant and significant part of American life. They survived into the nineteenth century, and then, in the Militia Act of 1903, their functions were formally subsumed into other agencies, like the National Guard and other law enforcement and military entities.

It was against this background that the Supreme Court weighed the challenge to the early form of gun control in the *Miller* case. McReynolds's opinion for the Court was almost entirely originalist in its reasoning. The opinion quoted the provisions of Article I dealing with the militia powers, and then stated, "With obvious purpose to assure the continuation and render possible the effectiveness of such forces, the declaration and guarantee of the Second Amendment were made. It must be interpreted and applied with that end in view." Indeed, if the Second Amendment were intended by its framers to give individuals a right to keep and bear arms, the initial militia clause would be both unnecessary and meaningless.

McReynolds went on to say that the framers believed militias would protect the rights of the people from an oppressive central government. "The sentiment of the time strongly disfavored standing armies; the common view was that adequate defense of country and laws could be secured through the Militia—civilians primarily, soldiers on occasion." He quoted William Blackstone and Adam Smith on the importance of militias and reviewed the state laws concerning them. "Most if not all of the States have adopted provisions touching the right to keep and bear arms," he wrote. "But none of them seems to afford any material support for the challenged ruling of the court below." For these reasons, justices concluded that the Second Amendment existed to preserve the rights of militias—not individuals—to possess arms.

After the unanimous and largely uncontroversial decision in *United States v. Miller*, the issue of the Second Amendment more or less disappeared from the national agenda for decades. During and after World War II, the United States entered a period of prosperity and safety. There was little call for gun control, and thus no reason to challenge the constitutional basis for it. That began to change in the 1960s, when assassinations and crime generally built political momentum for restrictions on gun ownership. Following the murder of Robert F. Kennedy, Congress passed the Gun Control Act of 1968, the last major piece of legislation of Lyndon Johnson's presidency. The bill's restrictions were modest—prohibiting the sale of most firearms through the mail, limiting certain high-risk people from buying guns. There was widespread support for the law, even from the National Rifle Association. In this period, part of what it meant to be tough on crime—a traditional Republican goal—was to endorse gun control. President Gerald Ford, a typical member of his party for his era, proposed gun control legislation. But Ronald Reagan, Ford's opponent for the Republican nomination in 1976, was staking out a different position.

Reagan worked opposition to gun control into a broader libertarian message. To him, gun control was just another big-government program that did more harm than good. Gun control punished law-abiding citizens while leaving firearms in the hands of criminals. What was more, Reagan hinted, gun control was prohibited by the Second Amendment. "The Second Amendment gives the individual citizen a means of protection against the despotism of the state. The rights of the individual are preeminent," Reagan wrote in *Guns & Ammo* magazine in 1975. "The Second Amendment is clear, or ought to be. It appears to leave little if any leeway for the gun control advocate." Reagan lost in 1976, but times were changing. The 1972 Republican platform had supported gun control, but the 1976 platform opposed it.

The political and legal branches of the conservative movement joined forces in support of a new reading of the Second Amendment. On May 21, 1977, a hard-line faction of the National Rifle Association staged a coup d'état at the annual meeting of the group, in Cincinnati. Out went the traditional emphasis on gun safety and in came a new focus on political action, especially in fighting gun control. The NRA financed a group called Academics for the Second Amendment, which advocated for the individual rights view in conferences and seminars. Still, this position remained well outside the legal mainstream, if not downright eccentric. The rule of the *Miller* case remained the unchallenged law of the land. Not even a lower federal court had embraced the view that the Constitution limited the ability of the government to regulate gun ownership. A few years after Warren Burger stepped down as chief justice, he said in an interview on PBS that the Second Amendment "has been the subject of one of the greatest pieces of fraud— I repeat the word 'fraud'—on the American public by special interest groups that I have ever seen in my lifetime."

Nevertheless, gun rights joined "family values" and the anti-abortion fight as key planks of the conservative agenda that in 1980 propelled Reagan into the presidency and the Republicans into the Senate majority. When Orrin Hatch, the Utah Republican, became chairman of the Subcommittee on the Constitution, he commissioned a report entitled "The Right to Keep and Bear Arms." In the preface he wrote, "What the Subcommittee on the Constitution uncovered was clear—and long lost—proof that the second amendment to our Constitution was intended as an individual right of the American citizen to keep and carry arms in a peaceful manner, for protection of himself, his family, and his freedoms." The chief author of the report was a Hatch staffer named Stephen Markman, who later joined the Reagan Justice Department. There, one of Markman's junior colleagues was Samuel Alito.

Crime spiked again in the early nineties, and the Clinton administration, in its early days, responded by passing what became known as the Brady bill, named after James Brady, Ronald Reagan's press secretary, who was wounded in the 1981 attempted assassination of the president. This complex piece of legislation included an interim provision that directed state and local officials to conduct background checks for prospective handgun purchasers. That portion of the bill was challenged, and in 1997, by a 5–4 vote, the Supreme Court found the temporary part of the law unconstitutional. Scalia's opinion for the Court in *Printz v. United States* concluded that the law amounted to an impermissible federal intrusion on states' rights.

Thomas joined Scalia's opinion for the majority but wrote a concurring opinion that examined the case in a different way. Thomas devoted his argument to the Second Amendment, which the Court had not addressed since the *Miller* case in 1939. He suggested that the Brady bill might be unconstitutional as a violation of the Second Amendment. "Marshaling an impressive array of historical evidence, a growing body of scholarly commentary indicates that the 'right to keep and bear arms' is, as the Amendment's text suggests, a personal right," Thomas wrote. Concluding with a flourish and referring to Joseph Story, a renowned figure from the early days of the Court, Thomas declared, "Perhaps, at some future date, this Court will have the opportunity to determine whether Justice Story was correct when he wrote that the right to bear arms 'has justly been considered, as the palladium of the liberties of a republic.' "

Thomas's opinion marked the near culmination of a remarkable political and legal undertaking—an example of the "living Constitution" in action, even if that was not how the protagonists described it. A small group of activists took a fringe and discredited constitutional interpretation, injected their considerable passion, intelligence, and financial resources, and nearly brought their ideas to success.

The actual culmination of their work would take a little longer.

8

LAWYERS, GUNS, AND MONEY

The Supreme Court can sometimes have the last word, but it never has the first. The executive and legislative branches of government can initiate action on any issue of their choosing. But the justices must wait for a case to come to them. Some or all of the justices may be itching to rule on a subject, but they have no chance to do so until an appropriate appeal arrives at their door. When it came to guns, that was what made Bob Levy so important.

Robert A. Levy was born in 1941 and grew up in modest circumstances in Washington, where his parents ran a hardware store. He went to college at American University, earned a PhD in business there as well, and went on to live the American dream. He founded a financial information and software firm, CDA Investment Technologies, and sold it for many millions of dollars in 1986. At that point, Levy thought carefully about what he would do with the second half of his life—and decided to start law school at the age of forty-nine. He chose to study at George Mason University, because it had a reputation for welcoming libertarian scholars and students. After graduating, Levy became a law clerk first for Royce Lamberth, of the federal district court in Washington, and then for Douglas Ginsburg, on the D.C. Circuit. (Levy may be the only law clerk in history who was older than the judges he clerked for. The security guards at the federal courthouse, noting Levy's judicial bearing and formidable bald head, would often greet him by saying, "Good morning, Your Honor." In chambers, Lamberth would put him in his place by reminding him to fill the water jugs in the jury box.)

When Levy completed his clerkships, he brought the same entrepreneurial spirit to law that he had to business. He had a special interest in the Second Amendment, which was the subject of a great deal of scholarly attention at the time, even though he himself never owned a gun. The NRA-funded Academics for the Second Amendment had been churning out copy, and even several liberal academics, including Laurence Tribe, Akhil Reed Amar, and Sanford Levinson, had looked with some sympathy on the individual rights theory of the Second Amendment. And Justice Thomas's concurring opinion in the *Printz* case had put the issue squarely on the Supreme Court's agenda.

There was also the matter of *United States v. Emerson*. The Brady bill made it a crime for individuals who were subject to domestic-violence protective orders to possess firearms. In 1999, a local court filed a protective order against Timothy Emerson, a doctor in Tom Green County, Texas, who was involved in a messy divorce. Later, a federal grand jury charged Emerson with violating the Brady bill, because he purchased a pistol while subject to the protective order. Emerson challenged the constitutionality of the law, on the ground that it violated the Second Amendment. A federal district court, relying heavily on Thomas's opinion in *Printz*, concluded that the Second Amendment did confer an individual right to bear arms and threw out the indictment. In 2001, the Fifth Circuit reinstated Emerson's indictment but again cited Thomas's opinion in calling for a new understanding of the Second Amendment.

The political momentum for a revived Second Amendment was building, too. By this point, John Ashcroft had become George W. Bush's first attorney general. A longtime member and favorite of the NRA, Ashcroft gave a full official endorsement of the theory that the Second Amendment granted individuals a right to keep and bear arms. In a letter read at the NRA annual convention in 2001, Ashcroft announced that the federal government would now advocate the individual rights theory in all litigation. But *Emerson* was actually a poor vehicle for testing the limits of the Second Amendment, because the constitutional issue was so closely bound up with the matter of domestic violence. Not surprisingly, the justices declined to hear the *Emerson* case.

Levy had clerked for Lamberth with a young lawyer named Clark Neily III, who then went to work for the Institute for Justice, a libertarian-leaning public interest law firm. (Levy was on the board.) Neily and a colleague, Steve Simpson, came to Levy with the idea of putting together a test case that would raise the Second Amendment issue for the Supreme Court. The scholarly articles, the Thomas opinion in *Printz*, the friendly Justice Department, the *Emerson* case—all suggested that the time was right. The problem was, the Institute for Justice didn't do this kind of work. Neily and Simpson asked Levy to finance the case himself, and he agreed. Levy also hired Alan Gura, an aggressive young lawyer from Virginia, who happened to have an interest in the subject but no experience at all with constitutional litigation or the Supreme Court.

The National Rifle Association was not amused by the attempt of Levy, Neily, Simpson (and later Gura) to horn in on what it considered its turf. Levy had a day job at the Cato Institute, the libertarian think tank in Washington, where he later became chairman of the board. One day he was visited there by Nelson Lund, one of his professors at George Mason, whose chair had been endowed by the NRA, and Charles Cooper, a former Reagan-era Justice Department official with close ties to the conservative movement. Their mission was to talk Levy out of funding the case. The pair told him that the issue was a loser. The law-and-order conservatives then on the Court, including Rehnquist and O'Connor, would never buy a wholesale revision of the Second Amendment. A bad ruling could set back the cause for years. Better to leave the issue to the NRA and its experienced team of litigators.

Conflicts over litigation strategy are common, even among ideological allies. Issues of timing, risk of adverse decisions, control of a case, and simple ego often lead to bitter feuds. The models for such ideologically driven legal crusades remain the work of Thurgood Marshall for civil rights in the forties and fifties and Ruth Bader Ginsburg for women in the seventies. Levy felt his work was in this tradition. Sometimes, though, it's almost as important to know when *not* to bring a case as when to press forward. Advocates have at times gone to extraordinary lengths to keep cases away from the justices. In 1997, after a white schoolteacher was laid off to save the job of a black colleague, a coalition of civil rights groups raised $300,000 to settle the case two months before it was slated to appear on the Supreme Court docket.

Especially on issues with high public profiles, the motives of the participants can be decidedly mixed. There were even conservatives who believed that at some level the NRA didn't *want* a favorable decision from the Supreme Court on gun rights; they thought NRA fund-raising depended on maintaining a sense of perpetual risk. Levy thought the

NRA was just protecting its turf, but his own fortune gave him the luxury of a single-minded focus: winning in the Supreme Court. Lund and Cooper denied that the NRA's motives were anything less than pure, but Levy decided to stay the course with his case.

Their best option, Levy's team realized, was under their noses in Washington. The District of Columbia had the strictest gun laws in the nation, banning possession of handguns even in private homes for self-defense. Over the years, gun cases had foundered in part because they had unsympathetic plaintiffs. In 1939, Miller was a bank robber; many years later, Emerson was accused of threatening domestic violence. Those were not favorable settings in which to raise Second Amendment claims. Gura and the others wanted to avoid such problems from the start. They decided to pick their plaintiffs almost as if they were casting a movie.

After months of research, the Levy team came up with six people who could, as a group, appeal to almost any judge. There were three men and three women, four whites and two blacks, five straight and one gay. The lead plaintiff, Shelly Parker, was an extremely charismatic African American woman. In February 2002, Parker had moved to the periphery of Capitol Hill and found her neighborhood overrun by drug dealers. She started a one-woman security patrol, walking the streets in an orange cap and reporting what she saw to the police. In response, drug dealers broke her car windows and drove into her back fence. She wanted a gun to protect herself and her home. Levy's team entitled the case *Parker v. District of Columbia.*

Despite all the careful planning, the case ran into a problem the team had not fully anticipated. For all that they were fighting to advance a conservative goal—gun rights—their case was still a kind of public interest litigation. Like civil rights plaintiffs, these six people were initiating a lawsuit in order to challenge a government action. Thanks to the conservatives on the Supreme Court, the legal rules on standing in such cases had been tightened a great deal in recent years. Applying those new rules, the D.C. Circuit held that the plaintiffs could not simply walk into the courtroom and demand a ruling on the gun control law. The circuit court said the plaintiffs had to have actually made an application for a gun license and been rejected in order to have standing to bring the case. This rule presented a catch-22. Under the D.C. law, you had to own a handgun first to apply for a permit—but it was illegal to buy a gun in Washington. Federal law, moreover, made it illegal to buy a gun in a state where you did not reside. So you needed a gun to apply for a license, but you couldn't buy the gun in the first place.

Five of the six plaintiffs (including Shelly Parker) had not applied for gun licenses, so the D.C. Circuit threw out their cases. But the litigation survived. The sixth plaintiff, Dick Heller, was a specially assigned District of Columbia police officer who helped protect the Federal Judicial Center. He was issued a gun to use at work, and he wanted to keep a private handgun at his home as well. Alone among the plaintiffs, Heller already had a gun, and he had actually sought a gun permit from the D.C. government and been denied. For that reason, the court found that only Heller had standing to bring the constitutional challenge to the law.

But one plaintiff was enough. The D.C. Circuit adopted for the first time the individual rights theory. The court held that Heller had the right to "keep and bear arms" under the Second Amendment and struck down the local law. The lawyers for the District of Columbia asked the Supreme Court to review the decision, and the justices agreed to hear it. In the manner of such things, the case had taken years. Finally, on March 18, 2008, as the highlight of John Roberts's third year as chief justice, the Supreme Court heard arguments in the case now known as *District of Columbia v. Heller.*

The government of the District of Columbia hired Walter E. Dellinger III, the former acting solicitor general in the Clinton administration and a veteran of Supreme Court litigation, to defend the gun law in front of the justices. Dellinger started with what he thought was his strongest material—the words of the framers themselves in 1787. In these debates, "every person who used the phrase 'bear arms' used it to refer to the use of arms in connection with militia service, and when Madison introduced the amendment in the first Congress, he exactly equated the phrase 'bearing arms' with, quote, 'rendering military service,' " Dellinger said. "And even if the language of keeping and bearing arms were ambiguous, the amendment's first clause confirms that the right is militia-related."

If the second clause of the amendment granted an individual right to bear arms, Dellinger was saying, then the first clause, the militia clause, would have no meaning at all—and the framers must have included the language for a reason. But Dellinger immediately ran into a problem with Anthony Kennedy, who would probably hold the swing vote.

Kennedy said he thought Dellinger was right that the militia clause could not be "extraneous." But that didn't solve the problem. In Kennedy's view, the two clauses were entirely separate and both valid. "In effect the amendment says we reaffirm the right to have a militia, we've established it, but in addition, there is a right to bear arms," Kennedy said. Later in the argument, Kennedy made his point even more clearly: "And in my view [the second clause] supplemented [the first clause] by saying there's a general right to bear arms quite without reference to the militia either way."

The debate continued in this vein as Dellinger, Gura, and Paul Clement, the solicitor general, argued the case. Clement expressed the Bush administration's view that the Second Amendment protected an individual right and that the D.C. law was unconstitutional. The conversation rarely strayed from the eighteenth century. What did "bear" and "arms" mean to the framers? What did Blackstone, the English law scholar revered by the framers, think about the issue? The questions and answers reached an almost comic level of obscurity: "Do you think the Second Amendment is more restrictive or more expansive of the right than the English Bill of Rights in 1689?" . . . "If we're going back to the English Bill of Rights, it was always understood to be subject to the control and limitation and restriction of Parliament." . . . "That view was taken by William Raleigh in his 1828 treatise. Raleigh was, of course, a ratifier of the Second Amendment." . . . "General Gage's inventory of weapons seized from the Americans in Boston included some 1,800 or so firearms and then 634 pistols."

At one point, David Souter had the temerity to return the conversation to twenty-first-century Washington, D.C., the ostensible focus of the case before the justices. "Can we also look to current conditions like current crime statistics?" he asked Gura.

"To some extent, Your Honor," Gura answered, "but we have certainly—"

"Well, can they consider the extent of the murder rate in Washington, D.C., using handguns?" Souter went on.

Gura conceded the rate was high.

Then Scalia jumped in, almost jovially: "All the more reason to allow a homeowner to have a handgun!"

Scalia had good reason for cheer, because even before the *Heller* case was decided, the argument alone represented a singular triumph for him. Before Scalia joined the Court, the lawyers in a case like *Heller* would have argued, in a general way, about how to apply the values reflected in the Second Amendment to the modern world. The justices would have sought to define a contemporary meaning of the Constitution. In contrast, Scalia often said that he believed in a "dead" Constitution—that its meaning was set for all time at the moment of its creation. The argument in *Heller* showed how much Scalia's originalist view had come to dominate the Court. When Scalia was appointed to the Court, twenty years earlier, there was simply no way that an argument would have dwelled at such length, and in such detail, on the text of the amendment or the intentions of the framers. Scalia had brought originalism to the Court, and he had come to define the terms of the debates, if not always to win them.

The split in *Heller* was the familiar 5–4—with Stevens, Souter, Ginsburg, and Breyer in their customary losing position—but this time the surprise came from the chief justice. Instead of giving the opinion to Kennedy to keep him on board, Roberts asked Scalia to write for the majority. In his two decades as a justice, Scalia had few important majority opinions to his name. At first, his views were too eccentric for Rehnquist to trust him to keep a majority together. But the Court, and the country, had moved Scalia's way, and now he reaped the reward.

Scalia turned *Heller* into a textualist and originalist tour de force. Literally word by word, Scalia deconstructed the meaning of the Second Amendment, using the sources available to the framers of the Constitution. (He cited Blackstone eight times.) He went back to the Glorious Revolution of seventeenth-century England, to uncover the roots of the constitutional right. "And, of course, what the Stuarts had tried to do to their political enemies, George III had tried to do to the colonists," Scalia wrote. "In the tumultuous decades of the 1760's and 1770's, the Crown began to disarm the inhabitants of the most rebellious areas. That provoked polemical reactions by Americans invoking their rights as Englishmen to keep arms. A New York article of April 1769 said that '[i]t is a natural right which the people have reserved to themselves, confirmed by the Bill of Rights, to keep arms for their own defence.'" In light of this history, which Scalia laid out in exhaustive detail, he concluded "the Second Amendment right is exercised individually and belongs to all Americans."

Scalia's greatest tribute came not from his allies but from his adversaries, particularly Stevens. Of course, Stevens disagreed with Scalia about the meaning of the Second Amendment. "The Second Amendment was adopted to protect the right of the people of each of the several States to maintain a well-regulated militia," Stevens wrote. "It was a response to concerns raised during the ratification of the Constitution that the power of Congress to disarm the state militias and create a national standing army posed an intolerable threat to the sovereignty of the several States." But to make his argument, Stevens relied on the same kind of evidence, and the same style of argument, as Scalia did for the majority. "Neither the text of the Amendment nor the arguments advanced by its proponents evidenced the slightest interest in limiting any legislature's authority to regulate private civilian uses of firearms," Stevens wrote.

Stevens, too, was talking like an originalist. The true measure of Scalia's success in *Heller* was that he had changed the terms of the debate. In the twentieth century, it was inconceivable that two justices would spend thousands of words excavating from seventeenth- and eighteenth-century sources the purported intentions of the framers. The Supreme Court did not operate that way in those days. Scalia changed that. It was left to Breyer to write the kind of dissent that the justices used to produce. He said the protections of the Second Amendment, even if Scalia was right about its origins, should not be absolute. Rather than look exclusively at the framers' debates in 1787 in Philadelphia, Breyer examined the records of the City Council of the District of Columbia in 1976, when it passed the gun control law. The council concluded, "on the basis of extensive public hearings and lengthy research, that the easy availability of firearms in the United States has been a major factor contributing to the drastic increase in gun-related violence and crime over the past 40 years." According to Breyer, it was not the place of the Supreme Court to "second-guess the Council in respect to the numbers of gun crimes, injuries, and deaths, or the role of handguns."

The ruling in *Heller* was announced on June 26, 2008, the last day of the term. As usual on the last day, the justices were tired and their nerves worn. Scalia's voice was hoarse as he began, but he still could not resist going for a laugh. "Our opinion is very lengthy, examining in detail the text and history of the Second Amendment," he told the hushed courtroom. "This summary that I'm giving will state little more than the conclusions. If you want to check their validity against the dissent's contrary claims, you'll have to read some 154 pages of opinions."

Soon enough, though, people did read all the pages. And some of the problems with the originalist view came into focus.

There was, for starters, the simple problem of historical accuracy. To the extent a historical debate can be settled, Stevens had the better argument about what the framers intended in the Second Amendment. Jack Rakove, a leading early-American historian at Stanford, joined by several other prominent academics, filed a brief in the *Heller* case that examined in depth the original meaning of the Second Amendment. It concluded, "Once explored, this context establishes that the private keeping of firearms was manifestly not the right that the Framers of the Bill of Rights guaranteed in 1789." (Rakove later observed that while Scalia devoted a great deal of his opinion to statements made decades *before* the ratification of the Constitution, it was Stevens who hewed more closely to the actual debates of the framers.)

At a minimum, the conflict between Scalia and Stevens underlined the difficulty of determining any single meaning of the intentions of the framers, more than two centuries after the fact. By eighteenth-century standards, the men who gathered were a diverse group. They had different ideas about what their work meant, as did the state legislators who ratified their work. On many provisions, they compromised; on others, they left their words intentionally vague. Often, there is no single "original intent" or "original meaning." Moreover, for all that the framers quarreled over the wording of the Constitution, they never indicated that they understood their *intentions* should bind future generations. All that mattered, they thought, was the Constitution itself.

Even Scalia's originalist approach could not settle all the issues in *Heller*. The Court concluded that the Second Amendment protected an individual's right to keep and bear arms, but that still raised the question: which arms? A true originalist would identify which arms the framers believed were protected and then find their twenty-first-century analogue. But here Scalia ran into a problem. In the eighteenth century, militias required civilians to obtain military weapons. In the Uniform Militia Act of 1792, Congress compelled militia members to purchase muskets, bayonets, and other weapons that were needed in military combat. The true originalist would, presumably, assert that the Constitution protected an individual right to possess military weapons. But Scalia limited his ruling for the Court in *Heller* to handguns. He said D.C. could not ban handguns because "handguns are the most popular weapon chosen by Americans for self-defense in the home, and a complete prohibition of their use is invalid." Scalia translated a right to military weapons in the eighteenth century to a right to handguns in the twenty-first. He never explained his rationale, but the reason was obvious. It would be intolerable to allow individuals to purchase tanks, bazookas, Stinger missiles, and other modern weapons of war. So, with little explanation, Scalia wrote those kinds of weapons out of the Second Amendment. He affirmed "the historical tradition of prohibiting the carrying of dangerous and unusual weapons" and noted further that "nothing in our opinion should be taken to cast doubt on long-standing prohibitions on the possession of firearms by felons and the mentally ill, or laws forbidding the carrying of firearms in sensitive places such as schools and government buildings, or laws imposing conditions and qualifications on the commercial sale of arms."

With those limitations, what was left of *Heller*? It forbade the federal government from banning the possession of handguns in the home. It was not clear that it did much else. It was clear, on the other hand, that for all its rhetoric and historical citations, Scalia's decision had little to do with the original meaning of the Second Amendment. It was an improvisation designed to reach a policy goal, which was, not coincidentally, one of the top priorities of the modern Republican Party.

Heller was, in the end, very similar to the decisions most hated by conservatives. In *Roe v. Wade*, Blackmun found a right to privacy that (in his view) protected a woman's right to abortion up to the time a fetus was viable. In *Grutter*, O'Connor said that (in her view) affirmative action in university admissions could continue for another twenty-five years. In *Heller*, Scalia discovered a Second Amendment that (in his view) said yes to handguns and no to machine guns. His view was strikingly similar to the one Barack Obama advocated on the campaign trail. Both Scalia and Obama endorsed a Second Amendment that protected individual rights to own handguns but with limitations on more dangerous weapons. The difference was that only Scalia pretended the framers had dictated the result.

Heller represented the culmination of a political, legal, and public relations offensive that was many years in the making. Scholars, lawyers, politicians, and activists created a new understanding of the Second Amendment that eventually commanded five votes on the Supreme Court. Notwithstanding his denials, Scalia had demonstrated precisely how the Constitution is not dead at all—but a vibrant, living thing. In other words, there was less to the originalism revolution than met the eye. Originalism was no more principled or honorable than any other way of interpreting the Constitution. It was, as *Heller* demonstrated, just another way for justices to achieve their political goals.

THE UNREQUITED BIPARTISANSHIP
OF BARACK OBAMA

On December 5, 2008, Roberts sent Obama an invitation. With characteristic care, the chief justice researched how he should address Obama and came up with: "Dear Mr. President-elect." The letter began:

> Through the years, our respective predecessors have occasionally arranged a pre-inaugural meeting between the President-elect and Members of the Supreme Court, so that colleagues in public service might become better acquainted.
>
> The Associate Justices and I would be pleased to see that sporadic practice become a congenial tradition. We cordially invite you and Vice President-elect Biden to visit us at the Supreme Court.
>
> If your schedule permits such a visit, you will receive a warm welcome from the Members of the Court as you prepare to undertake your important responsibilities on behalf of the American people.

Ronald Reagan and George Herbert Walker Bush had met with the justices shortly before they took office in 1981, and Bill Clinton followed suit in late 1992. (The punctilious William Rehnquist long remembered that Clinton was forty-five minutes late for his visit; Clinton had such a good time that he also stayed a half hour late.) Roberts's gesture was especially gracious, because both Obama and Biden had voted against his confirmation three years earlier.

At 3:45 p.m., on January 14, 2009, eight justices greeted the president- and vice president-elect in the West Conference Room of the Court. (Alito did not attend, even though he had been at oral arguments that morning.) Biden was the only person who knew everyone present. He had served on the Judiciary Committee since 1977 and had voted on the confirmation of all nine current justices. After a few initial pleasantries, Roberts made a pitch that he had coordinated with his colleagues. Judicial salaries had been stagnant for about a decade; lower-court judges were leaving the bench to pay for college tuitions. As a Washington veteran, Roberts knew that a personal appeal on this kind of issue would certainly have an impact and might make a difference. Greg Craig, an old Washington hand himself, and the White House counsel designate, had warned Obama that Roberts might bring up the topic. Obama said he supported a raise for federal judges, but he knew it would be a tough sell to Congress, especially in hard economic times. (The raise never happened.)

Roberts offered to show the pair his chambers, where the Court takes its votes in secret. They filed from the West Conference Room—which is one of the Court's public spaces, often used for receptions—through the Great Hall, with its busts of chief justices, into the private realm of the justices. Like most of his recent predecessors, Roberts keeps a small office directly behind the bench in the courtroom. It's next door to the conference room, which is still dominated by the massive desk where Charles Evans Hughes once presided.

The inner sanctum impressed Obama and Biden, as it does most everyone. The project to renovate the Court building, begun by Rehnquist, had nearly been completed. Warren Burger, in his day, had installed rows of fluorescent bulbs in the ceiling of the conference room, but Kennedy (the chair of the Court's building committee) had found historically accurate chandeliers as replacements. Double-paned windows (highly resistant to most kinds of ammunition) gave the room a soft glow and distinct hush. After inspecting the Hughes desk, Obama lingered by the simple rectangular wooden table, with its nine chairs, that is the tangible symbol of the work of the Court. Like the President's Oval Office, the Supreme Court's conference table represents the power of the institution—and its mystique may be even greater because it is seen, especially in person, by so few.

"Is this where they decided *Brown?*" Obama asked.

Indeed it was, Roberts told him.

Toward the end of the meeting, Kennedy mentioned that there was a basketball court on the top floor of the Court building. "We hear you're a basketball player," Kennedy told Obama. "We'd like you to come play on the highest court in the land."

"I don't know," Obama said. "I hear that Justice Ginsburg has been working on her jump shot."

Six days later, Roberts performed the oath ceremony with Obama at the Capitol, and seven days later they had their repeat performance in the Map Room, at the White House. On January 26, Roberts presided over the installation of the new leader of the Smithsonian Institution. "Those of you who have read it will see from the program that the Smithsonian some time ago adopted the passing of a key in lieu of the administration of an oath," Roberts said. "I don't know who was responsible for that decision. But I like him."

The work of the new administration began. On the morning of January 29, a raucous, almost giddy crowd filled the East Room, the location for the most formal and important occasions at the White House. Just after ten, the disembodied voice of an announcer silenced the audience. "Ladies and gentlemen," it said, "the President of the United States, accompanied by Mrs. Lilly Ledbetter."

Side by side, along the red carpet, Obama and Ledbetter walked slowly to the podium, while the audience stood, whooped, and hollered. "This is a wonderful day," Obama began. More applause. "First of all, it is fitting that the very first bill that I sign—the Lilly Ledbetter Fair Pay Restoration Act"—more applause, even louder—"that it is upholding one of this nation's founding principles: that we are all created equal, and each deserve a chance to pursue our own version of happiness."

The bill to overrule Alito's 2007 opinion in the Ledbetter case had been pending throughout the final year of the Bush administration, but Republicans had blocked it. In early January 2009, the new Congress finally passed the bill. The margins were 61–36 in the Senate and 247–171 in the House.

"Lilly Ledbetter did not set out to be a trailblazer or a household name," Obama told the crowd in the East Room. "She was just a good hard worker who did her job—and she did it well—for nearly two decades before discovering that for years, she was paid less than her male colleagues for doing the very same work. Over the course of her career, she lost more than $200,000 in salary, and even more in pension and Social Security benefits—losses that she still feels today.

"Now, Lilly could have accepted her lot and moved on. She could have decided that it wasn't worth the hassle and the harassment that would inevitably come with speaking up for what she deserved. But instead, she decided that there was a principle at stake, something worth fighting for. So she set out on a journey that would take more than ten years, take her all the way to the Supreme Court of the United States, and lead to this day and this bill which will help others get the justice that she was denied."

Behind the new President, Joe Biden wiped tears from his eyes. Ruth Bader Ginsburg did not attend the proceedings, but she followed the fate of the Ledbetter bill with considerable interest, and greater pride.

Obama took office facing a wider range of challenges than any other president since Franklin Roosevelt. There were two wars and an economic collapse; there were restless Democratic majorities in both houses of Congress eager to put their stamp on a variety of issues, including health care, immigration, and climate change. Considering these burdens, it would not have been surprising if the new administration treated the issue of judicial nominations as a less than pressing priority.

That is precisely what happened. Indeed, a variety of other factors combined to give the issue even less attention than it might otherwise have received. Greg Craig had not sought the job of White House counsel. During the Clinton administration, he had watched that office become bogged down in fending off investigations by hostile Republicans, and at the age of sixty-three he had no longing for such enervating duties. He'd rather have worked in the State Department. But Craig didn't believe in turning down requests from presidents, so he took the job. Obama also asked Craig to find a place on his staff for Cassandra Butts, one of the president's law school classmates, who had also worked on the campaign. Craig agreed, and she became the deputy general counsel in charge of judicial nominations.

The problems began almost immediately. Through his years with Senator Edward Kennedy and later in the Clinton State Department, Craig had developed a special interest in international human rights. He made a personal mission of fulfilling Obama's oft-repeated campaign promise to close the detention facility at Guantánamo Bay. Craig's fixation with Guantánamo brought him into conflict with Rahm Emanuel, Obama's chief of staff. Emanuel believed the president's top priority (as well as his own) was to push Obama's legislative agenda through Congress, starting with the economic stimulus bill and then health care reform. Emanuel regarded Guantánamo as a distraction that could only alienate members of Congress, where Obama's margins were tiny. In those first months, there were fifty-nine Democrats in the Senate, and Republicans were filibustering on virtually everything, meaning the president needed sixty votes to pass bills. Obama had to claw for every vote he could get, and Emanuel—who was famously profane and opinionated—thought Craig was making the president's job harder. Craig believed he was simply doing the work the president hired him to do. In short order, Emanuel and Craig loathed each other.

Butts did not have an easy time either. Craig had assembled a staff that was heavy on the qualifications that were valued at his law firm, Williams & Connolly. That meant an abundance of young, self-confident Supreme Court law clerks. Butts had gone to Harvard but she had spent much of her career on Capitol Hill, working longest for Congressman Richard Gephardt. In the recondite status hierarchies of the legal profession, Butts occupied a somewhat lower plane than the A students favored by Craig. There were tensions between Butts's and Craig's other underlings, who traded whispered complaints about arrogance and incompetence. Susan Davies, who worked under Butts on judicial nominations, had clerked for both Kennedy and Breyer and then served on Patrick Leahy's staff on the Judiciary Committee. Davies and Butts embodied the internal culture clash.

Butts, and thus Obama, also had difficulties with the Senate. By long-standing tradition, senators of the president's party controlled district court nominations in their states. It had been almost a decade since Democratic senators had had a chance to pick judges. Many were slow to put machinery in place to do so, and the senators also bristled at the Obama demand that they submit three names (instead of just one name) for every vacancy. The process stalled. Weeks, then months, passed.

George W. Bush had made a splashy show of his first set of judicial nominations. On May 9, 2001, Bush assembled his first eleven selections in a ceremony in the East Room. The group included two nominees to the D.C. Circuit, John Roberts and Miguel Estrada. (Democrats stalled

Roberts's nomination for two years before confirming him; Estrada was filibustered by Democrats and ultimately defeated.) Those two, as well as nominees like Terrence Boyle (a former aide to Senator Jesse Helms) and Jeffrey Sutton (a former Scalia clerk) indicated that Bush would work hard to put a conservative cast on the federal judiciary. The public nature of the occasion served as a clear demonstration of the centrality of judicial appointments in a Republican administration. It showed the voters and the Senate that Bush cared about his judges.

Obama took a different approach. He knew that Bush's high-profile announcement of his first nominees was intended, and taken, as a provocation to his political adversaries. Obama preferred to try to lower the political temperature. He thought it would be better to start with a single, uncontroversial choice that would burnish his postpartisan credentials. In this way, he could show his good faith to Senate Republicans and expect similar fair dealing in return. So Obama wanted a first nominee who was sure to have Republican support.

As it turned out, there was a perfect candidate lined up. On March 17, 2009, President Obama nominated David Hamilton, the chief federal district court judge in Indianapolis, to the Seventh Circuit court of appeals. Hamilton had been vetted with care. After fifteen years of service on the trial bench, he had won the highest rating from the American Bar Association; Richard Lugar, the senior senator from Indiana and a leading Republican, was supportive; and Hamilton's status as a nephew of Lee Hamilton, a well-respected former local congressman, gave him deep connections. The hope was that Hamilton's appointment would begin a profound and rapid change in the confirmation process and in the federal judiciary itself. What could go wrong?

Almost everything. Not for the last time, Obama misread the political environment in the Senate. As they put it in the White House, "Hamilton blew up." Conservatives seized on a 2005 case in which Hamilton ruled to strike down the daily invocation at the Indiana legislature because its repeated references to Jesus Christ violated the establishment clause of the First Amendment. Hamilton had also ruled to invalidate a part of Indiana's abortion law that required women to make two visits to a doctor before undergoing the procedure. By the time Patrick Leahy, the chairman of the Judiciary Committee, scheduled a vote on Hamilton, in June, the best he could muster was a straight party-line vote, 12–7, in favor of the nomination. (Months of delay followed. The nomination did not reach the Senate floor until November 19, and Hamilton was confirmed by a vote of 59–39.) Obama had chosen the Hamilton nomination to send a message, but he wound up receiving one instead. Republicans *cared* about the courts.

And as everyone knew, a Supreme Court vacancy was imminent.

No justice on the Court spent more time on the job, or enjoyed it less, than David Souter. Six days a week, sometimes seven, Souter would drive his battered car into the basement parking lot and trudge up to his chambers on the first floor. On weekends, he would occasionally forswear his three-piece suit. Souter lived in a modest apartment in an unlovely neighborhood. He didn't go to parties or even out to dinner. His world was mostly circumscribed by the jogging paths near his home and the corridors of the Supreme Court building. (In 2002, Souter did happen to attend a party to celebrate Strom Thurmond's one hundredth birthday. Afterwards, he told his law clerks, "If I am still on the Court at eighty-five, I want one of you to shoot me.") Even people who didn't know much about the Court knew that David Souter hated Washington.

There was truth in this, but it was far from the whole story. In some ways, Souter didn't mind having his unhappiness on the Court portrayed as a simple eccentricity, like his predilection for lunching on a cup of yogurt and an apple (including the core). *This is a guy who doesn't know how to use a computer or a cell phone—and, crazily enough, he doesn't like Washington either!* That kind of explanation obscured the more painful truth. Ironically, Souter liked Washington somewhat more in his later years on the Court, in part because he had his first serious girlfriend in years. It was true that Souter wanted to return to New Hampshire, but the reasons were harsher, and uglier, than a simple longing for the White Mountains. He abhorred the views of Roberts and Alito. Souter didn't like what the Republican Party—his party—was doing to the Court, or to the country.

Souter identified with a tradition in American politics and law that had almost vanished from public life: the moderate Republican. As Souter was moving up the ranks in New Hampshire, from attorney general to the state supreme court, his mentor was Warren Rudman. New England used to abound in moderates like Rudman—and Lowell

Weicker in Connecticut, Robert Stafford and Jim Jeffords in Vermont, and John Chafee in Rhode Island. On the Supreme Court, moderate Republicans had played crucial roles for decades: John Marshall Harlan II in the fifties, Potter Stewart in the sixties, Lewis Powell in the seventies, and Sandra Day O'Connor in the eighties, nineties, and beyond. As a group, they prized stability and venerated precedent. So did Souter, who liked to quote something that Rehnquist (hardly a moderate himself) used to say: "The law of the United States is like an ocean liner. You can't turn it on a dime." Scalia and Thomas, joined now by Roberts and Alito, thought otherwise and were trying to make that sharp turn in case after case. Moderate Republican ideas, like moderate Republicans, were disappearing from the Court as they were disappearing from the country.

For Souter, all his worries, all his distaste for the modern Court, had come together in a single case: *Bush v. Gore*. In the years since the decision, in 2000, there was a kind of informal agreement among the justices not to talk about it. They were used to disagreeing with one another, of course; that was the nature of the work. But the wounds of *Bush v. Gore* were so deep, the anger so profound on both sides, that it was thought best to avoid the subject altogether. Momentous Supreme Court cases tend to move quickly into the slipstream of the Court's history. In the first ten years after *Brown v. Board of Education*, the justices cited the case more than twenty-five times. In the ten years after *Roe v. Wade*, there were more than sixty-five references to that landmark ruling. By the time Obama became president, it had been nearly a decade since the Court, by a vote of 5–4, terminated the election of 2000 and delivered the presidency to George W. Bush. Over that time, the justices provided a verdict of sorts on *Bush v. Gore* by the number of times they cited it: zero.

Bush v. Gore broke David Souter's heart. *The day the music died*, he called it. It was so political, so *transparently* political, that it scarred Souter's belief in the Supreme Court as an institution. Scalia, in his public appearances, would often be asked a hostile question about *Bush v. Gore*, and he always said the same thing: "Oh, get over it!" Souter never did. After the election of 2004, Souter almost quit the Court in disgust. After all, he thought, George W. Bush told the people what he wanted to do with the Supreme Court, and he won the election, so perhaps he should just let Bush have his chance. Souter thought of Oliver Wendell

Holmes's mordant observation about the role of a judge in a democracy: "I always say, as you know, that if my fellow citizens want to go to Hell I will help them." A close friend in New Hampshire talked Souter out of quitting, but he was certainly ready to go by the time Obama won the election. Souter would not even turn seventy years old until later in 2009—still middle-aged for a Supreme Court justice—but he had had enough. Roberts and Alito were obviously intelligent and honorable men, Souter thought, but he didn't recognize their approach to the law. He thought it was time to let someone else try to figure it out.

Through former Souter clerks on his staff, Greg Craig learned that Souter planned to leave at the end of the 2008–09 term. Souter asked his clerks to find out from Craig what the best time for his announcement might be. Craig sent back word that late in the spring would be better than earlier; that way, Obama could build up some momentum with other judicial nominations before moving on to the Supreme Court. In any event, the formal announcement leaked out rather awkwardly. On the evening of April 30, Nina Totenberg of NPR and Pete Williams of NBC announced that Souter would be retiring at the end of the term. The following day, other news outlets confirmed the story, but there was still no official word from Souter or the Supreme Court. Craig decided simply to call Souter and ask him what was going on. Souter confirmed that he was retiring and would write his formal letter of resignation the next day.

Supreme Court resignation letters are an art form. The justices know that the letter will be widely distributed, so they make an effort to craft a meaningful valedictory. "It has been a great privilege, indeed, to have served as a member of the Court for 24 terms," O'Connor wrote in 2005. "I will leave it with enormous respect for the integrity of the Court and its role under our constitutional structure." (This sentence reflected what O'Connor intended: her pride that the Supreme Court had reined in George W. Bush's excesses in the war on terror.)

In contrast to O'Connor but in keeping with his singular style, David Souter wrote his letter with all the poetry of a phone bill:

Dear Mr. President,

When the Supreme Court rises for the summer recess this year, I intend to retire from regular active service as a Justice, under the provisions of 28 US.C. § 371(b)(1), having attained

the age and met the service requirements of subsection (c) of that
section. I mean to continue to render substantial judicial service
as an Associate Justice.

Yours respectfully,
David Souter

Souter's letter meant that he had served long enough as a federal
judge to retire at full pay. (Years earlier, Souter had made a series of
canny investments in New England bank stocks that multiplied in
value and left him, with Ginsburg, as the wealthiest justice, with a net
worth between $6 million and $27 million. But Souter remained at
heart a frugal New Englander, and if he was entitled to retirement pay,
he was going to take it.) Souter's letter meant further that he wanted to
continue sitting as a circuit court judge, as was his right, following his
resignation as a justice.

More importantly, the letter meant that a Democratic president
would have a chance to name a justice to the Supreme Court for the
first time in fifteen years.

During those fifteen years, conservative ideas about the judiciary and
the Constitution—especially originalism—enjoyed a great deal of
prominence. To many in the liberal camp, the nomination of a new justice, and the confirmation hearings to follow, offered an excellent opportunity to put forth an alternative, progressive legal vision. To them, the
point was not simply to confirm a Democrat but also to win the war
over the interpretation of the Constitution.

Neither Obama nor the people around him wanted any part of such
an undertaking. In the first place, that wasn't the president's style.
He wasn't looking to start fights that he didn't need to have. Moreover, Obama himself had basically middle-of-the-road ideas about the
Constitution, and he wanted a nominee with similar views. Finally,
given the crowded legislative calendar, Obama and his team wanted a
no-drama confirmation. His nominee should be confirmed with as little
disruption as possible.

But who should it be? Back in Chicago, the week after the election,
Obama had given his own list of four names to Craig and Axelrod:

Sonia Sotomayor, Elena Kagan, Diane Wood, and Cass Sunstein. A young staffer on the transition, Danielle Gray, now a member of Craig's staff, had drawn up the first memos about the candidates. Now, about six months later, the list had changed slightly.

Cass Sunstein had been a colleague of Obama's at the University of Chicago Law School, where he was perhaps the most accomplished, and certainly the most prolific, legal scholar of their generation. Sunstein moved to Harvard Law School and worked on Obama's campaign, where he met and later married Samantha Power, a human rights scholar and activist who had also become an adviser to Obama. Sunstein's interests were a lot like Breyer's—administrative law, government efficiency in all its forms. As a result, Obama had appointed him to a little-known but powerful job running the Office of Information and Regulatory Affairs at the Office of Management and Budget. Republicans knew Sunstein was a possible Supreme Court nominee, so they put him through an arduous confirmation process; he still had not been confirmed by the full Senate for his OMB job when Souter stepped down. Sunstein's eclectic views had the ability to offend both the left and the right, and he liked being where he was. Sunstein was removed from consideration.

Janet Napolitano was added. Like Bill Clinton before him, Obama had mused about the need for nonjudges on the Supreme Court. In this regard, the transformation on the Court had been enormous. Only one of the justices who decided *Brown* in 1954 had ever been a full-time judge. (Sherman Minton was a former senator who had served on the Seventh Circuit; Hugo Black had been a part-time judge on a police court in Alabama.) When Alito replaced O'Connor, for the first time in history all nine justices were former federal appeals court judges. The change owed much to the differences in the confirmation process over fifty years. When FDR appointed figures like Felix Frankfurter (law professor and activist who had spoken out in defense of Sacco and Vanzetti), William O. Douglas (head of the SEC), and Robert Jackson (attorney general), the Senate did little more than act as a rubber stamp. That was true, too, when Eisenhower nominated Earl Warren, then governor of California, to be chief justice. But as senators started to apply greater scrutiny, especially after Robert Bork's defeat in 1987, presidents started opting for safe nominees whose prior records were largely devoid of political expression. That meant judges, not politicians.

Napolitano had an extraordinary résumé—governor of Arizona,

attorney general of the state, United States attorney as well. (Obama's vetters took some sinister joy in noting, too, that one of Napolitano's clients during her brief career in private practice had been Anita Hill. The possibilities for lively lunchtime conversations at the Court were duly noted.) But the prospect of scouring a lifetime of public appearances by a politician was daunting. Plus, Napolitano was off to a strong start as secretary of homeland security—a job that, if it could not win reelection for Obama, might lose it for him. Napolitano stayed on the list but, through no fault of her own, remained a problematic and unlikely choice.

Kagan was only an outside shot for the Souter seat as well. She, too, had been a professor at Chicago, where she became acquainted with Obama, and had gone on to service in the Clinton White House and then a successful tenure as dean of Harvard Law School. But it had been only a month since she was confirmed as solicitor general, and she had not yet argued a case for the government in the Supreme Court. Indeed, Kagan had never argued a case in any court throughout her entire career. She might be a strong candidate someday—but for now she came off the list.

The field—the real field—quickly came down to two: Diane Wood and Sonia Sotomayor.

10

WISE LATINA

Sonia Sotomayor could have been genetically engineered to be a Democratic nominee to the United States Supreme Court. She had impeccable credentials: Princeton, then Yale Law School. She had ideal experience: big-city prosecutor, six years as a federal district judge (nominated by George H. W. Bush), and then a decade on the federal appeals court. She had, above all, a great story: raised amid poverty in the Bronx, with juvenile diabetes no less, she would make history as the first Hispanic on the Supreme Court. In light of all this, it looked like political malpractice for Obama *not* to nominate her.

There was only one problem. Barack Obama really liked Diane Wood.

When Wood was shuttling her three young children to music lessons in the late nineties, she already had a very busy life. She was a judge on the Seventh Circuit, a Clinton nominee confirmed in 1995, and she taught part-time at the University of Chicago Law School. Still, she sprang a question on her kids' violin teacher: "Do you know anyone who could teach me the oboe?" Wood spent the next decade in intensive study of that difficult woodwind. Today she sits in with local orchestras.

There was nothing conventional about Diane Wood. Even in the rarefied realm of law professors and federal judges, she had a rich, full, complicated life. She was born in New Jersey but came of age as a teenager in Texas, and she went to the University of Texas for college and

law school. (This alone was an advantage on a Supreme Court dominated by Harvard and Yale graduates. Wood was also a Protestant; at
that point, Stevens was the only Protestant remaining on the Court.) In
Wood's day, there were only a handful of women at the law school in
Austin, but Wood flourished. She clerked on the Fifth Circuit for Irving
Goldberg—a legendary Texas liberal—and then for Harry Blackmun
on the Supreme Court. She speaks French, Russian, and German.

After clerking, Wood went to work in Jimmy Carter's State Department, where she specialized in international trade and antitrust law.
She taught at Georgetown and then Chicago, until Clinton summoned
her back to Washington to work in the antitrust division of the Justice
Department. He put her on the Seventh Circuit in 1995. Along the
way, Woods married three times—"my many husbands," she referred
to them ruefully. After a brief marriage during law school, she was
with her second husband for twenty years. Dennis Hutchinson was a
fellow professor at Chicago and one of Obama's few good friends on the
faculty. In 2006, Wood wed Robert Sufit, a professor of neurology at
Northwestern.

On the Seventh Circuit, Wood achieved a rare accomplishment. She
was both an unapologetic liberal and a valued, even beloved, colleague
to the outspoken conservatives on the Court, Richard Posner and Frank
Easterbrook. In her opinions and copious scholarly work, she mounted
a vigorous defense of the living Constitution. In an era when originalism was ascendant and many liberals (especially those with ambitions
of serving on the Supreme Court) found it convenient to stay away from
the debate, Wood took on the subject with enthusiasm. As she stated in
the James Madison Lecture at New York University in 2004, the language of the Constitution "may legitimately be interpreted broadly, in a
manner informed by evolving notions of a decent society." She went on:

> First and most important is the idea that we should take seri-
> ously the fact that the text of the Constitution tends to reflect
> broad principles, not specific prescriptions. Neither James Madi-
> son, for whom this lecture is named, nor any of the other Framers
> of the Constitution, were oblivious, careless, or otherwise unaware
> of the words they chose for the document and its Bill of Rights.
> The papers they left behind leave no doubt that they hoped to be
> writing for the ages. There is no more reason to think that they

expected the world to remain static than there is to think that any of us holds a crystal ball. The only way to create a foundational document that could stand the test of time was to build in enough flexibility that later generations would be able to adapt it to their own needs and uses.

This was a direct challenge to the originalist notion that Madison's words should be interpreted only as he and his peers understood them. Wood applied this mode of analysis consistently—including on the question of abortion.

It was Wood's misfortune to have several abortion cases before her during her years on the Seventh Circuit. She voted to strike down so-called partial-birth abortion laws in Illinois and Wisconsin and rejected an informed consent law in Indiana. In all of these cases, her colleagues voted to uphold the laws. Worse yet for her chances was the case of *National Organization for Women v. Scheidler*, in 2001.

The facts underlying that decision were chilling. During the 1980s, anti-abortion groups affiliated with the Pro-Life Action Network engaged in repeated acts of violence against women's health clinics around the country. NOW used the federal racketeering law known as RICO to sue the group for damages and for an injunction to stop further attacks, and a jury found that the Pro-Life Action Network orchestrated 121 crimes involving acts or threats of violence. As NOW summarized some of the evidence, protesters at a clinic in Los Angeles beat a postoperative ovarian surgery patient over the head with their anti-abortion sign, knocking her unconscious and opening the sutures in her abdomen. In Atlanta, they seized a clinic administrator by the throat, choking and bruising her. They trashed a clinic in Pensacola and assaulted a staff member. The trial revealed a nationwide wave of terror. Wood's opinion upheld the jury verdict, the damage award, and the injunction against the group.

The Supreme Court reversed Wood's holding by a vote of 8–1. (Only Stevens dissented.) The reason was narrow. Indeed, the *Scheidler* case demonstrated how cases involving terrible injustices can turn into bloodless disputes about legal technicalities in the Supreme Court.

The justices held that the protesters did not "obtain" any of the clinics' equipment, so that meant their activity did not fit the definition of extortion under the racketeering law. The case went back to Wood and the Seventh Circuit, which again ruled for NOW, and for a second time in the same case, the justices overturned Wood's ruling, this time unanimously. (Alito did not participate.) It was true that these cases, as they arrived at the Supreme Court, concerned fairly arcane matters of federal statutory interpretation, not abortion law per se. But it was also true that Supreme Court confirmation fights did not concern such subtleties. In crude terms, the Supreme Court had twice reversed Wood's rulings on abortion—and even Ruth Bader Ginsburg did not support her position.

To which Greg Craig said, "Good for Wood! This is why we need someone like her on the Supreme Court." Wood was both a fighter and a thinker, and she could be the voice of their side against Scalia. As a veteran appellate judge, Wood would hit the ground running.

For neither the first nor the last time during his tenure at the White House, Craig was out of step with his colleagues. More importantly, Craig misread his boss. Obama wanted someone who could put together winning coalitions at the Court—more than he wanted someone who could write a good dissent. Obama liked and admired Wood, but the benefits of appointing her were, from a political perspective, unclear. Not so for Wood's leading competitor. The closer Obama looked at Sonia Sotomayor, the better—in every respect—she seemed.

In the brusque shorthand of political life, White House officials later described Sotomayor's story as "an American story." It was an extraordinary one.

Celina Báez and Juan Sotomayor were both born in Puerto Rico and came to the United States as part of the great migration that transformed New York during and after World War II. Celina worked as a telephone operator at a hospital, Juan as a tool-and-die maker in a factory. Their daughter, Sonia, was born in 1954, and they moved into an unfinished Bronxdale housing project in the South Bronx with the poetic name of Building 28. (Her brother, Juan, was born three years later.) Their lives were hard and soon got even harder. When Sonia was eight, she was diagnosed with type 1 diabetes. The following year, Juan Sotomayor Sr. died suddenly of a heart attack at the age of forty-two.

Celina was a striver, committed to bettering herself and making sure that her children could do the same. After her husband's death, she started speaking English at home; as a consequence, Sonia speaks Spanish fluently but her younger brother barely speaks it at all. Celina obtained a GED and then trained to become a practical nurse. The job paid better, and it taught Celina to manage her daughter's illness. She placed Sonia and Juan in highly regarded Catholic schools. The reasons were educational, not religious. In an oft-told tale, Celina invested in an expensive set of encyclopedias—supposedly the only one in the building—for her two children. The neighborhood was deteriorating, and Celina moved her family to Co-op City, the sprawling development near the Westchester border. While keeping her job at the hospital, caring for her own kids, and serving as a kind of unofficial doctor for her neighbors, Celina commenced studies to be a registered nurse. (The exodus of middle-class families like the Sotomayors in the seventies helped turn the South Bronx into a national symbol of urban decay.)

Sonia won a scholarship to Princeton, where she experienced immediate culture shock. After a rocky freshman year, she settled in and became successful, socially and academically. She wrote a thesis about Puerto Rico's independence movement, graduated summa cum laude, and won acceptance to Yale Law School. (Her younger brother became a physician.) For all her achievements, Sotomayor held no illusions about one of the reasons for her success. As she said in a speech after she became a judge, "I am a product of affirmative action. I am the perfect affirmative action baby. My test scores were not comparable to that of my colleagues at Princeton or Yale, but not so far off the mark that I wasn't able to succeed at those institutions." In any case, she thrived at Yale, too.

Toward the end of law school, Sotomayor happened to show up at a career-day presentation by Robert Morgenthau, the legendary Manhattan district attorney. After sizing her up, Morgenthau arranged for a job interview the next day, and she was quickly hired. Sotomayor worked her way up in the office and capped her career there with a victory in the tabloid-ready Tarzan Murderer case. Richard Maddicks was a familiar New York type in the seventies and eighties—the desperate junkie who preyed on his neighbors to support his habit. What distinguished Maddicks was his ability to jump from building to building while making his rounds, a circuit that produced seven shootings and four murders. In 1983, thanks to Sotomayor and a fellow prosecutor, Maddicks was convicted and received a life sentence.

Sotomayor tired of the never-ending misery in the criminal justice system and left the office after only five years to join a small private firm. (After graduating from Princeton, she had married her college boyfriend, whom she had known since high school; he was in graduate school in molecular biology for much of the marriage, and their commuting relationship didn't last. They divorced after seven years. She was later engaged, but did not marry again.) Like many other young lawyers, Sotomayor was guided both by altruism and by ambition. In 1980, she joined the Puerto Rican Legal Defense and Education Fund— a leading civil rights organization. While in private practice, Sotomayor was named to the State of New York Mortgage Agency board; the next year, thanks to Morgenthau, she gained a seat on the New York City Campaign Finance Board. In 1986, she toured Israel with a group of Latino activists. When George H. W. Bush was president, the New York senators divided the judicial appointments so that Al D'Amato received three appointments for every one for Daniel Patrick Moynihan. In 1992, Moynihan heard about Sotomayor and put up her name; at the age of thirty-eight, she was confirmed unanimously for a federal judgeship in lower Manhattan.

As with the Tarzan Murderer, a celebrated case brought Sotomayor wide public notice on the district court. A labor dispute had destroyed the 1994 major league baseball season, including the World Series, and the 1995 season was in jeopardy when the battle between the players and the owners wound up in her courtroom. On March 30, 1995, the union demanded that the owners continue free-agent negotiations and salary arbitrations while the two sides negotiated an agreement. Sotomayor told the lawyers that she didn't know the history of their case, but "I hope none of you assumed . . . that my lack of knowledge of any of the intimate details of your dispute meant I was not a baseball fan. You can't grow up in the South Bronx without knowing about baseball." She issued an injunction reinstituting free agency, the players went back to work, and the 232-day dispute soon ended. It was a classic Sotomayor moment—decisive and unequivocal. It was the kind of behavior that generally wins praise for male judges, if not always for their female counterparts. Certainly, it did not hurt that Sotomayor became famous as the judge who saved baseball.

Bill Clinton nominated her to the Second Circuit two years later, and she soon became known—even to Barack Obama, whom she had never met—as the Democrats' leading Supreme Court justice-in-waiting.

But that was only part of the story, especially for Obama. Although Sotomayor flourished on the Second Circuit, she kept her ties to the Bronx. She remained a frequent visitor to her grammar school and high school; she was godmother of five children, including the son of her dentist; she gave talks to Hispanic student groups all over the country. As a public figure, Sotomayor had a stump speech of sorts. The one she gave in 2001 at the University of California, Berkeley, was typical. These kinds of inspirational talks often consist of banalities, but not Sotomayor's. Her talk was serious and substantive—with a quietly radical message.

Sotomayor began with the customary paean to her roots, in her case as a "Nuyorican." "For me, a very special part of my being Latina is the *muchos platos de arroz, gandules y pernil*—rice, beans, and pork—that I have eaten at countless family holidays and special events," she said. "My Latina identity also includes, because of my particularly adventurous taste buds, *morcilla*—pig intestines—*patitas de cerdo con garbanzos*—pigs' feet with beans—and *la lengua y orejas de cuchifrito*—pigs' tongue and ears."

Soon enough, Sotomayor took aim at one of the hardest questions surrounding affirmative action. *Why* does it matter if there are more women, or minorities, on the bench? She quoted a former colleague on the Manhattan federal trial court, Miriam Cedarbaum, who "sees danger in presuming that judging should be gender or anything else based. She rightly points out that the perception of the differences between men and women is what led to many paternalistic laws and to the denial to women of the right to vote." Sotomayor went on, "Judge Cedarbaum nevertheless believes that judges must transcend their personal sympathies and prejudices and aspire to achieve a greater degree of fairness and integrity based on the reason of law."

But that wasn't Sotomayor's opinion. She embraced the view that women and minorities brought something different to the bench. "Our experiences as women and people of color affect our decisions," she said. "The aspiration to impartiality is just that—it's an aspiration because it denies the fact that we are by our experiences making different choices than others." She continued, "Whether born from experience or inherent physiological or cultural differences, a possibility I abhor less or discount less than my colleague Judge Cedarbaum, our gender and national origins may and will make a difference in our judging. Justice O'Connor has often been cited as saying that a wise old man and wise old woman will reach the same conclusion in deciding cases." But in the crucial passage in the speech, Sotomayor said she *disagreed* with O'Connor's view. "I would hope that a wise Latina woman with the richness of her experiences would more often than not reach a better conclusion than a white male who hasn't lived that life." According to Sotomayor, gender and ethnicity among judges made a substantive difference in results. "Personal experiences affect the facts that judges choose to see," she said. "My hope is that I will take the good from my experiences and extrapolate them further into areas with which I am unfamiliar. I simply do not know exactly what that difference will be in my judging. But I accept there will be some based on my gender and my Latina heritage."

Sotomayor, Wood, Kagan, and Napolitano had all submitted enormous volumes of material, including all their public remarks, to the White House as part of the vetting process. For Sotomayor, the "wise Latina" speeches, as they became known, immediately jumped out as problems. But how big?

Obama wanted the new justice confirmed in time for the first Monday in October 2009, which meant that he could not tarry in making his choice. The Senate went into recess in August, so the hearings had to take place by the end of July. Souter had quit on May 1; Obama needed to nominate someone by the end of the month. All four candidates came to the White House for interviews with the president; Kagan and Napolitano received the clear message, from Obama and others, not to get their hopes up. It wasn't their time.

Wood or Sotomayor? An abortion problem or an affirmative action problem? By that measure, Wood had the advantage. In rough terms, the public was about 60 percent pro-choice; on affirmative action, support was closer to 30. (There are wide variations depending on how the poll questions are asked.) As Obama knew better than most people, the acceptable discourse about race and identity was fairly narrow. It was fine to say, as Sotomayor did, that it was important for women and minorities to have role models. It was acceptable, too, to say that diversity was a strength in any institution. But O'Connor, with her understanding of public opinion, knew the limits of the idea. It was not acceptable to say that men and women judges (or blacks and minority judges) actually reached different, or better, opinions in cases because of their backgrounds. But that was what Sotomayor had said in her speeches—repeatedly.

Sotomayor had another problem on that score. As it happened, the Supreme Court had just heard an appeal from the Second Circuit on an affirmative action case where Sotomayor had been on the panel. In 2003, a group of New Haven firefighters took a standardized test for promotions. Whites passed the test at double the rate of blacks, and the local Civil Service Board, worried about being sued by the failed black applicants, invalidated the test. Instead, nineteen white firefighters and one Hispanic who passed the original test sued for their promotions. In a brief order, Sotomayor and two other judges on the Second Circuit ruled against the white firefighters and upheld the decision to throw out the test. White House soundings on Capitol Hill produced almost no support, even from liberals, for Sotomayor's position. "Diversity" was one thing, but blacks and whites should have to play by the same rules or, in this case, take the same test.

Obama sought advice from Biden, Craig, Butts, Susan Davies, and Biden's chief of staff, Ron Klain, who had worked on Ginsburg's and Breyer's nominations in the Clinton White House and was Biden's top aide in the Senate during the Clarence Thomas hearings. No staffer had more experience with Supreme Court nominations than Klain. There were sixty Democratic votes in the Senate. Either Wood or Sotomayor was likely to be confirmed. Obama simply had to make his choice.

The decision revealed a great deal about Obama. In his interview with Sotomayor, the president took particular note of how she had stayed in touch with her former neighborhoods in the Bronx. He sensed an authenticity in her, and no one had to remind the president of the political appeal of appointing the first Hispanic to the Supreme Court. If he had a chance to make history in this way, with an impeccably qualified nominee, Obama was going to do it.

There was something more, too. In a way, Obama thought that Soto-mayor's "problems" were also advantages. It was impolitic to say that race and ethnicity mattered, but the first black president, far more than most, knew how much they did. Obama was often described by others as "postracial," but he didn't see himself that way. After all, as a young man Obama had written an entire book about coming to terms with his racial identity. Around the same time as he was making his choice for the Supreme Court, Obama made an uncharacteristically indiscreet revelation. He was asked about an incident where Henry Louis Gates Jr., a renowned Harvard professor and friend of Obama's, was arrested on the front steps of his home in Cambridge. Gates was returning from a long overseas trip and found the front door to his home jammed. He struggled to open it, and a neighbor called the police, thinking a burglary was in progress. The police came and exchanged words with Gates, and he was arrested.

A few days later, a reporter asked Obama for his opinion. "Now, I've—I don't know, not having been there and not seeing all the facts, what role race played in that," Obama said. "But I think it's fair to say, number one, any of us would be pretty angry; number two, that the Cambridge police acted stupidly in arresting somebody when there was already proof that they were in their own home. And number three, what I think we know separate and apart from this incident is that there is a long history in this country of African Americans and Lati-nos being stopped by law enforcement disproportionately. That's just a fact." Obama quickly came to regret his remarks, which were indeed ill-informed about the specifics of the incident. (By way of apology, in the summer, he held a "beer summit" at the White House with Gates and James Crowley, the Cambridge police sergeant who made the arrest.) Still, the Gates incident was revealing. Obama had never been arrested, but he knew what it was like to be a black man facing the police. So, in a different way, did Sonia Sotomayor. That was more than fine with the president.

Heading into Memorial Day weekend, Sotomayor had been told she was the likely nominee but that she would hear the official word from the president probably on Monday. (White House officials had con-sulted several doctors and were assured that Sotomayor's diabetes would not prevent her from living a normal life span.) On the afternoon of the holiday, Obama called Klain and asked him to run the negatives on Sotomayor one more time. Klain rehearsed the expected attacks: intemperate, too liberal, too pro–affirmative action. Obama was unpersuaded by the case against her and told Klain he would make the formal offer that night.

In the meantime, Sotomayor—nervous and unable to tell anyone what was going on—went to her chambers on Memorial Day, if only to fill the time. Relatives called for updates, and there were none. Finally, she decided to return to her apartment in Greenwich Village and pack for the trip to Washington—just in case. At 8:10 p.m., Obama called her cell phone. When he made the offer official, Sotomayor began to cry.

"I want you to make me two promises," Obama said. "First, you have to remain the person you are. And second, to stay connected to your community." Happy to oblige, the nominee told the president.

Obama and his staff had been so caught up in the details of the selection process that they weren't prepared for what happened the next day, when he announced Sotomayor's nomination in the East Room. There were people, lots of them, weeping with joy. Many of them did not even know Sotomayor personally. Supreme Court nominations are cultural markers in the United States—Louis Brandeis in 1916, Thurgood Marshall in 1967, Sandra Day O'Connor in 1981. The dates are not coincidental, for they mark coming-of-age moments for Jewish Americans, African Americans, and women. May 26, 2009 was such a date for Hispanic Americans. In a White House hallway afterwards, Obama told Ron Klain, his designated naysayer, "I feel great about this now."

As recently as the nineties, Supreme Court nominees could be eased into the confirmation process, first with a round of courtesy calls on a few senators and then with several weeks to prepare for their hearings. Harriet Miers put an end to that. Miers had been George W. Bush's private attorney and then his White House counsel before he nominated her to replace Sandra Day O'Connor in 2005. (Bush initially named Roberts to take O'Connor's place, but then Rehnquist's death opened the chief justice position for Roberts.) Right after Miers's nomination, her handlers at the White House scheduled a few informal meetings with senators, who took the opportunity to test her knowledge on a

variety of issues. Miers performed disastrously, and she was soon forced
to withdraw as a nominee.

So there was nothing casual about Sotomayor's preparations for her
first meetings. (She eventually met with ninety-two senators, a substantial increase from prior practice.) Sotomayor had been a judge for the
past seventeen years, and she was more used to asking questions than
answering them. Plus, her docket in New York had not included some
subjects that were closest to the hearts of the senators—like national
security, gun rights, and the death penalty. She needed to study up, and
fast.

Like Cassandra Butts, who was still nominally the deputy counsel
in charge of judicial nominations, Sotomayor had gone to a prestigious
law school, but she had not operated in the universe of Supreme Court
law clerks. The nominee felt an edge of condescension from what she
called "the bright young things" on Greg Craig's staff. Matters were not
helped on June 8 when Sotomayor tripped at LaGuardia Airport and
broke her ankle. She was determined to keep to her schedule of meetings on crutches—and to avoid using painkillers—but it wasn't easy.
Eventually Sotomayor agreed to take some Aleve, but she remained in
pain for weeks. (In keeping with recent tradition, her future colleagues
on the Supreme Court greeted her nomination with a frosty silence. No
one called. Only Ginsburg, who as the justice responsible for the Second Circuit had known Sotomayor for years, wrote her a congratulatory
note.)

As her hearings approached, Sotomayor's ambitions narrowed. This
was not about explaining the Constitution or even winning arguments
but only about getting confirmed. It did not help that after her nomination, but before her hearing, the Supreme Court voted 5–4 to overturn
her decision in the New Haven firefighter case.

As Sotomayor had often said, her own career was a monument to the
success of affirmative action. She had a Hispanic and female take on the
Constitution. But at her hearings, she steered away from that controversial territory. Instead, Sotomayor's opening statement was a monument
to banality. "In the past month, many senators have asked me about my
judicial philosophy," she said. "It is simple: fidelity to the law. The task
of a judge is not to make the law—it is to apply the law." Of course,
all justices believe they are displaying fidelity to the law; the question
is how they interpret the law. Like other nominees since Robert Bork,

Sotomayor ducked questions about substantive issues—abortion and gun control especially—but her nonresponsiveness exceeded the norm. The Democrats had sixty votes; Sotomayor tried to run out the clock without making a mistake.

On the "wise Latina" issue, Sotomayor caved. When questioned closely on the matter by Jeff Sessions, the senior Republican on the committee, she first dodged the central contention of her speeches: "My record shows that at no point or time have I ever permitted my personal views or sympathies to influence an outcome of a case. In every case where I have identified a sympathy, I have articulated it and explained to the litigant why the law requires a different result."

"Well, Judge . . . ," Sessions interrupted.

"I do not permit my sympathies, personal views, or prejudices to influence the outcome of my cases," she said, ignoring the interruption.

In the end, Sotomayor just walked away from her previous position. "I was using a rhetorical flourish that fell flat. I knew that Justice O'Connor couldn't have meant that if judges reached different conclusions—legal conclusions—that one of them wasn't wise. That couldn't have been her meaning, because reasonable judges disagree on legal conclusions in some cases. So I was trying to play on her words. My play was—fell flat.

"It was bad, because it left an impression that I believed that life experiences commanded a result in a case, but that's clearly not what I do as a judge," she went on. "It's clearly not what I intended in the context of my broader speech, which was attempting to inspire young Hispanic, Latino students and lawyers to believe that their life experiences added value to the process."

From the perspective of the White House, Sotomayor's hearing was a clear success. Above all, she did nothing to jeopardize her chances of being confirmed. In a way, it was an Obama-like performance—progressive by implication, biographical rather than ideological. Sotomayor was a highly qualified nominee whose views appeared to mirror the careful inclinations of the president who appointed her. That's what Obama wanted in a Supreme Court justice, and that's what he received. On July 28, the Judiciary Committee voted 13–6 in her favor. (Only Lindsey Graham, Republican of South Carolina, crossed party lines to vote for her.) On August 6, the full Senate confirmed Sotomayor by a vote of 68–31. (Nine Republicans voted for her.)

Roberts and Alito had been sworn in at the White House—over the objections of John Paul Stevens, a fierce defender of the prerogatives of the judicial branch of government. Stevens thought such ceremonies should take place at the Supreme Court, because new justices should make clear that they now owed no allegiance to the president who appointed them. In a subtle but unmistakable sign of her inclinations in the battles to come, Sotomayor agreed with Stevens. On August 8, at the Supreme Court, she officially became the 111th justice in American history.

It was especially important for Sotomayor to take her place right away, because the Court was hearing a case before the traditional start of the year, on the first Monday in October. It was September 9, 2009, when Sotomayor ascended the bench for the first time and heard the chief justice call her first case. It also turned out to be the first case argued by the new solicitor general, Elena Kagan.

"We'll hear argument today in Case 08-205," Roberts said, "*Citizens United v. the Federal Election Commission.*"

PART

THREE

11

MONEY TALKS

The story of *Citizens United* includes several of the great themes of Supreme Court history, among them corporate power, freedom of speech, and the intersection of law and politics. The tale involves legislation and court cases of enormous complexity, but the struggle at its heart has been a fairly simple one. For more than a century, the partisans in these battles have sometimes seen fit to obscure or deny the ideological fissures, but the sides have remained more or less the same: progressives (or liberals) vs. conservatives, Democrats vs. Republicans, regulators vs. libertarians. One side has favored government rules to limit the influence of the wealthy in political campaigns; the other has supported a freer market allowing individuals and corporations to contribute as they see fit. The battles sometimes had unexpected consequences, but the motivations on either side never changed.

The saga began with one of the enduring mysteries in the history of the Supreme Court. In 1886, the Court heard a rather obscure and uncontroversial tax case called *Santa Clara County v. Southern Pacific Railroad*. The lawsuit concerned whether a railroad should have to pay taxes on fences adjacent to its tracks. What made the case famous was a remark by Chief Justice Morrison R. Waite, just prior to the oral argument. Waite told the lawyers, "The court does not want to hear argument on the question of whether the Fourteenth Amendment to the Constitution, which forbids a State to deny to any person within its jurisdiction the equal protection of the laws, applies to these corporations. We are all of the opinion that it does."

The argument proceeded, and the Court unanimously decided the case in favor of the railroad. The fences were not taxable. The justices never addressed the issue of whether corporations, for purposes of the Fourteenth Amendment, were persons. Still, just before the opinion was issued, J. C. Bancroft Davis, the clerk of the Supreme Court, wrote to Chief Justice Waite to ask him about his remark before the oral argument. Waite confirmed what he said, and Davis quoted the remark verbatim in his "headnote," or summary of the case. From the earliest days of the Supreme Court, these headnotes had been prepared by the staff of the Court, not the justices, and they have never been part of the official opinions of the Court. They have no formal legal significance; they are merely to assist readers of the Court's opinions. Still, the *Santa Clara* headnote became the wellspring for a crucial idea in the history of American law: under the Fourteenth Amendment, corporations had the same rights as people. In an opinion from 1978, then–Justice Rehnquist said of the *Santa Clara* case, "This Court decided at an early date, with neither argument nor discussion, that a business corporation is a 'person' entitled to the protection of the Equal Protection Clause of the Fourteenth Amendment."

All these years later, questions about the *Santa Clara* case abound. Why didn't Waite want to hear argument on this question? Why didn't the justices address the point in an opinion? Why did they leave this momentous issue to be settled by the clerk of the Court? The writer Jack Beatty, who examined the questions in detail, could not settle the matter with certainty: "Davis may have gotten it right, may have misunderstood what Waite said or meant, or may have understood yet gone ahead to make constitutional law on his own."

The historical context for the Court's decision was clear. In the aftermath of the Civil War, the Court remained what it had been before the war—a very conservative institution. During Reconstruction, Congress and the states passed three new amendments to the Constitution—the Thirteenth, Fourteenth, and Fifteenth—to give the newly freed slaves the full rights of citizenship. Almost immediately, the Supreme Court did much to undermine these new provisions, ultimately permitting the continued oppression of African Americans. At the same time, the justices became eager accomplices in the excesses of the Gilded Age. In a series of cases, including *Santa Clara*, the Court prevented any governmental restraints on the great new concentrations of wealth and power in commercial and corporate interests. Black people and poor people had few friends among the justices.

This time at the Court came just before the *Lochner* era, which was named after the most famous case of its day. In an early attempt to protect workers from exploitation, New York passed a law prohibiting bakery employees from working more than sixty hours a week. In the 1905 case known as *Lochner v. New York*, the Court declared the state law unconstitutional on the ground that it interfered with the "right of contract" of both the employer and the employee. "The general right to make a contract in relation to his business is part of the liberty of the individual protected by the Fourteenth Amendment of the Federal Constitution," Justice Rufus Peckham wrote for the 5–4 majority. In short, the New York law was an "unreasonable, unnecessary and arbitrary interference with the right of the individual to his personal liberty or to enter into those contracts in relation to labor which may seem to him appropriate or necessary for the support of himself and his family." In simple terms, the majority in *Lochner* turned the Fourteenth Amendment, which was enacted to protect the rights of newly freed slaves, into a mechanism to advance the interest of business owners.

The implications of *Lochner* were breathtaking. The Court basically asserted that all attempts to regulate the private marketplace, or to protect workers, were unconstitutional. In the words of the legal historian Morton J. Horwitz, *Lochner* "expressed, above all, the post–Civil War triumph of laissez-faire principles in political economy and of the view that 'the government is best which governs least.' " The concept of "judicial activism," if not that precise term, dates to this period at the end of the nineteenth and early part of the twentieth centuries. During this time, the democratically elected branches of government passed a variety of laws to protect workers and other individuals. But the Court imposed itself as a superlegislature, rejecting many of these laws as violating the right to contract and due process of law. The *Lochner* era at the Supreme Court reflected conservative judicial activism; later, in the Warren Court era, there would be liberal judicial activism when the justices began overturning laws that violated the rights of minorities and women.

The conservative extremism of the *Lochner* era at the Supreme Court, and its broader political implications, eventually generated a backlash. Around the turn of the century, disparate reform movements began gaining traction. Antitrust legislation, food safety rules, child labor laws, women's suffrage, a tax on income—all came together under the broad rubric of Progressivism. Theodore Roosevelt, who became president in 1901, made the movement his own.

Roosevelt won a landslide election in 1904, helped in part by vast campaign contributions by corporations. Roosevelt drew heavily from railroad and insurance interests and, in the last days before the election, made a personal appeal for funds to a group of wealthy businessmen, including Henry Clay Frick, the steel baron. Years later, Frick recalled of Roosevelt, "He got down on his knees to us. We bought the son-of-a-bitch and then he did not stay bought." Almost as soon as TR won the election, he turned his attention to passing the first campaign finance reform act in American history—trying to outlaw the very techniques he had just used to hang on to the presidency. Roosevelt put the effort to ban corporate money in politics near the top of his agenda. In his annual message to Congress on December 5, 1905, he recommended that "all contributions by corporations to any political committee or for any political purpose should be forbidden by law."

Roosevelt's efforts came to fruition in 1907 with the passage of the Tillman Act, named for the eccentric rogue "Pitchfork" Ben Tillman, the South Carolina senator who sponsored the law. To be sure, the act was a modest first step. The law barred corporations from contributing to campaigns and established criminal penalties for violations, but there was no enforcement mechanism. (The Federal Election Commission would not be created for decades.) Loopholes proliferated. For example, individuals could still give as much as they wanted to political campaigns and be reimbursed for the contributions by their employers. Nevertheless, the Tillman Act was a nod toward what Congress described as its goal: elections "free from the power of money."

That never happened. In subsequent decades, the power of money in politics only grew. After World War II, candidates campaigned principally by buying advertisements on television, and that strategy created an ever-increasing need for cash. Richard Nixon's obsession with campaign fund-raising was one of the principal motivations that led to the Watergate scandals.

Watergate prompted the second great wave of campaign finance reform. The major legislative enactment of this era was the Federal Election Campaign Act Amendments of 1974, which created much of the regulatory structure that endures today. This law enacted unprecedented limits on campaign contributions and spending, created the Federal Election Commission to enforce the act, established an optional system of public financing for presidential elections, and required extensive disclosure of campaign contributions and expenditures.

And Watergate, and its legislative fallout, brought the Supreme Court into the thick of the issue.

Shortly after the new law went into effect, a group of politicians, including James L. Buckley, then a senator from New York, and Eugene McCarthy, the former senator and presidential candidate, challenged the new rules as unconstitutional. To this point in the Court's history, few decisions dealt with the constitutionality of campaign finance regulation. The Tillman Act was never directly tested in the Supreme Court, and no one questioned the right of the federal government to restrict corporate political spending. But the 1974 reforms were challenged in court, and the resulting decision, known as *Buckley v. Valeo*, issued in 1976, has gone down in history as one of the Supreme Court's most complicated, contradictory, incomprehensible (and longest) opinions.

No one really knows who wrote it. It is signed per curiam—"by the Court"—a label the justices usually use for brief and minor opinions. In *Buckley v. Valeo*, however, the Court used it to signal a team effort of sorts. William Brennan is generally regarded to have written much of *Buckley*, but Brennan's biographers note that sections were also composed by Warren Burger, Potter Stewart, Lewis Powell, and William Rehnquist. Not surprisingly, in light of the multiple authors, the opinion is a product of several compromises. To add to the confusion, five justices also wrote opinions concurring in part and dissenting in part from the majority. (A quarter century later, *Bush v. Gore* was another per curiam opinion by the Court that reflected poorly on the institution.)

It is possible, however, to extract some meaning from the dog's breakfast that is *Buckley v. Valeo*. At the heart of the decision is a distinction between expenditures and contributions. The Court said that, under the First Amendment, Congress could not restrict campaign expenditures. Spending money was like speech itself because "every means of communicating ideas in today's mass society requires the expenditure of money." That included printing handbills, renting halls, and buying ads on television. It is a result of *Buckley* that wealthy candidates can spend as much as they want of their own money on their campaigns; it would be unconstitutional to limit their expenditures.

On the other hand, according to *Buckley*, limits on contributions were constitutionally permissible. The Court said that a campaign contribution served only as "a general expression of support for the candidate and his views, but does not communicate the underlying basis for the support." In the Court's view, limiting contributions did not really inhibit much political expression by the person giving the money. This was why the Court concluded that it was permissible for the law to limit how much an individual could contribute to any particular campaign.

In the 1974 law, Congress had tried to set up a tightly controlled system for financing campaigns: the government would monitor and regulate both the inflows and outflows of money. It is not clear that it would have worked as intended, but at least the proposal made a sort of holistic sense. Congress could essentially select a number for the overall price of a congressional (or presidential) campaign and then force candidates to live within that parameter. *Buckley* ended that system before it even started and imposed a different one of the justices' own creation. In the justices' system, contributions could be limited, but expenditures could not. The legislators who designed the law certainly did not think this distinction made sense. Both contributions and expenditures involve political expression, and campaigns clearly need both of them to function. At the same time, a system that sought to limit the power of money in campaigns would have to control both contributions and expenditures in order to make any real difference. (That is what Congress tried to do.) Instead, the Supreme Court's improvised hybrid drew a distinction where none may have existed, and for two generations that distinction has been the central feature of the constitutional rules of campaign finance. The bottom line was that money is speech.

Buckley v. Valeo created an entirely new area of law. With the vague and imperfect guidance from the Court, the federal government and the states had to construct their systems for regulating campaigns. Concurrently, candidates, their supporters, and their opponents began to act according to their understanding of the law. *Buckley* dealt only with candidates and elections, but it left unsettled the rules for "issue advocacy"—television commercials that were supposedly designed to change public opinion rather than the outcome of a single election. "Issue advocacy" was much less regulated than campaign spending, but the line between the two was less than clear, and easily exploited.

The law treated the financing of campaigns and "issue advocacy" very differently. Under *Buckley*, candidates had to rely only on tightly regulated campaign contributions to pay for ads. But advocacy groups could receive and spend unlimited funds, and issue advocacy advertisements could look a lot like political campaign commercials. Advocacy groups could run commercials saying "Call Joe Congressman and tell him he's wrong," and that would not count as a contribution to his opponent. Similarly, groups could avoid federal regulation by preparing "voter guides" that pointed out the contrasts between candidates in clearly partisan ways.

Like any other major change in the law, the post-*Buckley* world of campaign regulation prompted a group of lawyers to develop specialties in the new field. The most revealing career was that of James Bopp Jr. Over three decades, Bopp became one of the most important anti-abortion lawyers in America and one of the most vocal opponents of campaign finance laws. Bopp's twin goals reflected a true symbiosis.

Bopp was raised in Terre Haute, Indiana, and in 1970 graduated from Indiana University, where he headed the chapter of Young Americans for Freedom, the student group that propelled many Republican careers. He returned to the state to practice law after graduating from the University of Florida law school in 1973, the year of *Roe v. Wade*. Bopp decided to join the fledgling anti-abortion movement and was hired as general counsel to the Indiana chapter of the National Right to Life Committee. Two years later, Bopp became general counsel to the full National Right to Life Committee—and a key Republican partisan in the elections of 1980.

Bopp persuaded his colleagues to start a political action committee to give financial support to anti-abortion candidates, and the Right to Life group put out a series of "voter guides" before Election Day. These guides were credited with helping to create the landslide that put Ronald Reagan in the White House and twelve new Republicans in the Senate. The right-to-life voter guides were barely concealed works of advocacy, and the FEC later tried to ban them. Bopp won a First Amendment challenge to the prohibition, and began working actively to challenge campaign finance restrictions as well as abortion rights. Bopp's dual career was launched.

Bopp ultimately filed or defended 140 lawsuits around the country, challenging various kinds of campaign finance regulations as violations of the First Amendment. He argued two cases before the Supreme Court, winning one of them, before his friends at Wisconsin Right to Life asked him for help in another case in 2004. It was, in certain ways, similar to the work he had been doing for decades, with one very important exception.

In 1989, during his first term in the Senate, John McCain was one of the "Keating Five" who participated in unsavory dealings with Charles Keating Jr., a corrupt Arizona financier. McCain was never charged with any wrongdoing, but the humiliation of the experience led him to become a leader in the fight for campaign finance reform. More than a decade of work produced the Bipartisan Campaign Reform Act of 2002 (BCRA), which was sometimes pronounced "bic-ruh" but more often called the McCain-Feingold law. The law passed mostly because of Democratic support. President Bush signed it with great reluctance, early in the morning to avoid a public ceremony, and immediately announced his reservations about its constitutionality. So for the most part, the customary ideological split on campaign finance reform prevailed with McCain-Feingold. Indeed, by the time McCain ran for the Republican nomination for president in 2008, he had all but repudiated the law that bore his name.

One of the primary targets of the McCain-Feingold law was the increasingly meaningless distinction between candidate advertisements and "issue" advertisements. For many years, corporations and labor unions had spent millions on ads that denounced individual candidates but technically avoided the specific language that turned a commercial into a "campaign" ad. McCain-Feingold sought to address this problem by prohibiting corporate and labor union funding of any broadcast ads mentioning a candidate within thirty days of a primary or caucus or within sixty days of a general election.

The new law prompted Wisconsin Right to Life to come to Bopp with a problem. The state had two Democratic senators, Russell Feingold and Herb Kohl, who both supported abortion rights. In the run-up to the election of 2004, when Feingold was on the ballot, Right to Life wanted to run radio ads like the following:

PASTOR: And who gives this woman to be married to this man?
BRIDE'S FATHER: Well, as father of the bride, I certainly could. But instead, I'd like to share a few tips on how to properly install drywall. Now you put the drywall up . . .
VOICE-OVER: Sometimes it's just not fair to delay an important decision.

But in Washington it's happening. A group of senators is using the filibuster delay tactic to block federal judicial nominees from a simple "yes" or "no" vote. So qualified candidates don't get a chance to serve.

It's politics at work, causing gridlock and backing up some of our courts to a state of emergency.

Contact Senators Feingold and Kohl and tell them to oppose the filibuster.

Paid for by Wisconsin Right to Life, which is responsible for the content of this advertising and not authorized by any candidate or candidate's committee.

The advertisement was designed to criticize Feingold, but it did not specifically discourage a vote for him. In that way, it looked like an "issue" ad, but because it ran before an election, it was prohibited by the McCain-Feingold law. The political priorities of the right-to-life movement were also revealing. The Wisconsin group, which was dedicated to fighting abortion rights, was putting its money behind pushing President Bush's judicial nominations, which suggests how important federal judges were to the conservative movement. (When President Obama's judicial nominations were obstructed by Republican senators, there was no comparable energy expended on their behalf by Democrats.)

Bopp believed the McCain-Feingold ban on issue advertisements violated the First Amendment, but he had a problem. In 2003, in one of the last major opinions of the Rehnquist Court, the justices had upheld the great majority of McCain-Feingold against a constitutional challenge led by Mitch McConnell, a leading Republican in the Senate and a dedicated foe of all campaign finance reform. (The case was known as *McConnell v. Federal Election Commission*.) How could Bopp challenge a law that had already been upheld?

But the lawyer was fearless. Bopp knew that the 2003 Supreme Court case was a challenge to McCain-Feingold "on its face"—that is, a claim that the law was going to be unconstitutional in all circumstances. A new case would challenge the law "as applied" against Wisconsin Right to Life. He would claim that this specific application of the law violated the group's First Amendment rights. Bopp didn't wait around for the FEC (a notoriously slow-moving agency) to challenge his clients. Rather, he decided to bring a preemptive lawsuit challenging the ban on issue advertisements before elections.

Bopp knew that he had an important advantage over the failed 2003 challenge to the McCain-Feingold law. In that case, O'Connor had voted to uphold most of the law as part of a 5–4 majority. But she was now gone, having been replaced by Alito, so Bopp could count on the more friendly faces of the Roberts Court.

The Wisconsin Right to Life case was heard on April 25, 2007, the last day of arguments during Roberts's tumultuous second year as chief justice. It was the year of great conservative ascendancy—of Lilly Ledbetter's loss, of the approval of the late-term abortion ban, and of *Parents Involved*, the cases involving the integration of the Louisville and Seattle schools. By the time *Federal Election Commission v. Wisconsin Right to Life* was argued, all these other cases had already been decided (if not yet announced), so the liberals knew that they would lose. No one was more frustrated than Stephen Breyer.

A pattern had emerged over Breyer's years at the Court. He would arrive each fall, after a summer of travel and relaxation, full of the optimism that had been a trademark for the first half century of his adult life. But each year, as the defeats piled up and the Court turned away from him, he would grow more and more discouraged. On this final day of arguments in the fateful 2006–07 term, Breyer was spitting fire—at Jim Bopp.

What frustrated Breyer in the Wisconsin case was that he thought he had already won this particular battle in 2003, when the Court upheld McCain-Feingold in the *McConnell* case. Breyer had recently published *Active Liberty*, a book intended for a popular audience, which celebrated at length the importance of campaign finance reform. Now that achievement, like so many of Breyer's victories on the Court, looked as if it could slip away.

Breyer taunted Bopp—which amounted to baiting his conservative colleagues. "If we agree with you in this case, good-bye McCain-Feingold," Breyer said. "Maybe we should do it up front. That's what you advocate. Very well. Would you address that? Why should this Court only a year or two after it upholds McCain-Feingold, accept a position that either in fact or in theory overturns that case?"

Bopp tried to defuse the issue, but Breyer wasn't having it.

"That's what McCain-Feingold was about," Breyer went on. "They said in today's world these are the kinds of ads people run just to defeat people. And then they said, moreover, most of the campaign money goes on them. And then they said, moreover, if you let corporations and labor unions contribute to these, well, then they can contribute to the campaign.

"If you're prepared to say the Constitution requires us to let corporations and unions buy these kinds of ads, well, how could it be constitutional to have a statute that forbids them to contribute directly to the candidate, something that's been in existence only since, I guess, 1904?" (Breyer was referring to the Tillman Act of 1907.)

Breyer could see where the Court was going. If his colleagues were prepared to rule that the modest regulations of McCain-Feingold were unconstitutional, then the whole edifice of campaign finance reform would crumble. Laws that were in place since the beginning of the twentieth century were going to fall, too.

Bopp could afford to parry Breyer's questions, because he knew he had the votes. At one point, Bopp said that the ads in Wisconsin were not just to support or oppose candidates in elections but also to change the positions of existing officeholders.

"People should have the opportunity to engage in grassroots lobbying," Bopp said.

"Is that called democracy?" Kennedy asked him.

"We are hopeful, Your Honor," Bopp replied. One might argue that television and radio advertisements were hardly "grassroots lobbying," and one could say elections dominated by those commercials were not necessarily "called democracy." But those arguments were clearly failing before the Roberts Court.

In candid moments, justices often remark that outsiders ought to pay more attention to the time of year that any given opinion has been handed down. The Court begins hearing arguments on the first Monday in October, and decisions rendered in November and December are often unanimous or at least the product of good-natured bargaining on all sides. As the year progresses, however, nerves grow frayed and impatience becomes the norm. The issues are harder. There is less negotiating, and there are more separate opinions, which take longer to write. By the last day of the term, especially one as fraught as 2006–07, the justices can barely stand the sight of one another. That tone was reflected in the decision in *Wisconsin Right to Life*.

The opinions in the case are a patchwork mess, a typical late-term failure to agree on much of anything. But on the core issue, the split remained the same. Roberts, Scalia, Kennedy, Thomas, and Alito found the restriction on Wisconsin Right to Life unconstitutional; Stevens, Souter, Ginsburg, and Breyer would have upheld the ban on the commercials. Scalia, Kennedy, and Thomas, who had dissented in the McCain-Feingold case in 2003, wrote separate opinions rearguing their position that McCain-Feingold should be struck down. Alito more or less said the same thing.

That left Chief Justice Roberts to speak for the Court. He was still trying to prove that he was cautious and respectful of precedent, as he had claimed to be during his confirmation hearing. But now he was part of a majority that was gutting a four-year-old opinion and decades more of settled law. Roberts completed this mission with typical finesse, declaring, "The First Amendment requires us to err on the side of protecting political speech rather than suppressing it." Unlike the others in the majority, Roberts did not explicitly call for overturning McCain-Feingold, but he plainly indicated where the Court was heading. As for the *McConnell* case, the 2003 decision upholding the law, Roberts wrote, "We have no occasion to revisit that determination today."

Today. *Today.* The sentence was a model of near-total transparency. To those who know the language of the Court, the chief justice was all but announcing that five justices were preparing to declare the McCain-Feingold law unconstitutional. Not today—but, clearly, soon.

Souter wrote the pained dissent for the liberal quartet in *Wisconsin Right to Life* and announced at the outset that the Court's 2003 decision upholding McCain-Feingold was "effectively, and unjustifiably, over-ruled today." But that wasn't true, at least not "today." For the coup de grâce to be applied to the campaign finance laws of the past century, it would take a charter member of the vast right-wing conspiracy.

SAMUEL ALITO'S QUESTION

The most famous television commercial of the 1988 presidential race was not produced by either George H. W. Bush or Michael Dukakis. An independent committee called Americans for Bush ran a commercial featuring Willie Horton, a convicted murderer who had received a weekend furlough from a Massachusetts prison and then committed several grisly crimes. The stark images of the African American perpetrator, as shown in the commercial, caused a sensation. The Bush campaign always claimed it had nothing to do with the ad.

Floyd Brown was happy to take the credit. A burly native of Washington State, Brown had worked around the fringes of the conservative movement for years. (Like Bopp, Brown got his start in politics through the Young Americans for Freedom, in Brown's case at the University of Washington.) Brown had mastered the art of setting up a nonprofit, raising money, making a splash, and moving on. When the election was over, Americans for Bush had obviously outlived its usefulness. So Brown embraced the notoriety that came with authorship of the Willie Horton ad, and founded a new organization. He called it Citizens United.

At first, Brown worked from the Horton template. He would create highly partisan television commercials and then engage in direct-mail fund-raising to pay to broadcast them. In 1991, for example, Citizens United produced a commercial in support of the nomination of Clarence Thomas to the Supreme Court. (The ads consisted mostly of attacks on the characters of senators who sat on the Judiciary Committee.) With the election of Bill Clinton as president, Citizens United took off in a new direction.

Brown acquired a sidekick—a recent dropout from the University of Maryland named David Bossie. Crew-cut and intense, Bossie had a passion for conservative politics and, like Brown, an entrepreneurial bent. (A dedicated volunteer fireman, Bossie lived above his local firehouse in Maryland.) In 1992, Brown named Bossie his "chief researcher" and the pair narrowed their focus to the personal and financial affairs of Bill and Hillary Clinton. The duo produced a book tied to the 1992 campaign, *Slick Willie: Why America Cannot Trust Bill Clinton.*

Over the next several years, Bossie became, in effect, the agent for various Arkansas figures who claimed they knew of wrongdoing by the Clintons. David Hale, a municipal court judge in Little Rock, was under FBI investigation in Arkansas for misusing federal small business loans. Friends of Hale put him in touch with Bossie. Hale asserted that Clinton was involved in a web of corruption in the state. Bossie, in turn, introduced Hale to various Washington journalists who printed or broadcast his accusations. (Hale's claims were never verified.) Later, Bossie served as a similar intermediary for stories that raised questions about the White House aide Vince Foster's suicide.

Twice during the Clinton years, Bossie left Citizens United to work for Republicans in Congress—first on the Senate investigation of the Clintons' Whitewater land deal and then for Congressman Dan Burton, an Indiana Republican who was obsessed with Clinton's alleged misdeeds. (In an effort to show that Foster might have been killed, Burton conducted a demonstration in his backyard where he shot what he referred to as a "head-like object," which was either a watermelon or a pumpkin.) During Bossie's tenure with Burton, he became friendly with Clarence Thomas's wife, Virginia Thomas, who at the time was on the staff of Richard Armey, the Republican leader in the House. Ginni Thomas thought Bossie was a bit extreme in his views. Burton fired Bossie after it was revealed that he had doctored certain transcripts to eliminate exculpatory information about Hillary Clinton. Bossie then went back to work at Citizens United.

The careers of Bossie and Brown had been sources of particular interest to Sidney Blumenthal, a journalist who joined the White House staff in 1997. It was Blumenthal who prepared Hillary Clinton for her appearance on the *Today* show, on January 27, 1998, her first interview after the Monica Lewinsky scandal broke. Schooled by Blumenthal in the ways of Brown, Bossie, and others like them, Mrs. Clinton told Matt Lauer, "This is—the great story here, for anybody willing to find it and write about it and explain it, is this vast right-wing conspiracy that has been conspiring against my husband since the day he announced for president."

With the inauguration of George W. Bush, the public profile of Citizens United receded. Bossie, who had become president of the group, thought that it needed a niche to distinguish it from the other conservative organizations in Washington. Bossie's moment of insight came in 2004, when he saw advertisements for Michael Moore's movie *Fahrenheit 9/11*. Bossie saw that the documentary was doing a kind of double duty. *Fahrenheit 9/11* and the television commercials promoting it were political salvos against the reelection of President Bush as well as a potential source of profit. (*Fahrenheit 9/11* earned more than $200 million at the box office.) A nonprofit organization, Citizens United had a total budget of about $12 million a year, and the vast majority of those funds came from donations from individuals. A small portion of contributions—about 1 percent—came from for-profit companies. (This turned out to be important.)

Bossie determined to remake Citizens United into a movie studio, to produce conservative documentaries. The first, *Celsius 41.11: The Temperature at Which the Brain Begins to Die*, was a direct response to Moore and not especially successful. But Bossie kept making films, and some found an audience. All had conservative themes, and many were narrated by Newt and Callista Gingrich. They included: *Fire from the Heartland: The Awakening of the Conservative Woman*, starring Michele Bachmann; *The Gift of Life*, against abortion rights ("My mom was raped, and I was almost aborted. My life was spared for a purpose."); and *Rediscovering God in America* ("There is no attack on American culture more destructive, and more historically dishonest, than the relentless effort to drive God out of America's public square.").

In the period leading up to the 2008 election, the presidential candidacy of Hillary Clinton was an irresistible subject for Bossie, given his long history opposing her and her husband. In many respects, *Hillary:*

The Movie was typical of the Citizens United oeuvre. It included news footage, spooky music, and a series of interviews with fierce and articulate partisans. ("She's driven by the power, she's driven to get the power, that is the driving force in her life," said Bay Buchanan, the activist and sister of Patrick, the onetime presidential candidate. "She's deceitful, she'll make up any story, lie about anything, as long as it serves her purposes of the moment, and the American people are going to catch on to it," added Dick Morris. " 'Liar' is a good one," said Ann Coulter.) Bossie wanted *Hillary: The Movie* to come out in late 2007, to tie it to the presidential election in the way that Moore pegged *Fahrenheit 9/11* to the previous race. Citizens United offered a cable company $1.2 million to make *Hillary* available for free to viewers on a technology known as Video On Demand.

Over the years, Bossie had become familiar with federal election law, and he was concerned that his movie would run afoul of the same law that was at issue in the *Wisconsin Right to Life* case, especially since he planned to run commercials in states holding presidential primaries. The movie and commercials would have multiple purposes: to advance the conservative cause, to hurt Hillary Clinton's chances for victory, and to make the production a financial success. The question, then, was how the Federal Election Commission would classify *Hillary* and the advertisements for it. Under the FEC rules, if *Hillary* was deemed a work of journalism or entertainment, like *Fahrenheit 9/11*, then Bossie could show it any time he wanted; the FEC had a clear exception for those kinds of works. But if the FEC regarded *Hillary* and its commercials as an "electioneering communication," that is, "speech expressly advocating the election or defeat of a candidate," then it could not be broadcast within thirty days of a primary or sixty days of a general election.

Bossie hired Jim Bopp, who, as ever, favored an aggressive tack. He went straight to the FEC to get a ruling. As expected, the FEC ruled that the documentary amounted to an "electioneering communication" and thus could not be broadcast in the period before a primary. Bopp appealed to the federal district court in Washington. A three-judge panel agreed with the FEC, holding that *Hillary: The Movie* is "susceptible of no other interpretation than to inform the electorate that Senator Clinton is unfit for office, that the United States would be a dangerous place in a President Hillary Clinton world, and that viewers should vote against her."

Bossie was determined to take the next step: an appeal to the Supreme Court. But first he had a tough decision to make. Whom should he hire as his lawyer?

Bossie may have arrived in Washington as a flamethrowing outsider, but over the previous decade he had become part of the conservative establishment. He knew that Bopp had just won the *Wisconsin Right to Life* case before the justices, but he also recognized that his own financial life, and potentially his place in history, was on the line in the *Citizens United* case. Did he want to leave his fate in the hands of a lawyer from Terre Haute?

Bossie checked with some of his mentors in Republican law and politics. He called Michael Chertoff, who had led the Senate Whitewater investigation (and then gone on to be secretary of homeland security); Alice Fisher, a former Bush Justice Department official; Victoria Toensing and Joseph DiGenova, the famous team of married former prosecutors. All their advice was the same.

Hire Ted Olson.

Olson was already a legendary figure in conservative legal circles. Bossie first met him in the nineties, when Ted and his wife, Barbara, were outspoken fellow critics of Bill Clinton. As a private lawyer at the firm of Gibson, Dunn & Crutcher, Olson had argued and won *Bush v. Gore* and was rewarded by President Bush with appointment as his first solicitor general. (Barbara Olson was killed on the plane that crashed into the Pentagon on September 11, 2001.) Olson had argued dozens of cases before the Supreme Court, and he had a great deal of credibility with the justices. He knew how to win. So Bopp was out, and Olson was in.

Olson quickly shifted tactics in the case. As Bossie saw it, Bopp was a cause lawyer whose top priority was to change the law of campaign finance. While Olson supported the conservative movement, he was primarily a litigator devoted to winning one case at a time. In that spirit, Olson tried to narrow the issues in *Citizens United*, so that the Court would not have to take any dramatic steps in order to rule his way. By the time the case reached the Supreme Court, *Hillary: The Movie* had already played in a handful of theaters, so the only legal issue related to Video On Demand. Indeed, the issue was now so small as to be almost obscure. The McCain-Feingold law prohibited corporate spending on "electioneering" in the period right before presidential primaries. The legal question in the case was whether the law allowed the broadcast of this documentary on Video On Demand during the proscribed period because Citizens United received a small amount of money from corporations.

Olson opened his oral argument on March 24, 2009, with a flourish: "Participation in the political process is the First Amendment's most fundamental guarantee. Yet that freedom is being smothered by one of the most complicated, expensive, and incomprehensible regulatory regimes ever invented by the administrative state. In the case that you consider today, it is a felony for a small, nonprofit corporation to offer interested viewers a 90-minute political documentary about a candidate for the nation's highest office."

After that bit of rhetoric, Olson made a point of limiting his demands. For Citizens United to win its case, according to Olson, the Court did not have to declare anything unconstitutional. The justices simply had to rule that the McCain-Feingold law (BCRA) did not apply to documentaries or nonprofits. "A 90-minute documentary was not the sort of thing that the—the BCRA—that the Congress was intended to prohibit," he said. At one point, Scalia seemed almost disappointed by the modesty of Olson's claim.

"So you're making a statutory argument now?" Scalia said.

"I'm making a—" Olson started.

"You're saying this—this isn't covered by it," Scalia continued.

That's right, Olson responded. All he was asking for was a ruling that the law did not prohibit the broadcast by a nonprofit corporation. The ninety-minute documentary could run on Video On Demand. If the justices had resolved the case as Olson had suggested, *Citizens United v. Federal Election Commission* might well have been forgotten—a narrow ruling on a remote corner of campaign finance law.

But then the lawyer for the government stood up to defend the FEC's decision, and a single question changed the case and perhaps American history.

Whenever the federal government is involved in a case before the Supreme Court, the solicitor general handles the representation. In an age when the reputations of many government agencies have suffered, the office of the solicitor general has remained a symbol of excellence: small, elite, and deeply respected by its most important audience, the justices.

Since the position was created in 1870, some of the most distinguished lawyers in the country's history have served as solicitor general. William Howard Taft, before he became president and then chief justice, was an early SG, and Franklin Roosevelt put two of his solicitors general, Stanley Reed and Robert H. Jackson, on the Supreme Court. In the sixties and seventies, the office was consecutively occupied by Archibald Cox, Thurgood Marshall, Erwin Griswold, and Robert Bork. Kenneth Starr stepped down from a judgeship on the D.C. Circuit to be George H. W. Bush's SG.

For all that the solicitor general serves as the public face of the office, and as an important senior political appointee, the career employees act as its principal representatives to the Court. Only about two of the twenty-two lawyers in the office are political appointees, so most move seamlessly from one administration to the next.

Tradition holds the staff to a different standard than the hired guns who generally appear before the Supreme Court. The solicitor general's lawyers press their position before the Court, but in a way that hews strictly to existing precedent. They don't hide unfavorable facts from the justices. This is why, in many cases, even when the federal government is not a party, the Court issues what's known as a CVSG—a call for the views of the solicitor general. The lawyers in the SG's office are not neutral, exactly, but they are more highly respected than other advocates. They dress differently, too, wearing a morning coat, vest, and striped pants when they appear in the Supreme Court.

Malcolm Stewart, the lawyer in the solicitor general's office who argued the *Citizens United* case, reflected the best of the office. A graduate of Princeton and Yale Law School, he had clerked for Harry Blackmun in the 1989 term. He joined the solicitor general's office in 1993, and his career soared through three presidencies and more than forty oral arguments. He twice won a John Marshall Award, among the highest honors in the department. Shortly before the *Citizens United* argument, Stewart had been named a deputy solicitor general, the highest rank for a career lawyer.

The justices say that oral arguments rarely make a difference in the outcome of cases. But that may not have been true in *Citizens United*—because Stewart's appearance was an epic disaster.

The morning the case began, the justices were in their typical positions. Scalia was on the edge of his seat, ready to pounce. Ginsburg was barely visible above the bench. Breyer was twitchy, his expressions changing with whether or not he agreed with the lawyer's answer. As ever, Thomas was silent and withdrawn.

Samuel Alito appeared miserable, as usual. Alito liked the job well enough, but he was uncomfortable with its public aspects. He liked reading cases and making decisions. He disliked pomp and bureaucracy. (Alito didn't even like hiring law clerks. For years, he chose clerks who had worked for him on the Third Circuit, so he didn't have to interview new ones.) After Thomas, Alito tended to ask the fewest questions. But no one asked better ones. It was easy to tell which way Alito was leaning, because his questions were so hard to answer for the lawyer he was targeting. Alito had radar for weak points in a presentation, and in this case he saw a big hole in Malcolm Stewart's.

Alito recognized how broadly McCain-Feingold was written, and he wanted to push Stewart down its slippery slope. This was a case about movies and television commercials. What else might the law regulate? "Do you think the Constitution required Congress to draw the line where it did, limiting this to broadcast and cable and so forth?" Alito asked. Could the law limit a corporation from "providing the same thing in a book? Would the Constitution permit the restriction of all of those as well?"

Yes, said Stewart. "Those could have been applied to additional media as well."

The justices leaned forward. It was one thing for the government to regulate television commercials. That had been done for years. But a *book*? Could the government regulate the content of a *book*?

"That's pretty incredible," Alito responded. "You think that if a book was published, a campaign biography that was the functional equivalent of express advocacy, that could be banned?"

"I'm not saying it could be banned," Stewart replied, trying to recover. "I'm saying that Congress could prohibit the use of corporate treasury funds and could require a corporation to publish it using its PAC." But clearly Stewart was saying that Citizens United, or any company or non-profit like it, could not publish a book about a presidential campaign.

Kennedy interrupted. He was the swing justice in many areas of the law, but in campaign finance cases, Kennedy joined the conservatives. Sensing vulnerability on the subject of books, he joined Alito's assault.

"Well, suppose it were an advocacy organization that had a book," Kennedy said. "Your position is that under the Constitution, the advertising for this book or the sale for the book itself could be prohibited within the sixty- and thirty-day periods?"

Yes, said Stewart.

But neither Alito nor Kennedy had Roberts's instinct for the jugular. The chief justice wanted to make Stewart's position look as ridiculous as possible. Roberts knew just how to do it. He continued on the subject of the government's censorship of books, leading Stewart into a trap.

"If it has one name, one use of the candidate's name, it would be covered, correct?" Roberts asked.

"That's correct," Stewart said.

"It's a 500-page book, and at the end it says, and so vote for X, the government could ban that?" Roberts asked.

"Well, if it says vote for X, it would be express advocacy and it would be covered by the preexisting Federal Election Campaign Act provision," Stewart continued, doubling down on his painfully awkward position.

Through artful questioning, Alito, Kennedy, and Roberts had turned a modestly important case about campaign finance reform into a battle over government censorship. The trio made Stewart—and thus the government—take an absurd position, that the government might have the right to criminalize the publication of a 500-page book because of one line at the end. Still, the justices' questions raised important issues. Did the McCain-Feingold law in fact permit such an outlandish outcome? Could Congress pass any law to ban a book? And was Stewart right to acknowledge that it did?

Stewart was wrong. Congress could not ban a book. McCain-Feingold was based on the pervasive influence of television advertising on electoral politics, the idea that commercials are somehow unavoidable in contemporary American life. The influence of books operates in a completely different way. Individuals have to make an affirmative choice to acquire and read a book. Congress would have no reason, and no justification, to ban a book under the First Amendment.

As for Stewart's performance, his defenders pointed to the unique role of the solicitor general. A private lawyer could have danced around the implications of the law and avoided making any concession, but Stewart had a special obligation to be straight with the justices, even if the answers hurt his cause. Stewart's critics—and there were many—said that he had no obligation to try to answer an absurdly far-fetched hypothetical involving the censorship of books. By doing so, according to this view, Stewart wasn't being honest—he was being foolish. He should have asserted that the federal government had neither the obligation nor the right to stop the publication of a book. Like most arguments about the quality of advocacy, this one had no clear resolution. Evidently, though, the damage to the government's case had been profound.

Here again, the vagaries of the Supreme Court calendar played a part in the resolution of the case. Like *Wisconsin Right to Life*, *Citizens United* was argued near the end of the term, on March 24, 2009. There was not a lot of time for the justices to reach a consensus before June. At their initial conference, the vote was the same as in *Wisconsin Right to Life*, with Kennedy joining the four conservatives.

A private drama followed that in some ways defined the still new chief justice to his colleagues. Roberts assigned the opinion to himself. Even though the oral argument had been dramatic, Ted Olson had presented *Citizens United* to the Court in a narrow way. According to the Questions Presented in the briefs, the only real issue in the case was whether the McCain-Feingold law applied to a documentary, presented on Video On Demand, by a nonprofit corporation. The liberals lost that argument: the vote at the conference was that the law did not apply to Citizens United, which was free to advertise and run its documentary as it saw fit. The liberals expected that Roberts's opinion would say as much, and no more.

At first, Roberts did write an opinion roughly along those lines, and Kennedy wrote a concurrence that said the Court should have gone much farther. Kennedy's opinion said the Court should declare McCain-Feingold's restrictions unconstitutional, overturn an earlier Supreme Court decision from 1990, and gut the Tillman Act prohibitions on corporate giving to campaigns. But after the Roberts and Kennedy drafts circulated, the conservatives began rallying to Kennedy's more expansive resolution of the case. Roberts proposed to withdraw his own opinion and let Kennedy write for the majority. Kennedy then turned his concurrence into an opinion for the Court.

The new majority opinion—which transformed *Citizens United* into a vehicle for rewriting decades of constitutional law—shocked the liberals. Stevens assigned the main dissent to Souter, who was in the last weeks of his tenure on the Court. (He was actually working on the opinion when he announced his departure.) The Kennedy opinion reflected everything Souter had come to loathe about the Roberts Court—its disrespect for precedent, its grasping conservatism, its aggressive pursuit of political objectives. Worse yet, Roberts's approach to *Citizens United* contradicted a position he had taken earlier in the term. At the argument of a death penalty case known as *Cone v. Bell*, Roberts had berated at length the defendant's lawyer, Thomas Goldstein, for his temerity in raising an issue that had not been addressed in the briefs. Now Roberts—the chief justice—was doing precisely the same thing to upset decades of settled expectations.

Souter wrote a dissent that aired some of the Court's dirty laundry. By definition, dissents challenge the legal conclusions of the majority, but Souter accused Kennedy and Roberts of violating the Court's own procedures to engineer the result Roberts coveted. The dissent, had it been published, would have been an extraordinary, bridge-burning farewell to the Court by Souter.

Roberts didn't mind spirited disagreement on the merits of any case, but he worried that Souter's attack might damage the Court's credibility, or his own. So the chief came up with a stroke of strategic genius. He would agree to withdraw the majority opinion and put *Citizens United* down for reargument in the fall. For the second argument, the Court would write Questions Presented that left no doubt about the stakes of the case. The proposal put the liberals in a box. They could no longer complain about being sandbagged, because the new Questions Presented would be unmistakably clear. But—as Roberts knew—the conservatives would go into the second argument already having five votes for the result they wanted. With no other choice (and no real hope of ever winning the case), the liberals agreed to the reargument.

Rearguments were very rare. There had been none of this kind since Warren Burger's days as chief justice. So, on June 29, 2009, the last day of the term, the Court surprised the litigants—and the political world—by issuing the following brief order: "This case is restored to the calendar for reargument." The parties were directed to file new briefs on a single issue:

> For the proper disposition of this case, should the Court overrule either or both *Austin* v. *Michigan Chamber of Commerce*, 494 U.S. 652 (1990), and the part of *McConnell* v. *Federal Election Comm'n*, 540 U.S. 93 (2003), which addresses the facial validity of Section 203 of the Bipartisan Campaign Reform Act of 2002, 2 U.S.C. §441b?

Translated into English, the Court's order told the parties that the justices were considering overruling two major decisions in modern campaign finance law. Specifically, the Court was weighing whether to overturn its recent endorsement of McCain-Feingold. As every sophisticated observer of the Court knew, the Court did not ask whether cases should be overruled unless a majority of the justices already *wanted* those cases overruled. And Roberts and his allies were so impatient to overturn these precedents that they were not even going to wait for the first Monday in October. The second argument in *Citizens United* was set for September 9, 2009.

THE ROOKIE

On the morning of September 9, 2009, a car pulled into the Justice Department courtyard to take the government's team to the Supreme Court for the reargument of *Citizens United*. Elena Kagan, the solicitor general, took the front seat and three of her deputies piled into the back. She had been confirmed by the Senate a few days before the first *Citizens United* argument, and the reargument would mark her debut before the justices. Kagan, at the age of forty-nine, had never so much as argued a single case in any courtroom. *Citizens United* would be the first time.

"C'mon guys," she said to those in the back. "It's my first day. Psych me up!"

The deputies looked at one another, and after a lengthy pause Malcolm Stewart whispered, "Go get 'em."

"Ugh," Kagan said. "You guys *suck!*"—and the laughter broke the tension in the car.

At precisely ten, the chief justice called Ted Olson to the lectern. Like everyone else associated with the case, he could tell from the new Questions Presented that the Court was leaning his way—heading for a ruling that was far broader than the one he originally sought. Olson argued cautiously, as if protecting a lead.

The liberal quartet of justices, recognizing that their position was probably hopeless, did their best to raise the alarm with the public if not with their colleagues. Ruth Ginsburg, surprisingly astute at judging popular opinion, brought up one potential source of future controversy.

"Mr. Olson," Ginsburg said, "are you taking the position that there is no difference in the First Amendment rights of an individual? A corporation, after all, is not endowed by its creator with inalienable rights. So is there any distinction that Congress could draw between corporations and natural human beings for purposes of campaign finance?"

"What the Court has said in the First Amendment context, over and over again," Olson replied, "is that corporations are persons entitled to protection under the First Amendment." He might well have added that the principle of corporations as people went back to the strange case of *Santa Clara County* in 1886.

"Would that include today's megacorporations, where many of the investors may be foreign individuals or entities?" Ginsburg went on.

Olson was ready: "The Court in the past has made no distinction based upon the nature of the entity that might own a share of a corporation."

Kagan's first decision was apparent even before she began speaking. Like many other members of the SG's office (especially women), Kagan thought the woman's version of the morning coat looked ridiculous. Through intermediaries, she had asked the justices if they would mind if she appeared in a normal business suit. None objected, and that was what she wore.

"Mr. Chief Justice, and may it please the Court," Kagan began, "I have three very quick points to make about the government's position. The first is that this issue has a long history. For over a hundred years Congress has made a judgment that corporations must be subject to special rules when they participate in elections, and this Court has never questioned that judgment.

"Number two—"

"Wait, wait, wait, wait," said Scalia.

And so it went. Kagan knew she had probably launched herself on a suicide mission. Her best hope was to limit the damage, perhaps by persuading the Court to strike down this particular application of McCain-Feingold rather than invalidate the entire law. Or, as Kagan put it to Roberts, "Mr. Chief Justice, as to whether the government has a preference as to the way in which it loses, if it has to lose, the answer is yes."

Stevens tried to help Kagan along these lines, suggesting that the Court could resolve the case with a narrow ruling. For example, the justices could create an exception in the McCain-Feingold law for nonprofits like Citizens United or for "ads that are financed exclusively by individuals even though they are sponsored by a corporation." Grasping the Stevens lifeline, Kagan said, "Yes, that's exactly right."

"Nobody has explained why that wouldn't be a proper solution, not nearly as drastic," Stevens went on. "Why is that not the wisest narrow solution of the problem before us?"

Ginsburg did Kagan the favor of allowing her to undo some of the damage from Stewart's argument in March. "May I ask you one question that was highlighted in the prior argument, and that was if Congress could say no TV and radio ads, could it also say no newspaper ads, no campaign biographies?" Ginsburg said. "Last time the answer was, yes, Congress could, but it didn't. Is that still the government's answer?"

"The government's answer has changed, Justice Ginsburg," Kagan replied, and the well-informed audience in the courtroom laughed. "We took the Court's own reaction to some of those other hypotheticals very seriously. We went back, we considered the matter carefully, and the government's view is that although 441b does cover full-length books, that there would be a quite good as-applied challenge to any attempt to apply 441b in that context." Better late than never, perhaps, but the concession probably mattered little at this point. Especially for a first argument, Kagan was poised, self-confident, even relaxed—and doomed.

Kagan's new subordinates in the solicitor general's office were not surprised by her self-confidence. In theory, the solicitor general himself (Kagan was the first woman to hold the job) personally reviews every brief that goes out in his name. In reality, most solicitors general picked a few high-profile issues that interested them and basically passed off the others to the career lawyers. The SG staff quickly learned that Kagan had other plans.

On her first day as SG, almost as a courtesy, Kagan was presented with a final draft of the government brief in a numbingly tedious case called *Cuomo v. Clearing House Association*. (It concerned state versus federal rules regarding certain banking regulations.) The case was the type that most solicitors general gave only a cursory review. Kagan disappeared into her office with the draft and emerged hours later with a copy that seemed to have more scribbled corrections in red than typescript. Her staff knew that Kagan had not practiced law in two decades. She had never written a Supreme Court brief in her life. Furthermore, the lawyers regarded themselves, with good reason, as an elite within an elite. As Kagan's handiwork was passed around the office, the nearly universal reaction was, "What the *fuck*?"

Certainly there were no complaints about Kagan's work ethic. She was in the office seven days a week. One of her briefs went through fifty-four drafts. To prepare for her *Citizens United* argument, she read every case cited in every brief—which came to about three thousand pages of material. Kagan subjected herself to the same rigorous moot court ordeal that every member of the staff endured before a Supreme Court argument. To prepare for a thirty-minute argument before the justices, the advocate submitted first to an hour-long grilling from three line assistants, a deputy solicitor general, and the junior lawyer who worked most closely on the case. In addition, the SG invited to the moot courts any government lawyers who had a special familiarity with the issues in the case. Some moots had a dozen lawyers in the audience; some had forty. After the hour of rehearsal, there was then another hour spent analyzing the advocate's answers. And the lawyers in the SG's office went through this entire process twice before any argument. So did Kagan.

After what turned out to be a fairly brief period, Kagan's staff came to terms with the solicitor general's hyperactive red pen. The lawyers saw that Kagan was blunt, funny, occasionally obnoxious, and usually right. What they did not know was that Elena Kagan was working from a very specific model.

Elena Kagan grew up on West End Avenue, on the Upper West Side of Manhattan, at a time when its canyon of apartment buildings were occupied by more civil servants and social workers than, as was later the case, corporate lawyers and investment bankers. Like the Kagan family, the neighborhood was comfortable, not chic; Jewish, but not devout. When Kagan became a public figure, it was widely suggested that she had modeled herself after her father, who was described as a crusading public interest lawyer, rather than her mother, a schoolteacher. In fact, the reverse was true.

Robert Kagan had a real estate law practice based largely around the ongoing conversions of apartment buildings (like the Kagans' own) from rentals to cooperatives. It was true that he did some work for neighborhood groups, but Bob Kagan, a gentle and modest man, was no crusader. Gloria Kagan was another story altogether.

Decades after Gloria taught her last class at Hunter College Elementary School, there are dozens if not hundreds of her former students who still dream about her. Some, clearly, have nightmares. Then as now, Hunter was one of New York's handful of selective public schools, and it has attracted generations of multiethnic strivers. Gloria taught language arts and social studies to fifth and sixth graders. She tapped into her students' preadolescent ambition, demanding excellence and rigor. Some students wilted, but many thrived and ascribed life-changing powers to their diminutive teacher. Of course, Gloria came of age at a time when the professional options open to a woman pretty much began and ended with teaching school (and nursing). As many who knew both of them observed, Gloria Kagan *was* Elena Kagan, three decades too early.

Elena made the most of the opportunities that were denied her mother. Even at Hunter, where Kagan braved her mother's legend, she clearly wanted a life beyond the classroom. In her high school yearbook photo, Kagan posed in a judicial robe, with a gavel, and included a quotation from Justice Felix Frankfurter: "Government is itself an art, one of the subtlest of arts." She went to Princeton, where she ran the editorial page of the college newspaper, and graduated summa cum laude in 1981. (Kagan was the third consecutive Princeton undergraduate appointed to the Supreme Court, following Alito '72 and Sotomayor '76. A Manhattanite, Kagan also became the representative of a fourth New York City borough on the Court, with Sotomayor hailing from the Bronx, Ginsburg from Brooklyn, and Scalia from Queens. Currently, no justice comes from Staten Island, the fifth borough.) After a fellowship at Oxford, Kagan joined the class of 1986 at Harvard Law School.[*]

In certain respects, Kagan's career at law school resembled that of Obama, who arrived at Harvard five years later. Both plainly intended to put their educations to work in public life. Indeed, their law school experiences made it just as easy to predict a judicial career for Kagan as it was to foresee a political one for Obama. Because of an unaccountably poor grade in torts during her first year—the first and only B-minus

---

[*] Kagan and I were classmates and friends at law school.

of her life—Kagan did not make the law review based on grades. She earned a place through the writing competition. Also like the future president, Kagan avoided the faculty battles over Critical Legal Studies. Like Obama, Kagan was no radical, but rather a committed and serious Democrat. And like him, she sought out and went to work for Professor Laurence Tribe, the putative justice of the Democratic Supreme Court in exile (or in waiting.) Tribe chose only the best students to work for him, and only those who shared Tribe's politics—and his ambition—selected him as a mentor.

Here, though, the parallels to Obama end. Kagan had neither the temperament nor the inclination for introspection that led Obama to write *Dreams from My Father.* Kagan didn't need a whole book to outline her goals, and while she would never have been so vulgar as to voice the hope, as Alito did in his college yearbook, to "warm a seat on the Supreme Court," her basic ambition was the same.

After law school, Kagan's life more closely paralleled that of another future colleague—John Roberts. In every generation of lawyers, a few are widely assumed to be headed for great things, possibly even the Supreme Court. That was certainly true for Kagan and Roberts, who graduated from Harvard Law seven years before she did. The art of building a judicial career today requires talents of some subtlety, because the rules changed in recent years. In the pre–Robert Bork era, especially during the early part of the twentieth century, Supreme Court appointments went to major public figures—like Louis Brandeis, the Progressive intellectual; Felix Frankfurter, the impassioned defender of Sacco and Vanzetti; or Hugo Black and Earl Warren, politicians with national reputations. In that bygone time, a lifetime of controversy and accomplishment was all but mandatory for a potential justice. But the Bork hearings made an outspoken public career—a long paper trail, as it came to be known—more of a liability than an asset. Recently, judicial ambition has called for excellence, intelligence, and caution, all of which Roberts and Kagan had in abundance.

Today, there are just two career tracks for potential judges, one for Republicans and the other for Democrats. It is important to be identified enough with one party to have patrons, but not so closely that you have enemies. The challenge was to *be* partisan without *seeming* partisan. By clerking for Henry Friendly on the Second Circuit and then Rehnquist on the Supreme Court, Roberts committed to the Republican track. Kagan went the other way. She clerked for Abner Mikva—the same

D.C. Circuit judge who later implored Obama to work for him—and then for Thurgood Marshall, who, in the 1987–88 term, was near the unhappy end of his judicial career. In the period that followed, Kagan's career seemed a rather obvious marking of time until a Democratic administration came along. First, she spent a couple of years as an associate at Williams & Connolly. (Her duties sometimes included libel checks on the *National Enquirer* as well as its wackier cousin, the *Weekly World News.*) Next, she joined the faculty of the University of Chicago Law School. Kagan dutifully did some scholarly writing, mostly about the First Amendment, but her heart was never in the academic world. Later, in confirmation testimony, Kagan referred to herself (accurately, if immodestly) as "a famously excellent teacher," but not long after she secured tenure, in 1995, she left for a job in the counsel's office in the Clinton White House.

The job was the pivotal point in Kagan's career, just as the Reagan White House changed Roberts's life. Every office, even the West Wing, has its stars, and both future justices stood out from their peers, even in such lofty environs. Clinton used to say that anytime Kagan walked into the Oval Office, the average IQ in the room doubled. She spent two years as an associate White House counsel and two more as deputy domestic policy adviser. (Roberts also spent four years in the White House.)

As with most other presidential advisers, it was difficult to identify with precision how Kagan's own views affected the policies of the administration. This was true of Roberts, too. Certainly Kagan played an important role in negotiating the complex resolution of lawsuits and legislation involving the cigarette industry. (Not coincidentally, it was during Kagan's White House years that she finally defeated her own twenty-year cigarette habit.) Perhaps most importantly, the White House gave Kagan the chance to impress a generation of senior Democrats, many of whom would go on to important roles in the Obama administration. Her colleagues knew her politics—but those insights would be forever off-limits to Republicans. In the fog of government policy making, Kagan became known in the Clinton years mostly as a no-bullshit closer. Like most other staffers, she was probably more liberal than the president she served. A decade earlier, Roberts earned a similar reputation and was certainly more conservative than Reagan. These insights about the true views of Kagan and Roberts created no paper trail, but that didn't make them any less true.

The parallel between Roberts and Kagan became especially clear at the end of her tenure in the White House. In 1992, George H. W. Bush had nominated Roberts, who was then just thirty-seven, to the D.C. Circuit, the traditional stepping-stone to the Supreme Court. In June 1999, Clinton nominated Kagan, who was thirty-nine, to the D.C. Circuit. Both nominations suggest how highly the two were regarded by their respective presidents and parties, even at such young ages. But both nominations met similar ignominious fates. In 1992, the Democrats in control of the Senate stalled Roberts's nomination into oblivion. As for Kagan, even though the change of administrations was more than a year and a half away at the time she was chosen, the Republicans who held the majority used the same tactics to kill her nomination; Kagan never even received a vote in the Judiciary Committee.

For both Roberts and Kagan, the failed nominations appeared to be crushing disappointments. For both, as it turned out, it was the best thing that ever happened to them.

The nomination of Kagan to the D.C. Circuit, even though she failed to be confirmed, marked her as a potential Supreme Court justice. It was a tremendous honor and vote of confidence. With the Clinton administration winding down, though, Kagan faced a more immediate problem. She needed a job.

Kagan had exceeded the customary amount of time on leave to preserve her tenure at the University of Chicago Law School, but she had assumed that the job was still hers if she wanted it. She was wrong. Chicago fancies itself the most self-consciously intellectual of major law schools, and Kagan's modest record as a scholar counted against her. She was out. (Decades earlier, Scalia struggled to receive tenure at Chicago for similar reasons; the local mandarins thought, correctly, that he preferred Washington to academia.) So Kagan scrambled and found a visiting professor position at Harvard, essentially an audition for tenure. She produced a major law review article on administrative law, her teaching was as famously excellent as ever, and she won tenure after her second year.

The key moment in Kagan's early years on the Harvard faculty occurred when she had an opportunity to put her true skills to good use. Harvard had purchased hundreds of acres on the Boston side of the Charles River, and the new president, Lawrence Summers, was considering moving the law school there from its longtime home in Cambridge. The faculty regarded this possibility with horror. Robert Clark, the dean of the law school, named Kagan the head of a task force to study the possibility of the move—in reality, to kill it. Kagan summoned all of her bureaucratic finesse and delivered a report to Summers that all but buried the idea. Summers turned the land over to scientific projects instead, and Kagan became a hero to her colleagues on the faculty. Then Clark stepped down.

Summers, himself a former Clinton White House aide and then treasury secretary, had been a friend and colleague of Kagan's in Washington. Though Kagan was only forty-three in 2003 and had almost no administrative experience, Summers decided to take a chance on her as the first female dean of Harvard Law School.

What happened next was one of those rare intersections of the right person at the right time in the right place. The dour Robert Clark had presided over the law school through all its enervating internal wars. Kagan, young and ebullient, swept in and cleared the air. The booming economy, at least for lawyers, helped solve many of her problems. Liberals and conservatives had battled for years for places on the faculty but Kagan had the money to reach the perfect solution—she could hire both! She gave the students free coffee, and an ice rink to use in the winter, and they loved her. Kagan's own politics were, as ever, artful. She preserved the longtime boycott against military recruiters—employers that discriminated against gay people were not allowed to conduct official interviews on campus—but she arranged an enthusiastic welcome for the soldiers and veterans who were students. (She invented an annual Veterans Day dinner for active military students, veterans, and their spouses.) It was the kind of behavior that would look good at a confirmation hearing, and, eventually, it did.

To be sure, some of Kagan's behavior was calculated—a studied attempt to present a bipartisan image. But her enthusiasm for debate, for the give-and-take of intellectual life on campus, was real. At a Federalist Society banquet at Harvard, she welcomed the group with the words "I love the Federalist Society"—and won a raucous standing ovation. Then she added, with winning candor, "But, you know, you are not my people." Her elaborate celebration of the twentieth anniversary of Antonin Scalia '60 on the Supreme Court bench was doubtless sincere—as well as very savvy. Her tenure as dean was such a success that when Summers was forced out as president in 2006, Kagan was an obvious candidate to succeed him as president of the university.

Here, though, Kagan's politicking proved too clever for her own good. Summers's fall as president was precipitated by his comments about the underrepresentation of women in science that were widely denounced for ignorance and sexism. At that moment, Kagan was Summers's most high-profile female hire. As such, she could have been an important defender of his. But Kagan, perhaps sensing Summers's impending doom, was notably restrained in offering support for her embattled boss.

This came back to haunt her. Robert Rubin, the former treasury secretary, was also a leading member of Harvard's governing board, and he had pushed for Summers, his successor at Treasury, to be named president of the university. In Rubin's view, Kagan had shown great disloyalty and ingratitude to Summers when she left him twisting in the wind during the women-in-sciences flap. Accordingly, Rubin made it his personal mission to prevent Kagan from becoming president of Harvard, and indeed the job went instead to Drew Gilpin Faust.

With her progress blocked at Harvard, Kagan looked for other options. She made it clear that she was backing Obama for president in 2008 and that she hoped to join him in Washington. During the transition period after the election, Greg Craig, the White House counsel designate, made a recruiting trip to Cambridge and asked Kagan what she had in mind for herself. She knew that the job of attorney general had been promised to Eric Holder, so she told Craig she wanted to be deputy AG, the person who traditionally runs the day-to-day operations of the Department of Justice. Following the disastrous tenure of Alberto Gonzales, DOJ was demoralized—just like Harvard Law School when Kagan became dean. She knew how to bring people together in a large and complex organization.

Sorry, said Craig. Holder had promised the deputy job to someone else.

What about solicitor general? he asked her.

"I'm not an appellate lawyer," Kagan said, which was, if anything, an understatement. She had only ever been a "real" lawyer as a junior associate at Williams & Connolly. But Kagan had never run anything before she was a dean—and never worked at the White House before she went there either. SG was the most intellectually demanding job in the Justice Department, but Gloria Kagan's daughter never lacked for moxie. "If I'm asked to do it, I'll do it," she told Craig. In short order, she was.

And so, in 2009, a decade after Kagan failed to become a judge on the D.C. Circuit, she was given the job that was sometimes known as the tenth justice. If she had been confirmed to the D.C. Circuit, as she had hoped to be, she might well have had a long paper trail of controversial decisions that could have disqualified her from being considered for the Supreme Court. Instead, she had a sterling—and largely apolitical—record as the savior of Harvard Law School.

As for John Roberts, his failure to win confirmation in 1992 allowed him to spend a decade as a widely respected, highly paid, and largely apolitical appellate lawyer at Hogan & Hartson. To complete the symmetry between the two lives, in 2001 George W. Bush (like his father) nominated Roberts to the D.C. Circuit, and this time, after another long delay, Roberts was confirmed. The seat Roberts occupied was the very one that Clinton had tried, and failed, to fill with Kagan.

After the second argument of *Citizens United*, the votes were the same as after the first one. Kagan's advocacy had failed to break up the majority. Roberts, Scalia, Kennedy, Thomas, and Alito voted to overturn the judgment of the FEC, with Stevens, Ginsburg, Breyer, and Sotomayor (in place of Souter) on the other side. Because of the revised, and much broader, Questions Presented, Roberts was now well within his rights to lead the charge to bury decades of campaign finance law.

At the time of the first argument, in March 2009, it was not clear that *Citizens United* was going to be a blockbuster, so the case received a modest amount of attention. But everyone understood the stakes of the reargument. There was the inherent drama of Kagan's debut as solicitor general and Sotomayor's first case on the bench. (From the start, the new justice proved an able and vigorous questioner.) More importantly, the political implications of *Citizens United* were immense. The conservative movement had been fighting for decades to dismantle campaign finance rules. Figures as varied as Mitch McConnell, the Kentucky senator and personification of the GOP political establishment, and David Bossie, the bad-boy investigator, had the same passion for the issue. It was true that their side had some support from traditional liberal groups, like the American Civil Liberties Union (which takes an absolutist view on free speech issues) and some labor unions (which wanted to keep spending money in elections). Still, the ACLU was eccentric, and unions were losing power.

At its heart, *Citizens United* was a case about Republicans versus Democrats. Since the Progressive era, Republicans had been the party of moneyed interests in the United States. For more than a century, Republicans had fought virtually every limitation on corporate or individual participation in elections. Democrats supported these restrictions. It was a defining difference between the parties. So, as the chief justice chose how broadly to change the law in this area, the real question for him was how much he wanted to help the Republican Party. Roberts's choice was: a lot.

THE NINETY-PAGE SWAN SONG
OF JOHN PAUL STEVENS

Roberts assigned the opinion in *Citizens United* to Anthony Kennedy. It was another brilliant strategic move by the chief. Alito's replacement of O'Connor in 2006 had locked the Court into a consistent 4–4 conservative-liberal split and left Kennedy the most powerful justice in decades. On controversial issues—including abortion, affirmative action, civil rights, the death penalty, federal power, among others—Kennedy controlled the outcome of cases. For the previous fifteen years or so, O'Connor had most often held the swing vote, though she never controlled as many cases as Kennedy did.

There was a striking difference in the way that O'Connor and Kennedy handled their roles as the swing vote. O'Connor was a gradualist, a compromiser, a politician who liked to make each side feel like it won something. When O'Connor was in the middle in a case, she would, in effect, give one side 51 percent and the other 49. In *Casey*, she saved abortion rights; in *Grutter*, she preserved racial preferences in admissions for the University of Michigan Law School; in *Hamdi*, she repudiated the Bush administration's lawless approach to the detainees held at Guantánamo Bay. In each of these cases, as the author of or contributor to the opinions, O'Connor split the difference. Yes to restrictions on abortion but no to outright bans; yes to affirmative action but no to quotas; yes to the right of detainees to go to court but no to the full constitutional rights of American citizens. In describing her judicial philosophy, O'Connor liked to point to the sculpted turtles that formed the base of the lampposts outside the Supreme Court. "We're like those turtles," she liked to say. "We're slow and steady. We don't move too fast in any direction."

Anthony Kennedy was no turtle. Unlike O'Connor, he tended to swing wildly in one way or the other. When he was with the liberals, he could be very liberal. His opinion in *Lawrence v. Texas*, the 2003 decision striking down laws against consensual sodomy, contains a lyrical celebration of the rights of gay people. Similarly, in *Boumediene v. Bush*, the 2008 case about the rights of accused terrorists, he excoriated the Bush administration and the Congress. "To hold that the political branches may switch the constitution on or off at will would lead to a regime in which they, not this court, say 'what the law is,'" he wrote, quoting Chief Justice John Marshall's famous words from 1803 in *Marbury v. Madison*. No one relished saying "what the law is" more than Kennedy.

But in his conservative mode, Kennedy could be shockingly dismissive of women's autonomy, as in *Gonzales v. Carhart*, the 2007 late-term abortion law case. He also wrote the most notorious sentence in the majority opinion in *Bush v. Gore*, acknowledging that the Court acted for the sole benefit of George W. Bush: "Our consideration is limited to the present circumstances, for the problem of equal protection in election processes generally presents many complexities." Kennedy was not a moderate but an extremist—of varied enthusiasms.

All of the justices knew that Kennedy's views were most extreme when it came to the First Amendment. (Independently, several different justices would say Kennedy had "a thing" about the First Amendment.) In the Roberts Court, there was a broad consensus about protecting freedom of speech. Many areas of the law that had once been controversial, such as the suppression of dangerous or unpopular views, were resolved with little disagreement. Even in a legal system that protects free speech, though, the government had long been able to regulate speech in all kinds of ways. Copyright infringement was subject to civil and criminal remedies; extortion and other verbal crimes were routinely punished. Campaign contributions, if they were considered "speech" at all, had been regulated for more than a century.

But Kennedy had an almost Pavlovian receptivity to arguments that the government had unduly restricted freedom of speech—especially in the area of campaign finance. Throughout his long tenure, Kennedy had dissented, often in strident terms, when his colleagues upheld regulations in that area. And as the possessor of probably the biggest ego on the Court (always a hotly contested designation among the justices), Kennedy loved writing high-profile opinions.

Roberts knew just what he would get when he assigned *Citizens United* to Kennedy. After all, Kennedy had written an opinion for the Court after the case was argued the first time. During his confirmation hearing, Roberts made much of his judicial modesty, his respect for precedent, saying that he was just an umpire on the playing field of the law. If the chief had written *Citizens United*, he would have been criticized for hypocrisy. But by giving the opinion to Kennedy, Roberts sidestepped the attacks and still achieved the far-reaching result he wanted.

Kennedy did not disappoint him. "Speech is an essential mechanism of democracy, for it is the means to hold officials accountable to the people," he wrote for the Court in his familiar rolling cadence. "The right of citizens to inquire, to hear, to speak, and to use information to reach consensus is a precondition to enlightened self-government and a necessary means to protect it." These rhetorical flights were a long way from the gritty business of raising and spending campaign money.

Kennedy often saw First Amendment issues in terms of abstractions. At its core, *Citizens United* concerned a law that set aside a brief period of time (shortly before elections) when corporations could not fund political commercials. To Kennedy, this was nothing more than censorship: "By taking the right to speak from some and giving it to others, the Government deprives the disadvantaged person or class of the right to use speech to strive to establish worth, standing, and respect for the speaker's voice. The Government may not by these means deprive the public of the right and privilege to determine for itself what speech and speakers are worthy of consideration. The First Amendment protects speech and speaker, and the ideas that flow from each."

Citizens United was a simple case for Kennedy. "The Court has recognized that First Amendment protection extends to corporations," he wrote. This had been true since 1886, and speech, especially political speech, could never be impeded. "The censorship we now confront is vast in its reach," Kennedy continued. "The Government has muffled the voices that best represent the most significant segments of the economy. And the electorate has been deprived of information, knowledge and opinion vital to its function. By suppressing the speech of manifold corporations, both for-profit and nonprofit, the Government prevents

t the stroke of noon, on January 20, 2009, Chief Justice John Roberts adminis-ered the oath of office to President Barack Obama at the U.S. Capitol. Stumbles nd mistakes in the oath prompted an unprecedented "redo" of the oath the follow-ng day at the White House.

hief Justice John Roberts readministers the oath of office to President Barack)bama in the Map Room at the White House on January 21, 2009. The portrait of Benjamin Latrobe, architect of the Capitol.

PRESIDENT'S OATH

I, BARACK HUSSEIN OBAMA, DO SOLEMNLY SWEAR //

THAT I WILL FAITHFULLY EXECUTE THE OFFICE OF PRESIDENT OF THE UNITED STATES, //

AND WILL TO THE BEST OF MY ABILITY, //

PRESERVE, PROTECT AND DEFEND THE CONSTITUTION OF THE UNITED STATES. //

SO HELP YOU GOD? //

Chief Justice Roberts prepared this card in advance of the inauguration to guide how the oath would be administered. (Roberts added a comma after "ability.") Aides to Roberts sent this card to the congressional inaugural committee, but it never reached anyone on Obama's staff.

On January 14, 2009, the president-elect and vice president-elect visited the Supreme Court by invitation of the chief justice. Eight justices greeted them, and Samuel Alito chose not to attend. From left: Barack Obama, John Roberts, John Paul Stevens, Clarence Thomas, Ruth Bader Ginsburg, David Souter, Joseph Biden.

Obama signs the Lilly Ledbetter Fair Pay Act in the East Room of the White House on January 29, 2009, with a smiling Ledbetter herself (center, with blond hair and pin) looking on. This was the first piece of legislation Obama signed as president, and it overturned Justice Alito's opinion in *Ledbetter v. Goodyear Tire & Rubber Co.*

Antonin Scalia, shown here (right), with Stephen Breyer at a congressional hearing in 2011, has been a dominant conservative voice on the Court for decades.

Dick Heller, a District of Columbia police officer who challenged the D.C. law preventing individuals from keeping private handguns, signs autographs after the Supreme Court ruled that the Second Amendment gives Americans a right to keep guns in their homes.

After her confirmation, Sonia Sotomayor hugs her mother, Celina Sotomayor, during a reception in the East Room of the White House on August 12, 2009.

The current 4-4 conservative-liberal split on the court has made Anthony Kennedy (shown here) the most powerful justice in decades. His swing vote has controlled the outcome of many cases, including *Citizens United*.

The Obama administration's anger over the Supreme Court decision in *Citizens United* prompted Obama to rebuke the justices during his State of the Union address on January 27, 2010.

Justice Alito mouthed "not true" and shook his head as Obama described the consequences of the *Citizens United* decision during his 2010 State of the Union address. Justices (top row, from left) Alito, Sotomayor, (bottom row, from left) Roberts and Kennedy.

Obama's second Supreme Court nominee, Elena Kagan, shown here with Obama and Chief Justice Roberts, takes her place as the 112th justice of the Supreme Court in 2010.

After Elena Kagan's Supreme Court nomination was announced in 2010, *The Wall Street Journal* ran this photograph of Kagan playing softball while she was a professor at the University of Chicago Law School. The *New York Post* reran the photo with a headline suggesting she was a lesbian.

From left to right, Sonia Sotomayor, Ruth Bader Ginsburg, and Elena Kagan. This is the first time in history that three women have served on the Supreme Court at the same time.

President Obama and Secretary of State Hillary Clinton share a victory hug after the House of Representatives voted to pass health care reform in March 2010.

Virginia Thomas, wife of Justice Clarence Thomas, speaks out against Obama's health care reform law at a Tea Party rally outside the U.S. Capitol in 2010. Her activities raised concerns about the propriety of a justice's spouse being a leader in a political movement.

Clarence and Virginia Thomas at a Federalist Society meeting in Washington in 2007.

Solicitor General Donald Verrilli Jr. on the Supreme Court steps during a brief recess from oral arguments on health care reform in 2012. The justices gave Verrill a tough time but ultimately vindicated him by ruling in his favor.

The current members of the Supreme Court: (back row, from left) Sonia Sotomayor, Stephen Breyer, Samuel Alito, Elena Kagan, (front row, from left) Clarence Thomas, Antonin Scalia, John Roberts, Anthony Kennedy, and Ruth Bader Ginsburg.

their voices and viewpoints from reaching the public and advising voters on which persons or entities are hostile to their interests.

"If the First Amendment has any force," Kennedy concluded, "it prohibits Congress from fining or jailing citizens, or associations of citizens, for simply engaging in political speech."

McCain-Feingold and several Supreme Court precedents had to be overruled. The Constitution required that all corporations, for-profit and nonprofit alike, be allowed to spend as much as they wanted, any time they wanted, in support of the candidates of their choosing.

To John Paul Stevens, however, *Citizens United* was much more complicated, with immense implications for American politics.

Stevens would turn ninety shortly after the *Citizens United* decision came down. Better than most justices, he knew the potential cost of staying too long on the bench.

Franklin Roosevelt named William O. Douglas to the Court in 1939, and he served with cantankerous brilliance well into a fourth decade. In 1974, however, Douglas had a stroke, and he became physically and mentally disabled. Douglas refused to retire, and his colleagues had to wage an awkward campaign to persuade him to bow to the inevitable. When Douglas did finally leave the Court the following year, Gerald Ford appointed Stevens to take his place. Stevens wanted to avoid a similarly unseemly end to his own career and deputized his closest friend among the justices, David Souter, to let him know when it was time to go. It seemed like a reasonable plan. After all, Souter was nearly two decades younger than the man known to all at the Court as JPS.

But then Stevens outlasted Souter. JPS was a remarkable physical specimen. He still played tennis on many mornings. (A frequent golfer, too, he practiced putting on the carpet in his chambers.) For more than twenty years, Stevens and his wife had spent a good deal of time at their condominium in Fort Lauderdale, but he remained deeply engaged in the work of the Court. During the eighties, Stevens was nicknamed the FedEx justice, because he did so much work from Florida; later, he used e-mail. By the new millennium, Stevens's age, and his genial bearing, had earned widespread affection. Stevens had a midwesterner's inveterate politeness, which manifested itself during oral arguments. He would begin speaking by saying, "May I ask you a question?" or "May

I ask you this?" Frequent advocates found this tic amusing and endearing, a little like his inevitable bow tie.

In light of all this, it was possible, by the time of *Citizens United*, to think of Stevens as a kind of docile old uncle. After all, he was thirteen years older than Ginsburg, his closest contemporary, and he belonged to an entirely different generation than the rest of the Court. (Sotomayor was almost *two* generations younger than Stevens.) But Stevens was no harmless codger. He was, rather, a ferocious competitor who hated to lose. Life made him a tough combatant.

In the early part of the twentieth century, the Stevenses were prominent citizens of Chicago. The justice's grandfather James Stevens had gone into the insurance business, and, with the profits, he and his sons Ernest and Raymond bought land on South Michigan Avenue, where they built what was then the biggest hotel in the world, with three thousand rooms. The Stevens Hotel opened in 1927 and featured a range of luxurious services, including a bowling alley and a pitch-and-putt golf course on the roof. There was a big, stylized "S" over the main entrance.

The Depression hit the family hard. As chronicled in *John Paul Stevens: An Independent Life*, a biography by Bill Barnhart and Gene Schlickman, questions arose as to whether the Stevens family had embezzled funds from the insurance company to prop up the hotel. In January 1933, the *Chicago Herald-Examiner* reported, "The Stevens children were sent to bed so they could not see their father arrested." After Ernest Stevens was released on bail, according to the biography, four men brandishing a submachine gun, two shotguns, and a revolver ransacked the Stevens home in search of cash. Ernest and his wife, Elizabeth, and two of their children, William, age fifteen, and John, age twelve, as well as the family cook and two maids, were herded upstairs and held in a bedroom after one of the boys was forced to open a safe in the first-floor library. It remains unclear whether the intruders were police officers or gangsters (or both), but they found no secret stash of cash.

Later in 1933, the patriarch, James, had a debilitating stroke. A few days afterward, John's uncle Raymond committed suicide rather than endure the disgrace of a criminal prosecution. Ernest Stevens thus had to go to trial alone, and in the toxic environment of the Depression he was swiftly convicted. He faced ten years in state prison. Deliverance came in 1934, when his appeal reached the Illinois Supreme Court and the justices unanimously reversed his conviction. "In this whole record there is not a scintilla of evidence of any concealment or fraud attempted," the decision said. Still, the family never recovered its former wealth, and it lost control of the hotel. (It is now known as the Chicago Hilton and Towers; the "S" is still there.)

John Stevens rallied from the trauma of his teenage years and excelled at the Lab School of the University of Chicago. (Sasha and Malia Obama would later be students there, and the Obamas lived about a mile away from where Stevens grew up, on the city's South Side.) In 1937, he enrolled at the university, where he was the editor of the newspaper, a stalwart of the tennis team, the head class marshal, and a member of Phi Beta Kappa. Toward the end of his undergraduate career, the dean of students, Leon P. Smith, rather mysteriously suggested that he take a correspondence course. Stevens did. He later learned that Smith was an undercover naval officer who had been asked to see if he could get students interested in cryptography. At the end of November of 1941, the navy sent Stevens a letter saying that he had completed enough of the course that he was eligible to apply for a commission. Stevens enlisted the day before Pearl Harbor and spent most of the war at that navy base in Hawaii, analyzing intercepted Japanese radio transmissions.

After being discharged in 1945, Stevens raced through Northwestern Law School in two years, graduating as valedictorian. (He also acquired a new name. A professor told him that every lawyer should have something unique about them. Stevens thought his name, John Stevens, was particularly boring, and decided always to use his middle name, at least professionally.) John Paul Stevens earned a Supreme Court clerkship with Justice Wiley B. Rutledge, an FDR appointee whom Stevens always revered. When Stevens's colleagues wanted to needle him, they would cite one of Rutledge's opinions against him. (Kennedy referred to Rutledge three times in his *Citizens United* opinion.)

After his clerkship, Stevens returned to Chicago and took a job at one of the city's first religiously integrated law firms. In time, he became a renowned antitrust litigator. He and his wife, Betty, had four children, two of them adopted, and he took up flying a private plane as a hobby, which also enabled him to visit clients around the Midwest. Stevens probably would have lived out his life in prosperous obscurity if one of Chicago's periodic corruption scandals hadn't intervened. A local character, a wheelchair-bound frequent litigant named Sherman Skolnick, alleged that two justices on the Illinois Supreme Court had taken bribes in a political corruption case. The court formed an investigatory committee, which appointed Stevens as its counsel. In a series of dramatic hearings in 1969, Stevens established that the two judges had indeed taken bribes. Both resigned, and Stevens became a public figure. The next year, Senator Charles Percy, an Illinois Republican, put Stevens up for a judgeship on the Seventh Circuit. Richard Nixon agreed, and, in 1970, Stevens began his judicial career.

In 1974, Gerald Ford, seeking to demonstrate a renewed commitment to ethics at the Justice Department, named Edward H. Levi, the dean of the University of Chicago Law School, as attorney general. When, the following year, Douglas left the Supreme Court, Levi pushed for Stevens, his fellow Chicagoan, whose anticorruption credentials looked especially desirable in that post-Watergate moment. Ford nominated Stevens, who was then fifty-five, on November 28, 1975, and the Senate unanimously confirmed him just nineteen days later. (Soon after moving to Washington, Stevens divorced and remarried. His second wife, Maryan Mulholland Simon, an old friend from Chicago, was a dietitian, whose ministrations Stevens credited for his longevity.)

Like Souter and his mentors, Percy and Levi, Stevens was a moderate Republican. In his early years on the Court, he settled into the ideological center, which was bounded, on the left, by William Brennan and Thurgood Marshall and, on the right, by Rehnquist, then an associate justice, and Chief Justice Warren E. Burger. Stevens's voting record was roughly in line with those of fellow Republican appointees like Potter Stewart, Lewis Powell, Harry Blackmun, and O'Connor. But as they were replaced by more contemporary Republicans, Stevens often found himself described as a liberal. In some areas, he did move to the left, especially on the death penalty and racial issues. But his evolution into the leader of the liberal wing was mostly the result of the rest of the Court moving so far to the right.

Stevens became the senior associate justice after Blackmun stepped down in 1994, and over the next decade Stevens remained confident that he could pull together majorities for his side. Toward the end of the Rehnquist Court, Stevens had a string of good years, as O'Connor became a frequent ally, especially on issues relating to Guantánamo. Kennedy, too, joined Stevens's side on gay rights and death penalty cases. More often than his liberal colleagues, Stevens would vote to hear controversial cases. Ginsburg and Breyer, fearing disaster if the

Court took these cases, tended to vote not to take them in the first place.

But John Roberts and Samuel Alito sapped John Paul Stevens's optimism. In under five years, the pair of Bush appointees, joined by Scalia, Thomas, and usually Kennedy, had overturned or undermined many of the Court's precedents. Unlike his new conservative colleagues, Stevens, like Souter, was a classic common-law judge who thought that the law should develop slowly over time, with each case building logically on its predecessors. The course of *Citizens United* captured everything that offended Stevens most about the Roberts Court.

In some ways, Stevens's greatest objections were procedural. Like Ginsburg (and almost no one else), Stevens had a deep fascination for the mysteries of federal procedure. He was happy to wade into the subject on his own for hours. (Stevens was the only justice who generally wrote his own first drafts of opinions.) So it was especially galling that the Court converted *Citizens United* from a narrow dispute about a single provision in McCain-Feingold into an assault on a century of federal laws and precedents. To Stevens, it was the purest kind of judicial activism.

Or, as he put it in his dissenting opinion, "five Justices were unhappy with the limited nature of the case before us, so they changed the case to give themselves an opportunity to change the law." The case could and should have been resolved by simply ruling on whether McCain-Feingold applied to *Hillary: The Movie*, or at least to nonprofit corporations like Citizens United. And here Stevens aimed a dart not at Kennedy but at the chief justice: "The parties have advanced numerous ways to resolve the case that would facilitate electioneering by nonprofit advocacy corporations such as Citizens United, without toppling statutes and precedents." Which is to say, the majority has transgressed yet another "cardinal" principle of the judicial process: "If it is not necessary to decide more, it is necessary not to decide more." Stevens was quoting Roberts's oft-cited line from his tenure on the D.C. Circuit—and throwing it back in his face. In essence, Stevens was saying that Roberts was acting not like a mere umpire but like an imperious commissioner of baseball.

Stevens was just warming up. His dissent was ninety pages, the longest of his career. He questioned every premise of Kennedy's opinion, starting with its contempt for stare decisis, the rule of precedent. He went on to refute Kennedy's repeated invocations of "censorship" and the "banning" of free speech. The case was merely about corporate-funded commercials shortly before elections. Corporations could run as many commercials whenever they liked during other periods, and employees of the corporations (by forming a political action committee) could run ads at any time.

Stevens was especially offended by Kennedy's blithe assertion that corporations and human beings had identical rights under the First Amendment. "The Framers thus took it as a given that corporations could be comprehensively regulated in the service of the public welfare," Stevens wrote. "Unlike our colleagues, they had little trouble distinguishing corporations from human beings, and when they constitutionalized the right to free speech in the First Amendment, it was the free speech of individual Americans that they had in mind." Congress and the courts had drawn distinctions between corporations and people for decades, Stevens wrote, noting that, "at the federal level, the express distinction between corporate and individual political spending on elections stretches back to 1907, when Congress passed the Tillman Act."

Stevens was almost amused at Kennedy's fear that the government might regulate speech based on "the speaker's identity." As he wrote, "We have held that speech can be regulated differentially on account of the speaker's identity, when identity is understood in categorical or institutional terms. The Government routinely places special restrictions on the speech rights of students, prisoners, members of the Armed Forces, foreigners, and its own employees." Stevens, a former navy man, could not resist a generational allusion: he said Kennedy's opinion "would have accorded the propaganda broadcasts to our troops by 'Tokyo Rose' during World War II the same protection as speech by Allied commanders." (Stevens's law clerks, having never heard of Tokyo Rose, who made propaganda broadcasts for the Japanese, implored him to remove the dated reference, but he insisted on keeping it.)

Stevens's conclusion was despairing. "At bottom, the Court's opinion is thus a rejection of the common sense of the American people, who have recognized a need to prevent corporations from undermining self-government since the founding, and who have fought against the distinctive corrupting potential of corporate electioneering since the days of Theodore Roosevelt," he wrote. "It is a strange time to repudiate that common sense. While American democracy is imperfect, few outside the majority of this Court would have thought its flaws included a dearth of corporate money in politics." It was an impressive dissent, but that was all it was. Anthony Kennedy, on the other hand, was reshaping American politics.

At the stroke of ten, on the morning of Thursday, January 21, 2010, the nine justices emerged from behind the red curtain and the chief justice introduced the sole order of business for the day. "In case 08-205, Citizens United versus the FEC, Justice Kennedy has the opinion of the Court," Roberts said.

Kennedy took about ten minutes to announce the Court's judgment. Kennedy had been a law teacher even longer than he'd been a judge, and he relished these moments to define, in layman's terms, what the justices had decided. Only a handful of people ever had the chance to see these performances—the Supreme Court seats about five hundred people—and the words in the opinions, not the words from the bench, represented the judgment of the Court. Nevertheless, Kennedy took these occasions seriously, as a chance to put in his own words what he sometimes called "the poetry of the law." At the climax of his brief summary, Kennedy said: "The Government seeks to use its full power, including the criminal law, to command where a person may get his or her information or what distrusted source he or she may not hear. It uses censorship to control thought. This is unlawful. The First Amendment confirms the freedom to think for ourselves."

In a case of this magnitude, there was never any doubt that Stevens would read his dissent from the bench. He didn't read all ninety pages, but he still prepared a twenty-minute stem-winder. For once, though, the news was not what Stevens said but how he said it. He stumbled frequently, skipped words, and at times was hard to understand (as when he said, "As the corp, court has long resembled . . ."). For the first time in public, Stevens looked his age. He charged that the way the majority had handled the case was even worse than the legal outcome. "There were principled, narrower paths that a Court that was serious about judicial restraint could have taken," he said. "The path it has taken to reach its outcome will, I fear, do damage to this institution." After thirty-five years on the Supreme Court, it was clear that John Paul Stevens was about to walk away from a place he no longer recognized.

"WITH ALL DUE DEFERENCE TO SEPARATION OF POWERS"

At the White House, the tensions between Greg Craig, the president's counsel, and Rahm Emanuel, his chief of staff, festered throughout 2009. Likewise, the concerns about Cassandra Butts, Craig's deputy and ostensibly the person assigned to screen potential judges, grew more widespread. By fall, both were on their way out. In November, Butts left the White House for a job at the Millennium Challenge Corporation, a Bush-era foreign aid agency. To facilitate a graceful exit for Craig, Obama offered to nominate him to the D.C. Circuit. (Nearly a year into the administration, the president had still not filled a vacancy on the second most important court in the country, a fact that itself illustrated the dysfunction in the counsel's office.) But Craig turned down the judgeship and returned to private law practice at the end of the year.

In December, a few weeks before *Citizens United* came down, Robert Bauer took over as the new White House counsel. Just as Craig had devoted much of his life to human rights, Bauer had his own cause: campaign finance. Bauer had been in private practice for thirty years, but at his law firm he helped virtually every major Democratic politician navigate the complex rules about how campaigns should be run and paid for. In a way, Bob Bauer was the Jim Bopp of the Democratic Party. In the nineties, Bauer was a top outside adviser to Richard Gephardt, the Democratic leader in the House, as well as Tom Daschle, the party's leader in the Senate. When Obama was elected to the Senate in 2004, Bauer became his personal attorney.

Bearded, genial, and professorial, Bauer didn't look like what he was: a fierce Democratic partisan. Given his background, he was also uniquely well positioned to understand the implications of *Citizens United*. The initial news reports portrayed the Court's decision almost as an act of bipartisanship. These reports tended to stress that the decision freed both labor unions and corporations to make unlimited expenditures on behalf of candidates. Because unions generally supported Democrats and corporations backed Republicans, the decision was described as an equal opportunity act of deregulation.

Bauer knew this was nonsense. Unions had been shrinking for a half century. *Citizens United* gave them permission to spend millions of dollars they didn't have. On the other hand, corporations controlled most of the wealth in the country. Corporations, especially private corporations, skewed overwhelmingly Republican. Moreover, in crude terms, Republicans had more money than Democrats; anything that deregulated the political process was thus likely to help the GOP. It was clear to Bauer that *Citizens United* was a gift to the Republican Party.

Citizens United was also, Bauer knew, an invitation to chaos. From long experience, Bauer understood that candidates and political parties were subject to real scrutiny from the media and their constituents. People running for office worried about defending the sources of their campaign money and how they spent it. In contrast, *Citizens United* empowered interests that were largely immune from public attention. The decision authorized independent expenditures by companies and committees that were generally unknown. *Citizens United* did uphold disclosure requirements; it was constitutional to force campaigns and committees to reveal the sources of their funds. But that detail scarcely mattered in the real world. These disclosures tended to take place long after the fact, and donors had ways of camouflaging their identities in any case. Because of *Citizens United*, unlimited amounts of money would be funneled into shadowy organizations to spend on commercials right before elections. The damage would be done before anyone knew who funded or produced the ads.

So what to do? The dilemma in the Obama White House bore some similarity to those Franklin D. Roosevelt faced in 1935. (And the resemblance would become greater in short order.) During Roosevelt's first term, a conservative Supreme Court declared unconstitutional several signature initiatives of the New Deal, including the National Industrial Recovery Act. The decisions represented the final spasm of the *Lochner* era, the long period when the Court regarded economic regulations as violations of the right to contract, or to due process of law. At first, Roosevelt responded to these decisions by launching his ill-fated court-packing plan in 1937. That idea—to add to the number of justices on the Court—died an unmourned death, but FDR achieved the same result by other means. During his long presidency, he named eight justices to the Court, and his appointees buried *Lochner* and allowed a vigorous federal role in the national economy. In 2010, those options were not available to Obama. There was not even a single vacancy at the Court.

And the clock was ticking for the administration to respond. *Citizens United* came out on the morning of Thursday, January 21, 2010. Six days later, Obama was to give the State of the Union address. What should he say?

In every administration, the production of the State of the Union address is an elaborate operation. Cabinet officials press for mentions of their initiatives. Congressional leaders lobby for their priorities. Political advisers test ideas in polls. The process takes many weeks. In rough terms, the White House plans its year around the speech. By the time *Citizens United* was read and digested, the White House had a matter of hours to respond.

David Axelrod, the president's top political adviser, was enraged by the opinion. A former journalist in Chicago, Axelrod came into politics as a reformer, and he had a deep understanding of the procedural issues underlying how campaigns operated. Specifically, Axelrod had intimate familiarity with the business of television commercials—how time was purchased and how the ads affected campaigns. Better than anyone at the White House, even Bauer, Axelrod understood the implications of *Citizens United*. Of course, given his responsibilities, Axelrod thought it was politically advantageous for Obama to get in front on the issue. More importantly, Axelrod wanted to raise the alarm. He knew where the Court's decision would lead.

That still left the question of what Obama should say in his speech about *Citizens United*. A Supreme Court decision interpreting the Constitution can be overturned only by a new decision or by a constitutional amendment. A call for a constitutional amendment would be seen as extreme, not to mention futile. Still, there was a chance to make a difference in the margins of the decision. Since the Court's call for reargument in the spring of 2009, the president's Democratic allies in Congress had been making plans for a response. A handful of Democrats, including Senator Charles Schumer of New York and Congressman Chris Van Hollen of Maryland, came up with what they called the DISCLOSE (Democracy Is Strengthened by Casting Light on Spending in Elections) Act. Because Kennedy's opinion had upheld McCain-Feingold's requirement that contributors be identified, the proposed new law would strengthen that requirement. It was not much—there was not much that could be done—but it was enough for the president to endorse in his speech.

The wording proved difficult. Election reform issues are notoriously difficult to explain, and voters tend to tune them out. The issue grew so complicated that Emanuel convened a meeting in his office to settle what Obama would say. Axelrod, Bauer, Ron Klain, and a few others pored over the *Citizens United* decision—parsed it, sentence by sentence—to make sure they were on solid ground. Like Ruth Ginsburg, Emanuel recognized the political appeal of arguing that foreign corporations could start buying their way into American elections.

"How sure are we on this foreign corporations thing?" Emanuel asked the group.

Sure enough, he was told.

The justices' attendance at the State of the Union had been spotty at best in recent years. In the sixteen years before 2010, six was the largest number of justices to attend the event. From 2006 to 2008, just four attended. Two came in 2002. Rehnquist missed one year because his painting class met that evening; other times he just chose not to come. Breyer was the only justice to attend in 2001 and from 2003 to 2005. Breyer made it a point to attend every year. He thought that the justices' appearance was an important symbol that the Supreme Court was a part of the government and had respect for the coordinate branches. But even Breyer didn't make it in 2000. (He had the flu.) Not one justice did.

It was easy to see why they skipped the event. For decades, the State of the Union had been a highly political occasion, where the president laid out his accomplishments and agenda. The legislators in the president's party frequently jumped to their feet and cheered; those from the opposing party mostly sat in silence. The justices had to calibrate when it was appropriate to applaud. Generic patriotic appeals, yes; the president's priorities, no. A tribute to the troops, yes; a plea to cut taxes, no. All in all, it was easier to stay home.

During the discussion in Emanuel's office, as well as the president's own prep sessions, the propriety of challenging the Supreme Court had never come up. The group was so focused on pushing Obama's agenda that the issue of the justices' presence seems not to have occurred to anyone. The administration's anger about *Citizens United* was such that (even though no one said this specifically) the Obama team simply regarded the Supreme Court majority as another group of Republicans, deserving no greater deference than GOP senators or congressmen.

But once Obama reached the relevant portion of his speech, he was very much aware of the justices assembled in front of him. "It's time to require lobbyists to disclose each contact they make on behalf of a client with my Administration or Congress. And it's time to put strict limits on the contributions that lobbyists give to candidates for federal office," Obama said. Then, looking up at the justices, the president ad-libbed a revealing phrase: "With all due deference to separation of powers." Obama suddenly realized that he was attacking the Supreme Court and decided to soften the sentiment. Specifically, he said, "With all due deference to separation of powers, last week the Supreme Court reversed a century of law that I believe will open the floodgates for special interests—including foreign corporations—to spend without limit in our elections." The Democrats rose in a standing ovation. "I don't think American elections should be bankrolled by America's most powerful interests or, worse, by foreign entities." More partisan applause. "They should be decided by the American people. And I'd urge Democrats and Republicans to pass a bill that helps to correct some of these problems."

Had the matter been left there, that portion of the speech might have drawn little notice. But, as was customary, the network television pool had received an advance copy of the State of the Union, so the producer knew that the reference to the Supreme Court was coming. He ordered cameras trained on the justices before Obama's reference to them. Roberts, Kennedy, Ginsburg, and Breyer were in the front row, with Alito behind Roberts and Sotomayor behind Kennedy. As it happened, Alito was wedged into an especially partisan corner. To his right was the Obama cabinet; behind him were the Democratic leaders of the

Senate: Harry Reid, Dick Durbin, and Schumer. All three vaulted to their feet as Obama denounced *Citizens United*.

Alito had spent most of his life in New Jersey, in nearly total obscurity. (Before joining the Supreme Court, he had lived in Washington only during part of the Reagan administration.) Circuit judges are not celebrities. Alito was not used to being photographed. He detested the attention he received during his confirmation hearings. It did not even occur to him that he would be on camera. So he did not censor his reactions. When Obama said "foreign corporations" could spend without limit, Alito shook his head and mouthed, "Not true." And he went on shaking his head as Obama made his second reference to foreign influence. Alito's colleagues sat stone-faced. Behind him, Schumer was nodding his head as vigorously as Alito was shaking his.

Afterwards, both Obama and Alito received some criticism for their behavior. The president and the justice were said to have disrespected each other, but in fact Obama understated the consequences of *Citizens United*.

Alito's actions were also revealing. It was not a coincidence that Alito was the most irritated of the justices. After all, he was the only one who had snubbed Obama and Biden at their preinaugural visit to the Court. Alito was also the author of the *Ledbetter* decision, which Obama took such relish in overturning. The clash was a moment of great authenticity. Obama and Alito were both men of intelligence and integrity; they were also dedicated political adversaries. The Democratic president and the Republican justice were deeply divided on *Citizens United* and a host of other issues. The brief back-and-forth was a glimpse of the truth.

The drama almost obscured the question of which one of them was right. Did *Citizens United* pave the way for foreign corporations to spend without limit in American elections? (In the aftermath of the speech, Obama demanded a memo from Bauer to satisfy himself on the issue.) Kennedy's opinion explicitly refrained from ruling on the limits on foreign corporations. "We need not reach the question whether the Government has a compelling interest in preventing foreign individuals or associations from influencing our Nation's political process," he wrote. So Alito had a point: the Court did not specifically rule that foreign corporations could spend money in American elections.

But Obama and his speechwriters had chosen their words with care. The president said only that *Citizens United* was a decision "that I believe will open the floodgates" to the influx of foreign money. There was good reason for this belief. In response to Ginsburg's questions during the oral argument, Olson had said the Constitution required the government to treat American or foreign corporations the same way; the lawyer thought both should be allowed to spend money on political campaigns. Furthermore, *Citizens United* said American corporate money presented no special risk of corrupting the political system; there was ample reason to believe that the Court would reach the same conclusion about foreign contributions. Consequently, Obama was well within his rights to state that the rights granted in *Citizens United* would be extended to foreigners. Both Alito and Obama drew reasonable, though conflicting, conclusions from the text of *Citizens United*.

In any case, the electric moment at the State of the Union defined in the public mind what had otherwise been an abstraction: the Obama White House and the Roberts Supreme Court were at odds. If there was any doubt in the aftermath of Obama's speech, the conservative justices began publicly denouncing the State of the Union as an unbearably partisan occasion. In a Federalist Society event, Scalia said it had been a "juvenile spectacle." In a talk at a Florida law school, Thomas said, "I don't go because it has become so partisan and it's very uncomfortable for a judge to sit there." He added that "there's a lot that you don't hear on TV—the catcalls, the whooping and hollering and under-the-breath comments." In an appearance in New York, Alito said it was awkward "to sit there like the proverbial potted plant."

The issue presented a special challenge for the chief justice, who at once wanted to defend the integrity of his decisions but also sought to preserve the picture (misleading though it was) of an apolitical Supreme Court. Roberts's frustrations came out in a question-and-answer session with students at the University of Alabama School of Law several weeks after Obama's speech. Asked about the president's criticism, Roberts said, "I have no problems with that. On the other hand, there is the issue of the setting, the circumstances, and the decorum. The image of having the members of one branch of government standing up, literally surrounding the Supreme Court, cheering and hollering while the Court—according to the requirements of protocol—has to sit there expressionless, I think is very troubling." He went on, "To the extent the State of the Union has degenerated into a political pep rally, I'm not sure why we're there." Roberts's complaint was understandable, though he and the other conservative justices had no grievances when George W. Bush gave his State of the Union addresses.

Asked about the chief justice's remarks, Robert Gibbs, Obama's spokesman, voiced none of the traditional deference to the Court. "What is troubling is that this decision opened the floodgates for corporations and special interests to pour money into elections—drowning out the voices of average Americans," Gibbs said. The conflict between the White House and the Court was now out in the open.

For his part, Alito spent the next State of the Union in Hawaii.

On March 21, 2010, two months after the State of the Union, the House of Representatives passed Obama's health care reform law, bringing to fruition decades of work by Democratic presidents and legislators. It marked the signal accomplishment of the president's term. Obama's popularity, however, was already tumbling. The economic recovery was faltering. Unemployment was rising. And at the Supreme Court, the justices were waiting for John Paul Stevens to announce he was leaving.

Like Souter, Stevens was a Republican who became alienated from his party. As old as Stevens was, he might well have hung on if McCain had won the previous election. As much as Souter wanted to leave, he too might have remained on the Court in the same circumstances. Stevens had a special fondness for Obama because of their shared Chicago roots. Stevens's decision, long expected, came on April 9, almost exactly eleven months after Souter's. Stevens's letter reflected his plainspoken manner. "My dear Mr. President," Stevens wrote. "Having concluded that it would be in the best interests of the Court to have my successor appointed and confirmed well in advance of the commencement of the Court's next Term, I shall retire from regular active service as an Associate Justice . . . effective the next day after the Court rises for the summer recess this year."

In Stevens's final spring, the conservative decisions continued. Two years earlier, in *Heller*, the Court had overturned a District of Columbia gun ordinance on the ground that the Second Amendment gives individuals a right to keep and bear arms. Because that law was limited to D.C. (which is not a state), *Heller* addressed only the right of the federal government to pass gun control laws. In *McDonald v. Chicago*, the question was whether the new interpretation of the Second Amendment applied to states as well as to the federal government.

The case dealt with a constitutional concept known as "incorporation." By their express terms, most of the provisions of the Bill of Rights apply only to the federal government. For example, the text of the First Amendment states: "Congress shall make no law respecting an establishment of religion, or prohibiting the free exercise thereof; or abridging the freedom of speech, or of the press." The amendment says nothing about the states. But during the twentieth century, the Court decided that most of the provisions of the Bill of Rights applied against the states as well. This process, which was associated with Hugo Black during his long career on the Court, was known as "incorporation." How did the Court decide which rights should be incorporated? Over a series of cases, the justices determined whether the right was "fundamental to our scheme of ordered liberty," or "deeply rooted in this Nation's history and tradition." The issue in *McDonald* was whether the right of an individual to bear arms, under the Second Amendment, met this test.

Alito's opinion, for the five conservatives, said yes. The Second Amendment right was so fundamental and deeply rooted that it should apply against the states as well as the federal government. "Self-defense is a basic right, recognized by many legal systems from ancient times to the present day, and in *Heller*, we held that individual self-defense is 'the *central component*' of the Second Amendment right," Alito wrote. In a dissent that was alternately weary and anguished, Stevens pointed out that it was only two years earlier—2008—that the Court for the first time recognized any individual rights under the Second Amendment. "States have a long and unbroken history of regulating firearms. The idea that States may place substantial restrictions on the right to keep and bear arms short of complete disarmament is, in fact, far more entrenched than the notion that the Federal Constitution protects any such right," Stevens wrote. After just two years, how could the right be "fundamental"? To Stevens, the Second Amendment did not carry the same weight as freedom of speech and religion. He wrote, "It does not appear to be the case that the ability to own a handgun, or any particular type of firearm, is critical to leading a life of autonomy, dignity, or political equality."

The spring of 2010 was a tense and uncertain time at the Court. The reality of Stevens's impending departure was sinking in. He would be leaving after thirty-five years, just short of William O. Douglas's record tenure. Because Stevens had spent so much time in Florida, he was a remote figure, even to some of his colleagues. Nevertheless, he had gone out of his way to welcome Sotomayor in her first year and had struck up a friendship with Alito as well. Stevens had a polite and respectful relationship with Roberts, which was inevitably colored by their disagreements in almost every major case. Decades of legal duels had poisoned the relationship between Stevens and Scalia. Still, no sitting justice had known a Court without JPS. It was difficult, and a little painful, to imagine one.

A worse problem for the Supreme Court family was Marty Ginsburg's illness. He was universally beloved. As a law professor and high-powered lawyer himself, he could speak to the justices as a relative equal; as a gregarious and self-deprecating spouse, he could welcome their wives (and O'Connor's husband) as a peer as well. He was a terrific cook whose talents nearly everyone in the Court building enjoyed at one time or another. His cancer, once seemingly in remission, had returned. He died on Sunday, June 27, 2010, at the Ginsburgs' home at the Watergate. It was one day before the final day of the Court's term.

Most of the time, the real operations of the Supreme Court take place behind the scenes. Sometimes, though, the public has a window into the very soul of the institution. Monday, June 28, was such a day. The judicial, the political, the personal, and the ceremonial—all were on display.

Even on Monday morning, no one knew for sure how the day would unfold. As news of Marty's death spread, it was unclear whether Justice Ginsburg would appear in Court the following day. Most of her colleagues assumed not, especially since Jewish tradition calls for immediate burial of the dead. But since Ruth, as a girl, saw women excluded from the minyan for her father, she never paid a great deal of attention to the formal rituals of her religion. The funeral would be Tuesday, at Arlington Cemetery, with full military honors. (Several mourners saw an amused Marty Ginsburg wink in the selection of the location. He tended to discuss his tenure at Fort Sill chiefly as the time he learned to cook.) On Monday, Ruth went to work.

The audience in the courtroom almost gasped when she appeared from behind the curtain at the stroke of ten. Her hair was pulled back with a black ribbon, her eyes downcast. Roberts said, "It is my very sad duty to announce that Martin David Ginsburg, husband of our colleague Justice Ruth Bader Ginsburg, died yesterday, June 27, 2010, at home in Washington, D.C." The chief went on to give a brief summary of Marty's life, including his "sharp wit and engaging charm." Roberts was extremely good at this sort of speech, much better than Rehnquist, who tended to mumble and rush through ceremonial occasions. As Roberts spoke, Scalia wept. The Ginsburg and Scalia families had celebrated every New Year's Eve together since the two judges were on the D.C. Circuit together. To the amazement of their friends, the families had never let politics come between them.

But this was a working session of the Court—the most important one of the year. Alito read the first opinion, *McDonald v. Chicago*, the victory for gun rights. Breyer, as was his custom, grimaced and rolled his eyes as his colleague spoke, and then read his dissent from the bench. Ginsburg had the next opinion, a case that held that a Christian student organization at a public law school could not bar gay students from attending their meetings. Her voice was unaffected by her ordeal.

Roberts went last, in a case where the Court, 5–4, struck down a minor provision of the Sarbanes-Oxley law, which was passed in the wake of the Enron accounting scandal. The decision involved only a small piece of economic regulation, but Roberts's characteristically eloquent opinion gave a clear sense of which way he wanted the Court to move in the future:

> One can have a government that functions without being ruled by functionaries, and a government that benefits from expertise without being ruled by experts. Our Constitution was adopted to enable the people to govern themselves, through their elected leaders. The growth of the Executive Branch, which now wields vast power and touches almost every aspect of daily life, heightens the concern that it may slip from the Executive's control, and thus from that of the people. This concern is largely absent from the dissent's paean to the administrative state.

Of course, it was Breyer—bureaucracy's best friend on the Court— who wrote the dissent. And he read it from the bench, too, scolding Roberts that "judicial opinions are not tickets for one ride in one day on one train. They have principle in all this." It was an echo of the dissenting opinions in *Bush v. Gore*.

All that was left for the Court was to say good-bye to John Paul Stevens. Roberts read a letter, signed by all the current justices, as well as

Souter and O'Connor, saluting his long tenure and his commitment to justice. "Justice Stevens, we will allow you time for rebuttal," Roberts said with a smile.

Stevens said that when he joined the Court in 1975 he would have addressed the other justices as "Dear Brethren." Instead Stevens said, "Dear Colleagues, Collegiality and independence characterize our common endeavor. I thank you for your kind words. Far more importantly, Maryan and I thank each of you and each of your spouses—present and departed—for your warm and enduring friendship. It has been an honor and a privilege to share custodial responsibility for a great institution with the eight of you and with ten of your predecessors." With midwestern reserve, Stevens's voice never broke. Roberts then adjourned the Court until the first Monday in October.

A dinner had been arranged for that night, where the current and retired justices would pay tribute to Stevens on his final day on the bench. Both the chief justice and Stevens offered to cancel the event in deference to Marty Ginsburg's death, but Justice Ginsburg insisted that the event proceed, even though she herself chose not to go. Maryan Stevens was not well enough to attend, and it was, on the whole, a depressing occasion. The justices were tired, sad, grumpy, and frustrated.

No one, though, was as downcast as Sandra Day O'Connor.

FOUR

THE RETIRED JUSTICES DISSENT

She was still the most famous justice. She had been retired for five years, but she was stopped for autographs every day. Always—*always*—parents introduced their daughters to Sandra Day O'Connor. Some people wept. There were nine justices on the Supreme Court, but people recognized O'Connor more than any of them—which was not surprising, since she was the most influential woman in American history. And in keeping with her remarkable life, O'Connor figured out a new way to be a retired Supreme Court justice, too.

In recent decades, Supreme Court justices had all done the same thing in retirement: they died, usually sooner rather than later. But O'Connor was only seventy-five in 2005—not especially old for a justice—and in good health. She loved the job. She reveled in her role as the swing justice. But she decided to quit anyway.

It was because of her husband, John O'Connor. John had been a successful lawyer in Phoenix, but his career never really took off after Sandra was appointed to the Court and the couple moved to Washington in 1981. If John ever felt resentment for being an especially well-known trailing spouse, he never made it apparent. He was an enthusiastic, almost giddy, backer of his wife's career. (So was Marty Ginsburg for Ruth.) For many years, however, John had been displaying symptoms of what was eventually diagnosed as Alzheimer's disease. The signs were barely visible outside the O'Connor family at first, but his decline accelerated in the new millennium. In 2003, Sandra started bringing him to Court on most days; he sat on the sofa in her outer office while she worked. Then, in 2004, John started wandering away, which is a common and dangerous problem for Alzheimer's patients. The situation was becoming unmanageable.

So in the spring of 2005, O'Connor went to see Rehnquist, who was trying to recover from thyroid cancer. She explained that she was considering leaving the Court to take care of John. O'Connor knew that neither she nor Rehnquist wanted to leave the Court with two vacancies. Who should leave first? Was Rehnquist thinking of retiring?

It was an extraordinary moment in an extraordinary friendship. They had known each other for more than five decades. Law school classmates at Stanford, they both decided to settle in the nascent metropolis of Phoenix. There, they went to the same pool parties with their young families. Somehow, improbably, they both wound up on the Supreme Court, Rehnquist in 1972, O'Connor nine years later. Her insistent moderation cost him several of his most precious goals—like overturning *Roe v. Wade* and ending affirmative action. But the affection between them never dimmed.

O'Connor was expecting Rehnquist to say that he would step down; though she didn't know the details, O'Connor could tell that he was desperately ill. But the chief told his old friend that he was going to try to hang on. He did not plan to retire and hoped soon to return to work.

That left O'Connor with an excruciating dilemma. No one had loved her role as much as O'Connor had, and she was more than capable of continuing to do the job. She didn't want to leave. But she thought John needed her, and that trumped her other misgivings. Over the years, many male members of the Court had nursed their wives through illnesses, but few if any considered leaving the Court to provide the care. In a way, this decision made O'Connor one more kind of pioneer.

On July 1, 2005, O'Connor announced her decision to resign, to be effective upon the confirmation of her successor. None of her colleagues except Rehnquist knew it was coming. Without exception, they were stunned.

What followed was, to use a favorite O'Connor expression, "a mess." George W. Bush nominated Roberts to replace her. Then, over Labor Day weekend, Rehnquist succumbed to cancer, and Bush named Roberts to be chief justice. After Roberts was confirmed, Bush nominated

Harriet Miers to replace O'Connor. Miers was grievously underqualified, and her selection turned into a tragicomedy that took several weeks to open and close. Months after O'Connor announced her resignation, there was still no replacement. It was not until November that Bush sent Alito's name to the Senate.

O'Connor's frustrations mounted. The delays were maddening. O'Connor was a planner, a doer, a control freak of sorts. She was the kind of person who took it upon herself to choreograph her law clerks' lives as well as her own life. Three mornings a week, her female clerks were expected to join her for aerobics on the basketball court on the top floor of the building. (Male clerks were often instructed to lose weight by other means.) O'Connor arranged for special access to exhibits at the National Gallery, and attendance for clerks was not optional. In her Arizona days, O'Connor had proudly worn the nickname the Yenta of Paradise Valley, and later she was not shy about encouraging her clerks to experience the joys of married life. Now, finally, she wanted nothing more than to leave the Court and take care of her own husband, and circumstances kept conspiring to prevent her from doing so.

And now it was up to George W. Bush to reshape *her* Court. O'Connor had voted with the majority in *Bush v. Gore*, but she came to regard the presidency that she and her colleagues had delivered to the country as a disaster. On one of her final days on the Court, O'Connor was explaining her decision to leave to David Souter, as the two of them stood outside her chambers. "What makes this harder," O'Connor told Souter, "is that it's my party that's destroying the country."

O'Connor's bill of particulars against Bush was extensive. "He's destroying the military with adventures that we aren't prepared for," she said, for the war in Iraq was going poorly. "We've got colossal deficit spending, and the only way he got reelected was by getting states to vote on same-sex marriage.

"I thought Republicans stood for a strong military, a balanced budget—and Barry Goldwater never gave a damn who you slept with," O'Connor went on. "Bush repudiated all of that." Her Republican Party—and Souter's—was gone. Her alienation had deepened during the Terri Schiavo case. There, Republicans in Congress had rushed through a bill to force a federal judge to reexamine the case of a critically ill woman in Florida. This perverse turn on "pro-life" politics had a particularly ugly resonance for O'Connor, who was herself making decisions for the care of her husband.

At long last, on January 31, 2006, the Senate confirmed Alito and Sandra O'Connor could step down to be with John.

O'Connor's departure was bittersweet in the extreme. During the months between her announced departure from the Court and her actual retirement, John slipped completely into the grip of Alzheimer's. He no longer recognized his wife of nearly fifty-four years. O'Connor and their three sons made the painful decision to move John to a long-term-care facility in Phoenix.

O'Connor handled even that experience in a groundbreaking way. In November 2007, Veronica Sanchez, a television news reporter in Phoenix, called a local nursing home to do a report on "mistaken attachments" among patients with Alzheimer's disease. With this syndrome, patients can forget their relationships with their spouses and other family members and "fall in love" with the people they see every day, usually other patients. At the last minute, Sanchez's story fell apart, and she was directed to another facility, the Huger Mercy Living Center, where she was told two families had agreed to tell their story on camera. Sandra Day O'Connor's family was one of them.

Sanchez wound up interviewing the O'Connors' son Scott, who lives in Phoenix, and he allowed John to be shown on camera with the woman who was the object of his affection. The story caused a worldwide sensation. A few months later, O'Connor herself testified before the Senate Special Committee on Aging. She said Alzheimer's was "a subject that is very dear to my heart and to the hearts of the millions of American families who love and provide care to relatives who have Alzheimer's disease. As you know, I became one of these caregivers in 1990, when my husband, John, was diagnosed with Alzheimer's. Living with this disease has been sad and difficult for my entire family." (The date of John's diagnosis had never before been made public.) O'Connor asked the senators for additional funding for research on the disease and its effects on the families of its victims. John O'Connor died on November 11, 2009.

This kind of work was, of course, admirable and courageous, as well as politically uncontroversial. But O'Connor also had other ideas for how to spend an unquiet retirement.

In part, O'Connor did the traditional work of retired justices. She continued to sit occasionally as a judge on the various circuit courts of appeals. (When she did, the benches for spectators were always filled.) She also took up the cause of civics education in schools. Horrified that two-thirds of American adults could not name all three branches of government (and a third could not name even one), O'Connor started traveling around the country advocating that public schools restore civics to a more prominent place in their curriculums. She founded and became the public face of a nonprofit organization, iCivics, that produced lesson plans and Web games to promote civics education. During her tenure on the Court, O'Connor traveled more and gave more speeches than any of her colleagues, and her schedule barely slackened during her retirement.

O'Connor had another cause, too, which she called judicial independence. At one level, the issue seemed almost bland, like literacy or nutrition, the kind of concern that a First Lady might embrace. O'Connor had been the nation's best-known judge, so it might seem natural that she would go on to speak out on behalf of fellow members of her profession. In fact, judicial independence, especially O'Connor's version of it, was an intensely partisan subject—and the former justice had very much chosen sides.

The history of judicial selection has tracked larger themes in American history. The Constitution invested the president with the power to nominate all federal judges, with the "advice and consent" of the Senate. That system has never changed. However, in state courts, where the great majority of civil and criminal lawsuits are resolved, the systems had evolved a great deal over time. In the Jacksonian era, before the Civil War, most states moved to electing judges, which was perceived as a form of bringing democracy to the courts. By the Progressive era, this system was under criticism, because elections were largely under the control of political parties, which were often corrupt. Progressives created "merit selection" systems, which usually involved the appointment of judges by governors or even independent panels; these systems sometimes included retention elections, where voters had the right to evict judges every few years. The "Missouri plan," adopted in 1940, gave the power to nominate judges to an independent commission, and allowed the governor to select from the commission's list. Many states adopted a version of this plan. Thirty-nine states have judicial elections for at least some judgeships.

The politics of judicial elections changed in the 1980s. Business interests began lining up behind Republican candidates who promised to limit tort awards; plaintiffs' trial lawyers, with fewer resources, began subsidizing Democrats. Elections, especially for state supreme courts, started to cost millions of dollars. Overall, Republicans thrived, especially in the South. (Karl Rove first became famous because his campaigns turned the Texas Supreme Court from all Democratic to all Republican.) Later, social conservatives joined business conservatives in pushing for Republican judges—and for moving states from systems of appointed judges to those of elected judges.

In short, by the time O'Connor took up the cause of judicial independence, the partisan battle lines were clearly drawn on the issue. Republicans supported judicial elections; Democrats wanted appointive systems. O'Connor joined the Democratic side, loudly and passionately. Earlier in her tenure, she was more ambivalent about these issues, but her embrace of judicial independence paralleled her move to the left on a variety of other matters. O'Connor's passion for the issue reflected her own experience as an elected official—real-world experience that was keenly missed at the Court. She knew what it was like to raise money for elections, and she knew how money could corrupt the judicial process. It was not an abstraction to her. She understood how political decisions were made, and she could communicate the earthy reality in a characteristically direct way. Urging the members of a state bar association to lobby for more funding for the courts, she told them, "Make sure to drop in some sob stories. If things get really bad, buy some beer and Mexican food, and have them all over." (O'Connor herself, who enjoyed a scotch, was fond of quoting her husband: "You don't have to have a drink to have a good time, but why take the chance?")

O'Connor stepped into one of the hottest political fights in the nation in 2010. The previous year, the Iowa Supreme Court had ruled unanimously that the Iowa constitution required that same-sex couples be allowed to marry. Three of those justices happened to be facing retention elections in 2010, and a conservative Republican activist organized a campaign to defeat them. Alone among national public figures, O'Connor traveled to Iowa to defend the three judges. "Justice Souter and I both look at the Court as the one safe place where a person can have a fair and impartial hearing to resolve a legal issue, and we have to keep that," O'Connor said. "We have to address the pressures being applied to that one safe place . . . to have it where judges are not subject to outright retaliation." Despite O'Connor's efforts, all three of the Iowa justices were voted out of office. (In Iowa, O'Connor described her mission as supporting judicial independence, not same-sex marriage per se. Her views on gay rights had evolved enormously, too. In 1986, O'Connor had voted with the majority in *Bowers v. Hardwick*, which upheld a Georgia prosecution of a gay man for having consensual sex. In 2003, in *Lawrence v. Texas*, O'Connor was part of the majority that overturned *Bowers*. By 2010, there was little doubt that O'Connor favored full equality, including marriage rights, for gay people.)

In Nevada, also in 2010, O'Connor's venture into electoral politics turned into an embarrassment. Shortly before the election, she went to Las Vegas to support a ballot initiative that would have moved the state to a primarily appointive system for judges. Through a series of snafus, supporters of the initiative used O'Connor's voice on robocalls that went out to about 50,000 voters—in the middle of the night. (One woman called the local newspaper to complain that, since she had a son in intensive care, she thought the call meant that he had died.) Through the Supreme Court public affairs office, O'Connor put out a statement that she had not authorized the use of her voice in this way. In any event, O'Connor's side in the initiative lost.

The change in O'Connor's circumstances was striking. She had gone from being one of the most powerful people in the country to an itinerant speechmaker who was not nearly as sure in her footing as a political player as she had been as a judge. O'Connor placed herself in an awkward position by taking such an outspoken role in elective campaigns. She had retired from the Supreme Court but remained a federal judge. Conservatives complained that she had violated ethical norms. She hadn't—the rules were vague—but the questions were unpleasant. She weathered them and went right back out on the road. O'Connor could have done what most retired justices do—pick up an honorary degree here or there, teach a class every once in a while. But O'Connor saw what was happening to her country—and her Court—and she couldn't let go.

O'Connor had an unusual conversational tic. She divided the world into things (and people) that were "attractive" and "unattractive." The distinction had little to do with appearance, but more with O'Connor's general sense of how things would be perceived in the world. O'Connor kept up her politician's radar for public sentiment. When the Court abruptly changed course and overruled its prior decisions, that was unattractive. Colin Powell was attractive. John Ashcroft was unattractive.

John Roberts was the very definition of attractive. When he became chief justice, O'Connor already knew him as a skilled and accomplished oral advocate before the Court. She was dazzled, like so many others, by his graceful and learned testimony before the Senate Judiciary Committee. O'Connor overlapped with Roberts for only about four months on the Court—from October 2005 to January 2006—but it was long enough for her to be enchanted with his debut. She told the story of his graceful handling of the exploding lightbulb all the time and went so far as to write a gushy tribute to the new chief justice in *Time*. "The stars must have been aligned that January morning in 1955 when John G. Roberts Jr. was born in Buffalo, N.Y., because almost everything thereafter led him straight to the Supreme Court of the U.S.," the story began. The new chief justice had made the transition to the Court "seamlessly and effectively," she wrote, concluding, "I'm certain he will serve a long tenure in the role and be an effective leader not only for the Supreme Court but for all the federal courts in the nation."

Then O'Connor started seeing the decisions. It wasn't one, or two, or even three of them. Abortion, civil rights, women's rights—it was as if the Roberts Court had made a special project of targeting O'Connor's legacy in particular. Hers had been the crucial vote in *Casey* in 1992 to save the core of *Roe v. Wade*—and then *Gonzales v. Carhart* jeopardized it. O'Connor had preserved affirmative action in *Grutter* in 2003—and Roberts belittled it in *Parents Involved*, the Seattle school integration case. O'Connor had projected onto Roberts her idea of what a chief justice, and what a Republican, should be. But if she had chosen to look more closely, it was always clear that Roberts reflected his own era of the Republican Party, not O'Connor's.

In private, O'Connor had a disparaging word for what she saw in Roberts—*an agenda*. Rehnquist was different, she said. He had taken each case one at a time; he had not tried to force his vision of the Constitution on the Court. This was actually revisionist history on O'Connor's part. Rehnquist was just about as conservative as Roberts was, but Rehnquist didn't have the votes to enact his agenda. Roberts, in most cases, did. (In slightly different ways, O'Connor, Souter, Ginsburg, Breyer, and even Stevens all created a kind of posthumous cult of William Rehnquist. *He was moderate! He played fair! He respected precedent! Rehnquist was great! Those were the good old days!* These reimaginings of him had more to do with these justices' distaste for Roberts than with a realistic assessment of Rehnquist.)

Mostly O'Connor kept her views about the Roberts Court private. Given her wide circle of friends, frequent travels, and outgoing nature, her opinions were hardly a secret. But *Citizens United* prompted her to shed her public reserve. The main reason the retired O'Connor had come to favor an appointive judiciary over an elected one was to limit the power of money in campaigns. And here the Court was casting aside decades of limits on campaign finance. "This rise in judicial campaigning makes last week's decision in *Citizens United* a problem, an increasing problem, for maintaining an independent judiciary," O'Connor said at a conference at Georgetown University Law Center just a few days after the decision. "No state can possibly benefit from having that much money injected into a political campaign." Like *Carhart II*, the partial-birth abortion case, *Citizens United* illustrated the importance of the Alito-for-O'Connor shift on the Court. If she had remained, that 5–4 decision would have gone the other way.

But as she knew better than anyone, O'Connor had left the Court, and she had to live with the consequences of her decision. Her health was still good, but midway through her ninth decade, she was more prickly and less patient than she used to be. There were two questions that she especially disdained, and she was asked them all the time. The first was about *Bush v. Gore*. Did she think she voted the right way? "It wasn't the end of the world," she said, in a typical response, at a conference in Aspen. "They had recounts of the votes in four counties by the press, and it did not change the outcome at all. So forget it. It's over!" Her defensiveness invited speculation about the state of her conscience on the subject.

The other question was whether she regretted stepping down from the Court. To know O'Connor was to recognize that she did not traffic in regrets. The rancher's daughter had no truck with whining about what might have been. Asked about what the Roberts Court had done to her legacy, she said at one point, "What would you feel? I'd be a little bit disappointed. If you think you've been helpful, and then it's dismantled, you think, 'Oh, dear.' But life goes on. It's not always positive."

David Souter's life, on the other hand, was pretty close to always positive—or at least close to what he always wanted.

Just a few months before George H. W. Bush nominated him to the Supreme Court in 1990, Souter was confirmed as a judge on the First Circuit. (He had been a justice on the New Hampshire Supreme Court for several years.) If Souter had stayed on the First Circuit, he would have had chambers in Concord, gone down to Boston about once a month for arguments, and lived in his old family home in Weare. It was the life he wanted. Now, twenty years later, Souter finally had it.

By the time Souter returned to New Hampshire full-time, the old family farm house was literally disintegrating under the weight of all his books. So he bought a newer one closer to Concord and started the laborious process of moving his possessions. Efficiency was never a Souter strong suit, so he spent months shuttling between the two houses, not living entirely in one place or the other. As a retired justice, Souter was eligible to sit on the First Circuit, but that court was short-handed and Souter soon had a substantial caseload. The Supreme Court, however, only gave him a secretary based in Washington, not Concord, so his chambers on Pleasant Street were strewn with disorderly piles of papers and books. Souter didn't mind. He went running through the hills every morning. He retired at sixty-nine, and a year or two in New Hampshire made him look five years younger. (He did miss his friends in Philadelphia, where he had been the Third Circuit justice for many years. He thought about visiting, but Philadelphia (!) just seemed too far to go.)

Souter put the Supreme Court behind him—almost. In May 2010, he agreed to give the commencement address at Harvard and get a few things off his chest. Souter had watched with impatience as Roberts, in his confirmation hearing, had compared himself to an umpire, limited only to the mechanical process of calling balls and strikes. Likewise, Souter had spent a generation confronting the resolute certainties of Scalia and Thomas that they could find the answer to any legal question in the plain text or the original meaning of the Constitution. Souter did not believe there was any such certainty. (He didn't share his predecessor William Brennan's liberal certainties either.) Rather, Souter built his jurisprudence around embracing the complexities and contradictions built into the Constitution.

"The explicit terms of the Constitution, in other words, can create a conflict of approved values, and the explicit terms of the Constitution do not resolve that conflict when it arises," he told the crowd at Harvard, citing the Pentagon Papers case, where the values of a free press conflicted with the need for national security. "A choice may have to be made, not because language is vague but because the Constitution embodies the desire of the American people, like most people, to have things both ways." To Souter, originalism and textualism were based on false promises. "If we cannot share every intellectual assumption that formed the minds of those who framed the charter, we can still address the constitutional uncertainties the way they must have envisioned, by relying on reason, by respecting all the words the Framers wrote, by facing facts, and by seeking to understand their meaning for living people." *Their meaning for living people*, not the intent of the framers—those, in Souter's genteel way, were fighting words. In temperament and style of living, Souter was probably closer to the eighteenth century than any other justice, but he recognized the folly of trying to re-create the world of the framers and then render decisions as they would have done. In all the important ways, Souter was a modern man.

The Harvard speech was very much an aberration. Souter was out of the game, and happily so. When he was on the Court, Souter had longed to take the time to read (reread, actually) Proust and Dickens, and that was what he was finally getting around to doing.

One thing gnawed at him. Before he left Washington, he had meant to take something of the Court with him. He wanted a souvenir, a keepsake, that might remind him of his days as a justice, but he never found the right thing.

Then, some time after he returned to New Hampshire, Souter had an idea. When he was a boy, he had collected stamps, and the postmaster in Weare used to save copies of the new issues for him. He remembered that when he was about eleven years old, there was a three-cent stamp with a picture of the Supreme Court building. Souter burrowed into his files and found the stamp, and he noticed that it featured the windows where he had had his chambers for many years. Souter put the stamp in a frame. That was good enough for him.

SOFTBALL POLITICS

Stevens's announcement of his departure, in April 2010, was no surprise. Neither was Obama's reaction to filling a second vacancy on the Court. The president thought the nomination and confirmation of Sotomayor had been a great success. So he decided to start with the same list of candidates and make his choice in the same way he had selected his first justice.

From the perspective of the White House, however, the world now looked very different. Sotomayor was nominated during Obama's honeymoon, which was long over by the time Stevens retired. There had been no significant recovery from the devastating recession, and the blame for this failure was starting to attach to Obama. In January, Scott Brown had won a dramatic upset victory in the race for the late Senator Edward Kennedy's seat in Massachusetts. That election took the Democratic majority in the Senate below the filibuster threshold of sixty. That same month, the *Citizens United* decision had reminded the White House just how much harm the Supreme Court could do to them. In light of his political weakness, Obama wanted to place the right justice on the Supreme Court while also looking to avoid a big fight in the Senate.

The three losing finalists for the Souter seat had been Kagan, Diane Wood, and Janet Napolitano. As before, though, Napolitano was doomed by her success as secretary of homeland security. Obama liked the job she was doing there, and nominating a politician, with a history of public positions on controversial issues, was problematic in the best of circumstances. Since she was out, Obama wanted to consider more options.

Merrick Garland joined the finalists. Bill Clinton had put Garland on the D.C. Circuit in 1997, and he had been a moderate liberal on that Court for more than a decade. He was viewed as an easy bet for confirmation, if not an especially politically advantageous choice. With the uncertainty surrounding the coming midterm elections, Obama was looking at a substantially reduced Democratic majority in the Senate during the second half of his term. It was wise to keep Garland in reserve in case he needed Republican support for confirmation. "I need a play I can run in 2011 or 2012," Obama said to an adviser.

Garland had graduated from Harvard College and Harvard Law School, and after his name leaked as a possible nominee, Obama received some criticism for educational snobbery. With Stevens leaving, the Supreme Court would consist of five products of Harvard Law School and three of Yale. (Ginsburg's law degree came from Columbia, though she spent her first two years at Harvard.) Was that a healthy thing? Were there only two law schools in the whole country? Obama wanted some diversity.

He added Sidney Thomas to the list. Thomas had an impeccably non–Ivy League pedigree. He was a graduate of Montana State University and the University of Montana Law School whom Clinton nominated to the Ninth Circuit in 1995. A protégé of Max Baucus, the state's senior senator, he was also among the most liberal judges on the most liberal appeals court in the country. (Some in the White House did relish the idea of a liberal "Justice Thomas" on the Supreme Court.) The White House made a point of leaking the fact that Thomas had been brought in for an interview with Obama, but he was never a realistic candidate.

Again, the real choice came down to Diane Wood and one other candidate, this time Elena Kagan.

Kagan went into the contest with what might be called the John Roberts advantage. Through his work in the Reagan White House, Roberts knew many of the most important Republican lawyers in the country. It was true that Roberts hadn't written much when he was appointed to the Supreme Court, but that didn't matter a lot, because these people *knew* him. They had been in that gilded foxhole together. Roberts didn't have to prove his conservative or intellectual bona fides. He was an insider.

So was Kagan. In the Clinton White House, she had worked closely with Rahm Emanuel, who was currently the White House chief of staff. Kagan and Cynthia Hogan, Biden's chief counsel, had been associates together at Williams & Connolly, and then Hogan had hired Kagan to assist Biden in the Ginsburg confirmation hearings in 1993. (That meant Biden knew Kagan as well.) Ron Klain, Biden's chief of staff, was a law school peer of Kagan's and one of her closest friends. Danielle Gray, the young lawyer who wrote the first vetting memos on Supreme Court candidates, had been her student at Harvard. As for Wood, the brother of Susan Davies, the deputy White House counsel, had once been a law clerk for her, but that could scarcely compare to Kagan's lineup of friends and advocates.

Wood did have one important supporter: Barack Obama. He liked her. He appreciated her cerebral nature and even temperament. He was impressed that Wood had worked so successfully with conservatives on the Seventh Circuit. After all, this Supreme Court was full of Republicans and likely to remain that way for years; any Obama nominee would have to build coalitions to win cases. Obama started asking his advisers: How many five-to-fours could Wood swing to her side each year? How many could Kagan? Garland? No one could say for sure, of course, but the question illustrated what mattered to Obama. *Citizens United* had demonstrated with great clarity the implications of losing these close decisions. Obama didn't want someone who could write eloquent dissents. He wanted someone who could *win*.

So: Wood or Kagan? Neither one of them offered the kind of compelling biographical story that Sotomayor did. Both Wood and Kagan grew up middle-class and became law professors. Nothing very striking there. The prospect of three women on the Supreme Court for the first time was appealing, but that didn't help him choose between the two finalists. In fact, Obama was amused at his advisers' increasingly desperate attempts to draw distinctions between them. (In response to one argument for Wood, Obama said, "Your pitch is that she is a regular person, and she plays *chamber music*?")

As the discussion continued, Obama's native caution came to the fore. Choosing Wood meant a fight over abortion in the Senate. She had also made critical remarks in speeches about the Bush administration's war on terror, and these comments would be used to portray her as weak. With fifty-nine Democrats in the Senate, Wood would probably win, but was the struggle really necessary? Could Obama get the justice he wanted without the heartburn? When Wood came for her second interview, Obama told her, "You realize that there is a political dimension to this decision." Correctly, Wood recognized that was not a promising sign.

Kagan's backers also played the age card. Kagan was born in 1960; she had just turned fifty. Wood was born in 1950; she was about to turn sixty. (Her supporters pointed out that Wood's *mother* was still in excellent shape.) A younger nominee probably meant a longer tenure—and a greater legacy for Obama on the Supreme Court. In the end, though, Margaret Witt might have tipped the balance.

Margaret Witt enlisted in the air force in 1987 and enjoyed a sterling record as a flight nurse, first on active duty and later in the reserves. Like many gay people in the military, she avoided questions about her personal life. But in 2004, the estranged husband of a woman Witt was seeing reported her to the air force. After an investigation, Witt was discharged in 2007 under the policy known as "Don't Ask, Don't Tell." From her home in Washington State, Witt, who was by then a major, launched one of the many legal challenges to the policy.

Obama ran for president on the promise that he would repeal "Don't Ask, Don't Tell." The policy was enshrined in a law, so Obama could not change it without congressional approval. Preoccupied with other matters, Obama did not press legislators on the issue during his first year in office. So lawsuits like Witt's proliferated. Witt lost in the district court, but then she won a major victory in the Ninth Circuit. The question became whether the government should appeal the Ninth Circuit's ruling to the Supreme Court.

As solicitor general, Kagan had to determine the government's position on Witt's appeal. Like most others in the Obama administration, Kagan opposed "Don't Ask, Don't Tell." She thought Congress should repeal the law, but there was little question in her mind that it was constitutional. And Kagan thought the Ninth Circuit's decision was clearly wrong. She believed the government should ask the justices to overturn the decision.

At the Justice Department and the White House, many people—most, in fact—disagreed with Kagan. The president was already facing charges from his supporters in the gay community that he had betrayed his promises. "Don't Ask, Don't Tell" was manifestly unjust. If the Ninth Circuit made it a little harder to discharge gay service members, then so much the better. Pushing his appeal would be a needless insult to some of the president's biggest fans—and a disgrace to honorable members of the armed forces like Margaret Witt. With the administration split, there's only one thing to do. The president has to decide.

So, during her first year as solicitor general, Kagan made the case to Obama that he should approve an appeal of the Ninth Circuit's decision. Her friends warned her of the risks of taking an unpopular opinion to the White House. Everyone knew she was a candidate for the Supreme Court, and it wouldn't pay to alienate the president on a touchy issue like this one. But Kagan thought the dispute was about the rule of law. There are right ways to change the law and wrong ways. What the Ninth Circuit did was the wrong way.

Obama rejected Kagan's advice. The government let the Ninth Circuit decision stand. But Kagan had impressed the president. Obama had a strange affinity for people who disagreed with him. It was often said that, in staffing his administration, Obama treated supporters of Hillary Clinton better than his own backers. Kagan's polite but resolute defense of a losing cause resonated with the president. In addition, she presented no political problems on abortion or national security. She was probably an easy confirmation. She was young. (As for Margaret Witt, after her victory in the Ninth Circuit, she won her trial in the district court. The government ultimately settled with her, giving her full retirement benefits. Congress repealed "Don't Ask, Don't Tell" in December 2010.)

On Monday, May 10, 2010, Obama introduced Kagan as his nominee. The moment had little of the drama of Sotomayor's, but the rollout was smooth and free of controversy. The president called Kagan "one of the nation's foremost legal minds," which was hyperbolic, given her modest record of scholarship. Obama also praised her "openness to a broad array of viewpoints" and her "fair-mindedness." These would be important themes for her confirmation strategy, based largely (and accurately) on her role in taming the ideological conflict at Harvard Law School. (Sotomayor broke the traditional silence of current justices toward nominees and called Kagan to congratulate her.)

Kagan's nomination became the subject of a peculiar media phenomenon. The day after she was announced, the *Wall Street Journal* ran a large front-page photograph of her playing softball when she was a teacher at the University of Chicago Law School, in the early nineties. Two days later, on May 13, the *New York Post*, which, like the *Journal*, was owned by Rupert Murdoch's News Corporation, ran the same photograph, with a full-page headline that read, "Does This Photo Suggest That High Court Nominee Elena Kagan Is a Lesbian?"

The issue had a close historical analogy. In 1990, when David Souter was nominated to the Supreme Court, he was, like Kagan, fifty years old and never married. For a brief time, the issue of his sexual orientation came up in the press. (This was when the myth arose that Souter always lived with his mother. That was not true, but the insinuation of such an arrangement was the point.) Johnny Carson, who was still on the air, made a few mild jokes about Souter. "He's lived in the same house his whole life," Carson said. "And he's never gotten married—which explains why he's lived in the same house his entire life!" The issue, such as it was, of Souter's private life was soon dropped. Given the relatively small number of news and entertainment outlets in 1990, and their relative timidity about exploring such issues, the story faded away.

The big difference in 2010 was the Internet. Once the softball picture was widely circulated, the story took on a life of its own. It wasn't just critics of Obama who were speculating about her sexuality. Andrew Sullivan, a prominent blogger of eclectic views, and himself a gay man, made Kagan's sexuality a major focus. "If Kagan is straight, why have so many people simply assumed she's gay?" Sullivan wrote in an early post. "The kind of 'I'm-out-but-not-really-out' straddle cannot work any more in national public discourse." Later he wrote, "We know she is Jewish, and it is a fact simply and rightly put in the public square. If she were to hide her Jewishness, it would seem rightly odd, bizarre, anachronistic, even arguably self-critical or self-loathing. And yet we have been told by many that she is gay . . . and no one will ask directly if this is true and no one in the administration will tell us definitively." Other bloggers responded to Sullivan, who continued to pursue the story, which wound on for thousands of words. On *The Colbert Report* (another institution that did not exist in 1990), Stephen Colbert did a segment mocking the *Journal* and the *Post* for creating and then reporting the rumor about Kagan's sex life—but the overall effect was to keep the issue in circulation.

Kagan's advisers in the White House struggled with how, and whether, to respond. Was being gay an "accusation" that had to be denied? Would a denial suggest that being gay was somehow sinister or wrong? Did addressing the rumor dignify it and extend the story? How does one "prove" that someone is gay or straight anyway? Was it better to say nothing at all? For her part, Kagan just seethed.

In short order, the administration reached a consensus: Kagan should be seen by the public as what she was—a heterosexual. The truth mattered. Ron Klain, Kagan's friend from law school, hit on the disclosure strategy that the White House ultimately adopted. During her second and third years of law school, Kagan was roommates with Sarah Walzer and Walzer's boyfriend (now husband), John Barrett. They had e-mailed Klain and volunteered to be "witnesses" for Kagan's heterosexuality. Klain asked Walzer to give a single interview on the subject of Kagan's personal life. It would be with *Politico*, an online publication that was widely read in political circles but with limited circulation outside the Beltway. Walzer agreed, and she spoke to *Politico*'s Ben Smith.

The resulting story, which ran under the headline "Elena Kagan's Friends: She's Not Gay," was excruciating but effective. "I've known her for most of her adult life and I know she's straight," Walzer told Smith. "She dated men when we were in law school, we talked about men—who in our class was cute, who she would like to date, all of those things. She definitely dated when she was in D.C. after law school, when she was in Chicago—and she just didn't find the right person." Walzer had founded a pioneering social service agency on Long Island, but her role in the story was that of giggly best friend. Walzer recalled "discussion about who she might be interested in—the usual girl talk stuff—talk about how to get his attention." This was "less along the lines of how to wear your hair," Walzer said. "It's an ongoing challenge for very smart women—there are not very many men who would choose women who are smarter than they are." The story accomplished its purpose. The issue faded.

Kagan had a very different experience from Sotomayor preparing for her confirmation testimony. Sotomayor had bristled at the "bright young things" in the White House counsel's office who insisted she become fluent in the full range of constitutional law. Her prep sessions were tense and laborious (and she was in constant pain from her broken ankle). Kagan, on the other hand, was completely familiar with the world of Supreme Court law clerks. Discussing cases was as natural as breathing for her.

As with Sotomayor, the White House team recognized that Kagan's "courtesy calls" on senators were serious auditions. Duly prepared, she was ready to answer (or duck) questions about abortion, affirmative action, *Citizens United*, and a whole range of other issues. But they rarely came up. Instead, over and over, the senators asked her about her position on guns. Sotomayor had much the same experience. It is difficult for people outside the day-to-day operations of the political system to understand the pervasive obsession with gun rights in the contemporary Republican Party, and among many Democrats as well. More to the point, it was especially hard for Kagan and Sotomayor to fathom, since both had spent their entire lives in urban enclaves, where the only gun owners tended to be cops and criminals.

In making the rounds, Kagan also suffered from a postconfirmation backlash among Republicans against Sotomayor. In 2009, Sotomayor had promised senators that she would have an open mind in the *McDonald* case, which was then pending. There, the Court ultimately ruled 5–4 that states, like the federal government, had to respect an individual's right to bear arms. Republicans were so used to winning on gun issues—national Democrats had basically thrown in the towel on gun control—that they were offended that Sotomayor had the temerity to vote with her liberal colleagues. Consequently, many senators found Kagan's promise of an open mind unpersuasive. In the course of the meetings, Kagan confessed that she had never gone hunting, which in turn won her several invitations to join various senators on their expeditions. Kagan demurred, but she did promise, if she was confirmed, to ask Justice Scalia if she could tag along with him.

The most important news for Kagan's prospective vote in the Senate came shortly after her nomination. The National Rifle Association announced its opposition to her and, more importantly, indicated that her confirmation would be a "scored" vote for the senators. A perfect NRA voting record was extremely important to many senators, and now it was clear that a vote for Kagan would ruin any such rating. Kagan had real hopes of picking off a substantial number of Republican votes. When she worked at the White House, she had good relation-

ships with John McCain and Orrin Hatch. Making the rounds on Capitol Hill after her nomination, Kagan had especially friendly meetings
with Richard Lugar and Lindsey Graham. The decision by the NRA
to score the vote essentially killed Kagan's chances of winning over
more than a handful of Republicans. In particular, Hatch, of Utah, and
Lugar, of Indiana, were looking at possible primary challengers who
were going to argue that they were insufficiently conservative. There
was no point in their taking a risk on this vote, especially since Kagan
was likely to be confirmed anyway. (Lugar lost his primary in 2012;
Hatch survived his race later that year.)

The Kagan and Sotomayor nominations showed how politicized the
confirmation process had become. After all, there was no doubt that
Kagan was intelligent and ethical enough to be a Supreme Court justice.
Perhaps, on those grounds alone, she should have won overwhelming
confirmation in the Senate. As recently as 1993, Ginsburg had received
ninety-six votes, and her background, which included extensive work
on behalf of the American Civil Liberties Union, was far more politically controversial than Kagan's. The same point could be made about
the opposition to Alito, who won by only 58–42, despite formal qualifications that were as good as or better than Kagan's. By 2010, it was
clear that the days of confirmation with ninety-plus votes for anyone
were over.

In a way, the politicization of the process was healthy, or at least
revealing. The Supreme Court is not an honor society for smart people.
It's the final arbiter on scores of the most controversial political issues
in the United States, including gun control. The NRA was under no
obligation to indulge the persistent myth that qualities like intelligence
or integrity mattered most for a Supreme Court justice. Ginsburg had
intelligence and integrity; so did Scalia. What mattered far more was
their ideology, which compelled them to see the Constitution in very
different ways. Based on the available record, it was a reasonable conclusion that Kagan would be hostile to the NRA's interests. Opposing her
confirmation was the rational thing for the NRA to do.

Still, as Kagan headed into her hearings, her prospects looked bright.
There was no hint of opposition from any of the fifty-nine Democrats
in the Senate and no talk of filibuster from the Republicans. The arith-

metic looked stacked in her favor. As with other recent Supreme Court nominees, Kagan's job in testifying was to stay out of trouble.

There was some irony in Kagan's embrace of the say-little approach that had become the norm for prospective justices in the post-Bork era. In 1995, when Kagan was still a junior professor, she wrote a 10,000-word article for the *University of Chicago Law Review* cogently laying out the absurdities of contemporary confirmation hearings. They were "a vapid and hollow charade," she wrote. "When the Senate ceases to engage nominees in meaningful discussion of legal issues, the confirmation process takes on an air of vacuity and farce, and the Senate becomes incapable of either properly evaluating nominees or appropriately educating the public." For current nominees, Kagan wrote, "the safest and surest route to the prize lay in alternating platitudinous statement and judicious silence."

That, of course, was the route that Kagan took. Confronted with her article at the hearing, Kagan hedged. "I do think that much of what I wrote in 1995 was right, but that in some measure I got a bit of the balance off. I skewed it too much toward saying that answering is appropriate even when it would, you know, provide some kind of hints," she said. "And I think that that was wrong. I think that, in particular, it wouldn't be appropriate for me to talk about what I think about past cases—you know, to grade cases—because those cases themselves might again come before the court." In one respect, Kagan's 1995 article did anticipate the kind of justice she would become—because the bracing, colloquial writing style quickly showed up in her opinions.

The Kagan hearings were significant more for what the senators said than for what the nominee did. It was clear that originalism had become official Republican policy—an enormous achievement for Antonin Scalia, who essentially introduced the idea to the wider world only about two decades earlier. As Senator John Cornyn, of Texas, framed the issue, constitutional law amounted to a contest between "traditionalists" who feel bound "to a written Constitution and written laws and precedent" and judges who believe in "empathy, as the president has talked about it, or a living Constitution, which has no fixed meaning." Tom Coburn, of Oklahoma, said that any view of the Constitution except "original intent is going to give a lot of people in this country heartburn, because what it says is our intellectual capabilities are better than what our original founding documents were, and so we're so much smarter as we've matured that they couldn't have been right. And that's dangerous territory for confidence in the Court."

Like Obama himself, Kagan did little to fight back against these notions, but there was a cost to their silence. Left unrefuted, originalism began to look like the status quo. There was no one to say that an eighteenth-century document that embraced slavery, that ignored women, and that limited the right to vote was an imperfect guide in resolving contemporary problems. No one made the argument that it was impossible to determine precisely what the framers meant in every provision (or that they often disagreed with one another about what the words meant). No one said the Constitution's values might be as important as its specific words, or that the framers never wanted or expected later generations to honor their precise understanding of their words, or that the Supreme Court's own interpretations of those words over time had value, too. Instead, the field was left to the Cornyns and Coburns. For Kagan, it was safer to glide frictionlessly to confirmation. There was only one moment that anyone would remember from Kagan's hearing. In an awkward introduction to a question about the terrorism arrest of Umar Farouk Abdulmutallab on December 25, 2009, on a Northwest Airlines flight to Detroit, Lindsey Graham asked Kagan where she was on that Christmas Day. Kagan didn't understand the question at first, but then after Graham clarified it, she started laughing. "You know, like all Jews, I was probably at a Chinese restaurant," Kagan said. The answer brought down the house and may rank as the most famous utterance by a Supreme Court justice since 1964, when Potter Stewart gave this definition of hard-core pornography: "I know it when I see it."

On August 5, 2010, Kagan was confirmed by a vote of 63–37.

THE TEA PARTY AND
THE JUSTICE'S WIFE

The confirmation of Elena Kagan was just about the last piece of good news Barack Obama received in 2010. The legislative horse trading that was necessary to pass health care reform offended many voters. The oil spill at the Deepwater Horizon drilling rig in the Gulf of Mexico took many long weeks to control. Above all, the economy failed to improve. Most of the political energy in the country during the period belonged to the Tea Party.

In certain respects, the Tea Party merely reflected the contemporary Republican Party; it was antitaxation, antiregulation, and anti-abortion. But the Tea Party was distinctive in other ways. Initially, it was largely a grassroots movement prompted to action by a spontaneous cry from CNBC's Rick Santelli. On February 19, 2009, from the floor of the Chicago Mercantile Exchange, Santelli denounced Obama's mortgage assistance plan as "promoting bad behavior" and rewarding "the losers." He called for a Chicago Tea Party in July. From this spark, legions of conservatives began speaking out at town hall meetings held by members of Congress in their home districts. The protesters raised various issues at the meetings, but their most frequent target was Obama's health care reform plan.

The Tea Party remained a decentralized movement, without a single leader or platform, but it is possible to generalize about some of its distinctive qualities. Its partisans often spoke out against "elites," like the highly educated president and the similarly credentialed experts in his administration. Members of this movement thought they could understand the issues facing the country as well as anyone else. As Theda Skocpol and Vanessa Williamson observed in their broad study,

"Tea Party skepticism about experts is part and parcel of their direct approach to democracy, their belief in citizen activism." In particular, these activists thought they could interpret the Constitution better than the law professor president.

The Tea Party cared deeply about the Constitution. They passed out copies at rallies. They referred often to the Tenth Amendment (which refers to states' rights) and the commerce clause (which limits the scope of federal legislation) and cited Supreme Court decisions, often with derision. More than any other conservative movement of the last several decades, the Tea Party embraced a party line about the Constitution. Above all, Tea Party members were originalists, dedicated to restoring the modern government of the United States to the views, as they understood them, of the eighteenth-century framers. In this respect, the Tea Party reflected the broad triumph of originalism, which was also seen in the questions at Kagan's confirmation hearing. Originalism had not yet fully triumphed at the Supreme Court, but it had become the quasi-official legal theory of the Republican Party.

Many of the key figures in the Tea Party movement were fascinated, even obsessed, by the text of the Constitution and its origins in eighteenth-century Philadelphia. Glenn Beck, the radio and television personality who was initially the personification of the movement, talked incessantly about the Constitution and wrote a book called *The Original Argument: The Federalists' Case for the Constitution, Adapted for the 21st Century.* As Beck wrote:

What the Federalist Papers offer to us today is a guide to understanding the Founders' core constitutional principles, the theories behind their words, the whys, where, and how of the foundation of America:

- Why smaller government makes better government
- Where federal power ends and state power begins
- How government should be organized and operated to maximize efficiency and minimize the risk of another monarchy.

Mark R. Levin, a radio talk show host and lawyer and another Tea Party favorite, wrote a series of best sellers devoted to supposed liberal perfidies about the Constitution. His first, published in 2005, was called *Men in Black: How the Supreme Court Is Destroying America* and featured such chapters as "Al Qaeda Gets a Lawyer," "Socialism from the Bench," and "Liberals Stack the Bench." As soon as Obama was elected, Levin wrote *Liberty and Tyranny*, his most successful book, which included a paean to the *Lochner* era on the Supreme Court, when the justices repeatedly struck down social welfare legislation. To Levin and the Tea Party, small government was not just a policy preference but a constitutional command. Modern justices, and Obama himself, "are an arrogant lot who reject the nation's founding principles," Levin wrote. "They teach that the Constitution should not be interpreted as the Framers intended. . . . No literate person can comprehend the Fourteenth Amendment to mean what the [liberals] in academia claim it to mean." In the political arena, Michele Bachmann, the Minnesota congresswoman embraced by the Tea Party, often described herself as a "constitutional conservative"—as if the views of the movement were mandated by the Constitution itself.

In fact, the Tea Party version of originalism went well beyond anything most of the current justices believed. Tea Party partisans insisted, like the conservative justices of the 1930s, that the Constitution forbade the regulation of the national economy. They rejected decades of cases that called for at least some separation of church and state. They believed that power should be concentrated in the states, rather than the federal government, in defiance of Supreme Court precedents that went back a century. In short, the constitutional interpretations of the Tea Party conflicted with those of every Supreme Court justice who had served on the Court since World War II—except for one: Clarence Thomas.

On September 12, 2009, tens of thousands of opponents of Obama's agenda, especially his proposed health care reform, gathered in protest at the west front of the Capitol. FreedomWorks, the conservative organization led by Dick Armey, the former Republican leader of the House, helped organize the rally, and Armey was by that point an orchestrator, if not an actual leader, of the Tea Party movement. "Give me liberty or give me death," Armey told the crowd. "Well, Barack Obama is trying to make good on that."

The September 12 rally, and the Tea Party movement, had a transformative effect on the life of Virginia Lamp Thomas. Ginni Lamp grew up in Omaha, in a wealthy family prominent in Republican politics. She went to Creighton, in her hometown, for college and law school and moved to Washington to work for a Republican congressman, Hal Daub. In 1985, she moved to the United States Chamber of Commerce, where she fought regulations on businesses. At a conference on affirmative action sponsored by the Anti-Defamation League, Lamp met Clarence Thomas, who was then chairman of the EEOC in the Reagan administration. They married in May 1987.

During the Clinton administration, Ginni Thomas went to work for Armey, who was then the House majority leader under Speaker Newt Gingrich. Ginni was already a well-known figure in the conservative world. She was not a theoretician or a writer but an organizer, a connector of people with jobs and ideas. The work matched her temperament, which was outgoing and jovial. In 1998, she went to work at the Heritage Foundation, one of the leading conservative think tanks in Washington. Between George W. Bush's election in 2000 and his inauguration, Ginni was assigned the job of matching conservatives with political jobs in the new administration. She served as the think tank's liaison with the Bush White House.

Shortly before Obama won the presidency, Ginni Thomas took a position in Washington with Hillsdale College, a small liberal arts institution in rural Michigan. The school had no formal religious affiliation, but it had been described by the *National Review* as "a citadel of American conservatism." Thomas ran a speaker series for the college in Washington, called the Center for Constitutional Studies and Citizenship. After she was named to the post, she stated that Hillsdale students "always study our Western heritage, American history, and the Constitution. Maybe some of what they learn at Hillsdale will rub off." Thomas brought in conservative speakers on such subjects as "The Meaning and Intent of the Second Amendment" and "The Constitutional Roots of the Free Enterprise System." For her first three decades in Washington, Ginni Thomas was a behind-the-scenes player, her name known mostly by other conservatives in the capital.

But after the Tea Party's rally on September 12, 2009, Ginni Thomas took on, for her, an unprecedented public role as a fiery and outspoken leader in the conservative cause. She told Fox News that she decided to move to the front lines "because of the march on Washington on September 12th, and seeing and being inspired by the real people who came and spent their own money to get to Washington." She started Liberty

Central, a nonprofit at the forefront of conservative advocacy. According to tax records, it was funded by two donations: one of $500,000, the other of $50,000. Under then-current law, she was not obligated to disclose the identities of her contributors, and she never did so. Liberty Central had a website, but mostly the organization appeared to exist to support Ginni Thomas's travels.

Thomas spent much of 2010 on a coast-to-coast campaign against the Obama administration. As she said in an introductory video on her website, "If you believe in limited government, individual liberty, free enterprise, national security, and personal responsibility, and have felt these principles are under attack from Washington, then you've come to the right place." In a later interview, she said, "I've never seen, in my thirty years in Washington, an agenda that's so far left. It's a radical, leftist agenda that grabs a lot of power to Washington so that Washington elites can pick the winners and losers."

All who know Clarence and Ginni Thomas remark on the depth of their love for each other. They travel the country together, often in the large motor coach that the justice calls "the bus." He is a devoted football fan, and sometimes they go to see Dallas Cowboys games or those of the Nebraska Cornhuskers. (Justice Thomas adopted the team of his wife's home state.) On other occasions, they just set out and drive, usually stopping in Walmart parking lots, which allow such large vehicles to stay overnight.

The couple also share political views. In his own speeches, Justice Thomas expresses himself in terms similar to those of his wife. Answering questions at a law school in Florida, he said, "The government has to be limited, so you have separations of powers, and some of the other enumerated powers that prevent the government from becoming our ruler. I don't know if that's happened already." Ginni Thomas's contempt for "elites," which she shared with the Tea Party at large, also mirrored a theme in Justice Thomas's writings. Dissenting from O'Connor's opinion in *Grutter*, upholding the affirmative action program at the University of Michigan Law School, Thomas wrote, "All the Law School cares about is its own image among know-it-all elites." In a concurring opinion in *Parents Involved*, the 2007 case that invalidated school integration plans in Seattle and Louisville, he added, "If our history has taught us anything, it has taught us to beware of elites bearing racial theories." In his autobiography, he described the ordeal of his confirmation hearings as a time when "America's elites were arrogantly wreaking havoc on everything my grandparents had worked for and all I'd accomplished in forty-three years of struggle." More than any other justice, perhaps more than any other public figure, Clarence Thomas helped inspire the Tea Party movement.

For the Thomases and the Tea Party movement, there was one issue that defined their political views in the Obama era: opposition to the president's health care reform plan.

Health care reform was a major issue in the presidential election of 2008. Until Lehman Brothers failed, the candidates talked about health care more than any other issue. It was one of the few areas of substantive disagreement between Hillary Clinton and Obama, and it came up often in the many debates between the two. Clinton supported an individual mandate—a requirement that all Americans purchase health insurance, with government subsidies for those who could not afford it on their own. Obama opposed the mandate, pointing out in a television advertisement before the Pennsylvania primary: "What's she not telling you about her health care plan? It forces everyone to buy insurance, even if you can't afford it. And you pay a penalty if you don't."

Once Obama locked up the nomination, however, his view changed. As the Princeton scholar Paul Starr reported in his account of the health care battle, Obama recognized that the insurance industry would not cooperate in the reform process unless there was a mandate. Obama understood that the government could not force insurers to accept individuals with preexisting conditions unless the risk pool included virtually every American; he needed an individual mandate to make the numbers work. As Obama told Neera Tanden, the longtime Clinton adviser who became Obama's campaign policy director for the general election, "I kind of think Hillary was right."

So when Obama and senior Democrats unveiled their health care reform ideas, shortly after the election, they all included an individual mandate. It was the heart of the plan, and as during the primaries, the proposal was intensely controversial. Conservatives stated that the plan amounted to a "government takeover" of health care. The issue dominated American politics well into the summer of 2009.

But the most significant aspect of the debate was something that was never said. Although the individual mandate had been a matter of major public controversy for two years, *no one suggested that the proposal was unconstitutional.* Not a single public figure raised the issue. No one wrote an op-ed piece; no one in Congress gave a speech on the subject. Of course, the Obama plan was opposed with great passion. Thousands of people, including some of the best political and legal minds in the country, devoted their professional lives to defeating the Obama plan. Yet not one of them came up with the argument that the plan was unconstitutional.

That silence is significant. If there had been a plausible argument that Obama's plan (or Clinton's plan) for an individual mandate was unconstitutional, it stands to reason that *someone* would have mentioned it during those many months. No one did. The reason was obvious. The federal government had a long and intimate regulatory connection to the health care industry. Medicare and Medicaid were central parts of Lyndon Johnson's Great Society, and there had been no doubt of their constitutionality for decades. Obamacare, as some called it, was simply an extension of this well-established federal role.

Furthermore, the individual mandate had been a central part of health care proposals for many years, often from conservative sources. The idea first came to wide public attention in 1989, when it was proposed in a plan sponsored by the conservative Heritage Foundation. For many years, Newt Gingrich himself supported the individual mandate. In 1993, he said on *Meet the Press,* "I am for people, individuals—exactly like automobile insurance—individuals having health insurance and being required to have health insurance." He repeated his support for the idea as recently as 2005. Gingrich never suggested the idea—his idea—was unconstitutional. In 2006, Governor Mitt Romney used the individual mandate as the centerpiece of his health care reform plan for Massachusetts—also without controversy about its constitutionality.

Finally, though, as the debate about Obama's plan reached its crescendo, someone came up with the constitutional argument. Peter Urbanowicz had been deputy general counsel of the Department of Health and Human Services under George W. Bush, and during the summer of 2009, he was a health care consultant in Washington. Following the debate in the press, he realized there was an angle that he thought had been neglected. Working with Dennis G. Smith, a former colleague at HHS who now worked for the Heritage Foundation, he decided to write up his thoughts for the Federalist Society website.

The two authors posted "Constitutional Implications of an 'Individual Mandate' in Health Care Reform" on July 10, 2009, asserting that "this individual mandate, if passed, would be an unprecedented federal directive that might call into question the constitutionality of such an action under Congress's taxation or interstate commerce 'regulatory' authority."

The Federalist Society article was written in three thousand carefully chosen, lawyerly words, but the effect on the health care debate was electric. David B. Rivkin Jr. and Lee A. Casey, who had worked in the Reagan and George H. W. Bush administrations, wrote an op-ed piece in *The Washington Post* translating the Urbanowicz-Smith article into more colloquial language. Randy Barnett, a law professor at Georgetown, soon became the public face of the argument that Obama's proposal was unconstitutional. Republican members of Congress added this objection to their bill of particulars against the individual mandate.

But no one made the case against Obama's plan with greater passion than Virginia Thomas.

In February 2010, Virginia Thomas said: "We all know we're at a big fight in our historical times and I wanted to join a lot of you on the front line. I've been with think tanks, and I've been behind the scenes, but I do want to partner with the Tea Party movement and the people we can find there who have all the right instincts." In March, Obama signed the health care law. In April, Ginni Thomas stated: "Let me tell you, there's a war going on, and Washington wants to make it look real complicated, real technical. It's not so complicated, it's not so technical. . . . You know what it comes down to? Are we gonna be self-governed by a Constitution that starts with 'we the people,' or are we gonna be ruled by elitists who want to govern our cradle-to-grave lives?" On Fox News, in May, Ginni added: "The audacity of power grabbing that I'm seeing right now in cap-and-trade, health care, the stimulus plan, it's corrupt. It's a big power grab. It's picking winners and losers from Washington; it's abhorrent to our founding principles." At the Steamboat Institute in Colorado, in August, she said: "We need a constitutional audit to help set up a system where Congress can reconsider different functions, and programs, and agencies. . . . I think we need a big spending reduction and no new taxes. . . . I think we need to repeal Obamacare." In Florida, noting her support for Republicans running for office in the midterm elections, she claimed, "We support the more constitutionally inclined candidate."

On occasion, especially in television interviews, Ginni was asked about her husband's view of her activities. At a Dallas appearance, she said, "My husband and I do really different things, by the way, but there was a tornado over our wedding when we got married. God knew that we were both troublemakers coming together. I do policy, he does law, and I don't understand that world and I'm glad God didn't tell me to do that, because I don't know how to do that." Justice Thomas, too, often drew the same law-versus-policy distinction when he was questioned about his wife's work. Actually, both Thomases overstated Ginni's ignorance about legal matters. After all, she was a lawyer, and she, too, invariably invoked the Constitution as the authority for smaller government.

As the midterm campaign of 2010 built toward its climax, Ginni Thomas's activities became so prominent that she drew some journalistic scrutiny. On Saturday, October 9, the *New York Times* ran a front-page story headlined "Activism of Thomas's Wife Could Raise Judicial Issues," which was a straightforward account of Ginni's political campaign.

At 7:31 that morning, Ginni decided to make a phone call.

THE THOMAS COURT

The Clarence Thomas–Anita Hill hearings remain one of the great set pieces of recent American history. Even two decades later, the facts are familiar. Anita Hill, also a graduate of Yale Law School, worked on Thomas's staff at the Department of Education and then at the Equal Employment Opportunity Commission. According to her testimony, Thomas made a series of crude advances to her, which included references to pornographic movies starring Long Dong Silver and utterances like "Who has put pubic hair on my Coke?" Thomas denied her allegations categorically and denounced the hearings as a "high-tech lynching for uppity blacks who in any way deign to think for themselves." On October 15, 1991, Thomas was confirmed in the Senate by a vote of 52–48.

Neither the Judiciary Committee nor any other government office has seen fit to reexamine the controversy, although a good deal of evidence has since emerged about the protagonists and their testimony. Near the end of the hearings, several other women who had worked for Thomas were prepared to corroborate Hill's testimony that Thomas had a history of making female subordinates uncomfortable with personal and sexual talk. The group included Angela Wright, Rose Jourdain, and Sukari Hardnett; other associates of Thomas's, among them Kaye Savage and Fred Cooke, would have sworn to the nominee's long-standing interest in pornography, again corroborating Hill's account. But Joseph Biden, then the chairman of the Judiciary Committee, decided not to call these witnesses. In 2011, Lillian McEwen, a Washington lawyer who had a long-term romantic relationship with Thomas before he met Ginni, published a memoir, *D.C. Unmasked & Undressed*. She, too, remarked on the justice's "strong interest in pornography." She also said that Thomas had designated certain colleagues as prospective sexual partners. In short, virtually all the evidence that has emerged since the hearings corroborated Hill's testimony.

Over the last twenty years, Clarence and Ginni Thomas built their lives away from such troubling reminders. They conducted their social and political lives in protected spaces. Ginni made many speeches, but only in front of supportive conservative crowds. Justice Thomas spoke at law schools and Federalist Society events, where he generally received a warm welcome. In Washington, the couple was a pillar of the conservative movement, socially as well as professionally. They threw parties at their home for like-minded friends and acquaintances. The Thomases hosted at their home, and the justice officiated at, the third wedding of Rush Limbaugh. (Thomas attended, but did not preside at, Wedding No. 4.) Other friends included the radio talk show host Mark Levin. Thomas was also close to Harlan Crow, a Dallas business-man and supporter of conservative causes who funded a museum in Thomas's hometown of Pin Point, Georgia. According to *Politico*, it was Crow who made the $500,000 contribution to Liberty Central, Ginni's Tea Party organization. Justice Thomas apparently spoke to a Federalist Society event that was part of the conference of conservative funders sponsored by Charles and David Koch, who are leading benefactors of the Tea Party movement. In addition, the justice was also a regular at Bohemian Grove, the annual all-male conclave in Northern California. In his social life, Thomas clearly differed from his frequent ally Scalia, who was well known for his friendship with Ginsburg, his ideological opposite and a fellow opera buff. ("I'm not really a Washington-type person," Thomas said at a law school appearance. "I don't sort of like hanging out at the opera and that sort of thing.") Even in the current highly polarized political environment, many members of Congress shared friendships across the aisle. But the Thomases chose to live in a bubble where everyone believed Thomas had told the truth in 1991. In fact, Ginni may have thought everyone else did, too.

All of which may explain her telephone call on October 9, 2010. At 7:31 a.m., she left a voice mail for Anita Hill, at her office at Brandeis University, where Hill teaches. "Anita Hill, it's Ginni Thomas. I just wanted to reach across the airwaves and the years and ask you to con-sider something. I would love you to consider an apology sometime and some full explanation of why you did what you did with my husband." She went on: "So give it some thought. And certainly pray about this and hope that one day you will help us understand why you did what you did. O.K., have a good day."

Hill reported the call to the Brandeis police, and its contents soon leaked to the press. News of the bizarre voice mail revived interest in the Thomas-Hill matter, which had been dormant for years; much of the publicity noted the abundant evidence that Hill, not the future justice, told the truth at the hearing. Many in the media mocked Ginni's phone call. In an interview with the Daily Caller, a conservative website for which she later became a "special correspondent," she insisted her voice mail was "a private matter" that was "probably a mistake on my part."

The controversy, especially the ridicule of his wife, took a toll on Justice Thomas, as he made clear in an emotional appearance at a Federalist Society event at the University of Virginia School of Law, in February 2011. "This is about our country, and one of the things I want to do is I want to go to my grave knowing that I gave everything I have to trying to get it right. And all I ask of you all, especially those of you who are still in school, is you give it your best," Thomas said. "I watch my bride who, in doing the same things, when she started her organization, she gives it 24/7 every day, in defense of liberty. You know, and maybe that's why we're equally young and we love being with each other because we love the same things; we believe in the same things. So, with my wife and the people around me what I see unreinforced is that we are focused on defending liberty. So, I admire her and I love her for that because it keeps me going." In conclusion, he said, "My bride is with me, Virginia Thomas, and some of you may know her. But the reason that I specifically bring it up: there is a price to pay today for standing in defense of your Constitution."

For those whose picture of Thomas remains frozen at the time of his confirmation hearings more than two decades ago, the justice today is a startling sight. His jet-black hair is almost completely white. He has gained a great deal of weight. (An injury long ago ended his days on the basketball court.) His gait is weary, and he looks older than his sixty-five years.

To the broad general public, Thomas was largely known only for two things. The first, of course, was the drama of his showdown regarding Hill. The second was his silence on the bench. Thomas last asked a question during oral argument in February 2006. No justice in the modern history of the Court has gone as long as a single year without asking a question; Thomas is well into his seventh consecutive year. In his public appearances, Thomas has often been asked about his silence; sometimes he has brought it up himself. Over time he has refined his answer, usually saying that he thinks the other justices ask too many questions and that the lawyers should be given a chance to speak for a time without interruption. At an appearance at a Hillsdale College dinner in Washington, in 2007, he said, "My colleagues should shut up!" At a law school talk in 2010, Thomas was asked what might change his mind about a case. "If my colleagues would let me talk," he said with a small laugh, then added, "assuming that improbability."

Thomas had a point. During his tenure on the Court, the other justices became notably more aggressive, and lawyers sometimes had trouble getting a word in edgewise. Even the chief justice, at an appearance in West Virginia in 2011, expressed the view that he and his colleagues might be talking and interrupting too much. "I am probably one of the prime offenders," Roberts said. Obviously, though, Thomas's reaction to this problem was extreme. He would certainly be allowed to ask questions if he tried.

What made his silence even more peculiar was his behavior in the courtroom, especially in recent years. The justices all sit in high-backed leather swivel chairs, and Thomas set his so that he can recline so far that he appears almost to be lying down. He stares at the ceiling. He rubs his face. He does not appear to be listening. He closes his eyes and looks as if he has fallen asleep. The overall effect is rude, if not contemptuous.

The conventional view of Thomas is that he is silent because he has nothing to say. Many believe that he is just a cipher for his fellow originalist, Scalia. Others think Thomas is not up to the job.

This stereotype is wrong in every particular.

In 1993, during the early days of the Clinton administration, Congress passed the gun control law known as the Brady bill. The complex piece of legislation included an interim provision that directed state and local officials to conduct background checks for prospective handgun purchasers. That portion of the bill was challenged, and in 1997, by a vote of 5–4, the Court found that part of the law unconstitutional. Scalia's opinion for the Court in *Printz v. United States* concluded that the law amounted to an impermissible federal intrusion on states' rights.

Thomas joined Scalia's opinion for the majority but wrote a concurring opinion that examined the case in a different way. Thomas devoted his opinion to the Second Amendment, which had not been addressed by the Supreme Court since the *Miller* case in 1939; the parties in *Printz* had not raised a Second Amendment claim at any stage of the proceedings. But Thomas used the case to undertake an extensive discussion of the Second Amendment and to suggest that the Brady bill might well be unconstitutional because the "right to keep and bear arms" is "a personal right."

In his *Printz* opinion, Thomas caught—and propelled—the intellectual wave that was building for a new understanding of the Second Amendment. His prominent endorsement of the individual rights theory spurred other judges, as well as academics and politicians, to take that view more seriously. The judges who embraced it in the *Emerson* case in the Fifth Circuit cited Thomas's opinion. Robert Levy and his colleagues who created the *Heller* case were also inspired, in part, by Thomas. In time, even Barack Obama followed Thomas's lead on this issue. It took eleven years for the full Court to embrace Thomas's interpretation of the Second Amendment. In 2008, Scalia wrote the opinion for the Court in *Heller*—which struck down the D.C. gun control law and adopted the new view of the Second Amendment—but it was Thomas who first put the issue on the Court's agenda.

He has played this role—as conservative intellectual pathbreaker—in many areas of the law. His hostility to campaign finance regulation, and his First Amendment absolutism, anticipated *Citizens United*. Like his intellectual heirs in the Tea Party, Thomas had a special hostility for government attempts to level the playing field in the political arena. For this justice, the Constitution mandated laissez-faire government. He first laid out his views on free speech in *McIntyre v. Ohio Elections Commission*, a case early in his tenure. In 1988, Margaret McIntyre distributed unsigned leaflets at public meetings in a small town in Ohio. According to Ohio election laws, she was required to put her name on any material she distributed, and McIntyre was ultimately fined a hundred dollars for breaking this rule. In a 1995 opinion by Stevens for a seven-justice majority, the Court overturned the fine as a violation of McIntyre's right to free speech. For the Court, Stevens weighed the interest of the state in protecting the integrity of campaigns versus the individual's right to express herself and concluded that the state's restrictions went too far.

Thomas wrote a concurring opinion that laid out a template that he and to some extent the Court have followed ever since. The opinion was an originalist tour de force, with extensive discussion of anonymous speech as conceived by the framers of the Constitution. "In light of the Framers' universal practice of publishing anonymous articles and pamphlets," Thomas wrote, it was clear "that the Framers shared the belief that such activity was firmly part of the freedom of the press. It is only an innovation of modern times that has permitted the regulation of anonymous speech."

Thomas believed that the First Amendment prohibited regulation of campaign advertising, contributions, or expenditures. He put his position clearly in a dissent to a decision, in 2000, that upheld a Missouri law that limited individual contributions to local campaigns to a total of $1,075. "In my view, the Constitution leaves it entirely up to citizens and candidates to determine who shall speak, the means they will use, and the amount of speech sufficient to inform and persuade," he wrote.

By 2010, in *Citizens United*, the opinion was Kennedy's, but the victory was Thomas's. Kennedy adopted several Thomas tropes—that corporations and people have the same rights to free speech under the First Amendment and that limitations on expenditures amounted to limitations on speech. Remarkably, Thomas wanted more. Kennedy's opinion upheld the rule that directed corporations and others to disclose how much they had contributed to political campaigns; Thomas said such rules amounted to an unlawful intrusion on the First Amendment. Returning to a theme first expressed in *McIntyre* fifteen years earlier, Thomas said, in a separate opinion in *Citizens United*, that the First Amendment protected anonymity as much as speech itself. Ever alert to contemporary conservative political developments as much as to eighteenth-century history, Thomas asserted that harassment of contributors to Proposition 8 in California, which banned same-sex marriage in 2008, demonstrated the dangers of mandatory disclosures. "These instances of retaliation sufficiently demonstrate why this Court should invalidate mandatory disclosure and reporting requirements," he wrote. On this issue, Thomas had not persuaded a majority of his colleagues—yet.

He was not a conventionally influential justice. Unlike, say, Kennedy or O'Connor (or Roberts or Stevens), Thomas wrote few important opinions for the Court. Rehnquist and later Roberts recognized that Thomas's views were so extreme that they could not assign controversial opinions to him and expect a majority of his colleagues to agree. Rather, Thomas's influence was that he introduced new ideas to his colleagues. Through sheer doggedness and, of course, the arrival of like-minded justices, especially Roberts and Alito, Thomas saw his views (if not his exact words) pass into law.

He relished outraging his ideological adversaries. His views on the Eighth Amendment's ban on cruel and unusual punishment remained so eccentric that they found little favor even on this more conservative Court. In 2008, in *Baze v. Rees*, a badly splintered Court upheld lethal injection as a method of execution. In the lead opinion for the Court, Roberts said that the evidence in the case showed that lethal injection was not "cruelly inhumane" and thus not a violation of the Eighth Amendment.

Thomas concurred, in an opinion that read like a treatment for a slasher movie. As always, he began by asserting that the relevant constitutional provision must be "understood in light of the historical practices that led the Framers to include it in the Bill of Rights." To that end, Thomas surveyed eighteenth-century executions that were, apparently, cruel and unusual even in those days. There was burning at the stake, " 'gibbeting,' or hanging the condemned in an iron cage so that his body would decompose in public view, and 'public dissection.' " Thomas went on, "But none of these was the worst fate a criminal could meet. That was reserved for the most dangerous and reprobate offenders—traitors." Their punishments involved "embowelling alive, beheading, and quartering." One death sentence in England called for the condemned to be "drawn on a hurdle to the place of execution, where you shall be hanged by the necks, not till you are dead; that you be severally taken down, while yet alive, and your bowels be taken out and burnt before your faces—that your heads be then cut off, and your bodies cut in four quarters."

The point of this grotesque catalogue was to assert that the Eighth

Amendment prohibited methods of execution that were also forms of torture—nothing more. Such a standard meant that Thomas ignored decades of precedent. Over the years, the Court had vetoed the imposition of "hard and painful labor," rejected disproportionate sentences for minor crimes, abolished the death penalty for rape, and outlawed life sentences for juveniles convicted of crimes other than murder. Under Thomas's narrow reading of the Eighth Amendment, all these cases would be wrong; under his understanding of stare decisis, all would be overturned.

It is Thomas's approach to stare decisis—the rule of precedent—that most distinguished Thomas from his colleagues, even Scalia. "You have to remember that we are the court of last resort," he told the students at the recent speech in Florida. "I always ask people, 'What would you do with *Plessy v. Ferguson*, which was sixty years old?'" That case, from 1896, affirmed the racial doctrine of separate but equal, until it was effectively overruled by *Brown v. Board of Education* in 1954. "If it's wrong, the ultimate precedent is the Constitution. And it's not what we say it is, it's what it actually says, and I think we have to be humble enough to say we were wrong," Thomas said.

All justices would like to see some precedents overturned, and certainly, in the modern era, all agree that the Court was right to overturn *Plessy* in *Brown*. Thomas differed with his colleagues in the sheer number of cases he wanted to overturn. He paid far less deference to prior rulings than anyone else on the Court. As he said, "If it's wrong, it's wrong, and we are obligated to revisit it."

This is a different approach from the traditional conservative position, which stressed the importance of stare decisis—of relying on precedent. As Roberts put it during his confirmation hearings, "Adherence to precedent promotes evenhandedness, promotes fairness, promotes stability and predictability. And those are very important values in a legal system." (Whether Roberts, as chief justice, actually honored that sentiment was another question.) Thomas, though, made little pretense of relying on the words of his colleagues and his predecessors when their interpretations conflicted with his own understanding of the Constitution's text.

From the moment he arrived on the Court, he was a committed originalist; he believed the Constitution should be interpreted as the words were understood by the men who wrote it. "When faced with a clash of constitutional principle and a line of unreasoned cases wholly divorced from the text, history, and structure of our founding document, we should not hesitate to resolve the tension in favor of the Constitution's original meaning," Thomas wrote in an opinion from 2005. Scalia was the figure most often associated with this school of thought, but he referred to himself as a "fainthearted originalist." Scalia meant that other factors besides his own understanding of the intent of the framers, especially the long-established precedents of the Court, influenced his resolution of constitutional disputes. "If a constitutional line of authority is wrong, Thomas would say let's get it right," Scalia told a reporter in 2004. "I wouldn't do that. He does not believe in stare decisis, period." In other words, there is nothing fainthearted about Thomas's convictions about the meaning of the Constitution. His understanding of the framers' intent trumps everything.

Thomas's approach to the Eighth Amendment underlined some of the problems with his approach to the Constitution, and with originalism. Only two justices, Thomas and Scalia, built their jurisprudence around originalism (one of them faintheartedly), so its full adoption would require the trashing of dozens, if not hundreds, of Court precedents. Further, notwithstanding Thomas's enduring certainties, it was difficult to know what the framers would have thought of any given situation in the modern world. (Alito, a conservative but not a full-fledged originalist, captured this problem nicely in the oral argument about a California law on violent video games. Following up on a series of questions by Scalia, Alito said to the lawyer, "I think what Justice Scalia wants to know is what James Madison thought about video games. Did he enjoy them?") It was true, too, that the framers often disagreed profoundly with one another, making a single intent behind any constitutional text even more difficult to discern. The twenty-seven amendments (each with its own framers) created another overlay of opinion. For all of Thomas's conviction, originalism was just another kind of interpretation, revealing as much about Thomas as about the framers' intentions.

Ginni Thomas's outspoken criticism of Obama, and especially his health care plan, prompted a new round of questions about Justice

Thomas's ethics. Based on Ginni's activities, seventy-four members of Congress called on Thomas to recuse himself from any legal challenges to the health care law. To make matters worse, he was compelled to amend several years of the financial disclosure forms that Supreme Court justices must file each year. The document requires the justices to disclose the source of all income earned by their spouses. Thomas failed to list Ginni's work for Hillsdale College and at the Heritage Foundation.

The Supreme Court operates in a peculiar ethical netherworld. The federal statute governing judicial conflicts of interest covers only lower-court judges. On the question of recusal, the law is clear that such a decision is entirely up to Thomas; the Supreme Court basically operates on an honor system. The tradition among the justices has been to avoid recusal if at all possible. Recusals at the Supreme Court raise the distasteful possibility of 4–4 ties, because, unlike in the lower courts, there is no mechanism for bringing in substitute judges.

Thomas was clearly within his rights to ignore calls for his recusal in the health care case. Ginni Thomas had been a political activist for decades, even before she met Clarence Thomas. This was her job; she was not obliged to quit because her husband became a judge. The Thomas family had no obvious or direct financial stake in the outcome of the health care case. The attempt to drive Thomas off the case was politically motivated. Democrats perceived Thomas as hostile to the health care law and thus tried to get rid of his vote. (To Thomas's good fortune, the leader of the effort was Representative Anthony Weiner, who was soon forced to resign because of a sex scandal.) As for Thomas's failure to list Ginni's employment on the disclosure forms, the error seemed sloppy rather than sinister. Her work was widely known, and, in any event, the law did not establish a punishment for mistaken filings.

If Ginni's activities did not disqualify her husband from the case, they were still extremely significant—and highly complementary to Justice Thomas's agenda on the bench. In their own ways, Ginni and Clarence Thomas helped build the intellectual infrastructure opposing President Obama's agenda. Ginni did her best to derail the health care plan when it came up for a vote in Congress. Justice Thomas had his chance when the law came before the Supreme Court. Even more than gun control and campaign regulation, the health care case reflected the issues at the core of Thomas's judicial career.

Early in the New Deal, the Supreme Court struck down several of President Roosevelt's signature initiatives as violating the commerce clause of the Constitution. If the law did not directly affect commerce "among the several states," in the words of Article I, the Court said that Congress had no right to pass it. FDR responded to these setbacks with his infamous court-packing plan, but a change of heart by Justice Owen J. Roberts in 1937, followed by Roosevelt's own appointments to the Court, transformed the understanding of that provision. In a series of cases, the justices gave Congress essentially unlimited power to regulate the national economy. In 1942, the Court said in *Wickard v. Filburn* that the federal government could regulate the amount of wheat grown on a farm, even if none of the wheat was sold across state lines, or even if no wheat was sold at all. The opinion stated that since the production of wheat, taken in aggregate, did affect interstate commerce, the regulation was permissible. After that, the issue of the commerce clause more or less vanished from the Supreme Court's docket for decades—until Thomas and the Tea Party brought it back to life.

Tea Party partisans embraced the ideas of the pre–New Deal Court and rejected *Wickard* and the decades of decisions that followed. As the journalist Kate Zernike wrote in her book *Boiling Mad: Inside Tea Party America*, "In the originalist view, and the Tea Party view, the perversion of the Constitution took off during the presidency of Franklin Delano Roosevelt."

On this issue, as ever, Thomas led where the conservative movement soon followed. In 1995, the Court, in an opinion by Chief Justice Rehnquist, finally struck down a law as violating the commerce clause. In *United States v. Lopez*, the Court rejected legislation that made it a crime to possess a gun near a school. Rehnquist's opinion said, in essence, that mere possession of a gun in or near a school was so totally unconnected to the national economy that Congress had no right to prohibit it.

Thomas agreed—and then some. In a concurring opinion, he said, "I write separately to observe that our case law has drifted far from the original understanding of the Commerce Clause. In a future case, we ought to temper our Commerce Clause jurisprudence." Even Rehnquist had acknowledged the long line of cases that said the commerce clause was satisfied if the activity in question "substantially affects" interstate commerce. In his characteristically lengthy and detailed opinion, Thomas also said that the early New Deal Court—which was nicknamed the Nine Old Men—was right, and all the justices over the following six decades were wrong. "From the time of the ratification of the Constitution to the mid 1930's, it was widely understood that the Constitution granted Congress only limited powers, notwithstanding the Commerce Clause," he wrote. If a majority of the justices agreed with Thomas, Social Security and the National Labor Relations Act, to say nothing of Medicare and Medicaid, might all be unconstitutional.

On March 23, 2010, President Obama signed his health care law, which was formally known as the Patient Protection and Affordable Care Act, or ACA. That same day, Kenneth Cuccinelli, the attorney general of Virginia, filed the first of many legal challenges to the law. Federal judges around the nation began passing judgment on the constitutionality of "Obamacare." One of the first, and certainly the harshest, verdicts came from Judge Roger Vinson, of the federal district court in Pensacola. He struck down the law in its entirety, relying several times on Thomas's concurring opinion in *Lopez*. Vinson said that the Obama administration's position would allow the federal government to "penetrate the recesses of domestic life, and control, in all respects, the private conduct of individuals." These words, of course, would have fit just as well in a speech by Ginni Thomas as in an opinion by her husband.

20

"DEMOCRACY IS NOT A GAME"

On November 2, 2010, Republicans routed Democrats in the midterm elections. The GOP won control of the House of Representatives, with a gain of sixty-three seats, and cut the Democrats' margin in the Senate to fifty-three to forty-seven. The results amounted to a repudiation of Obama's agenda.

The following morning, the justices heard an archetypical case of the Roberts era. It provided a chance for the Court to lower the barrier between church and state, and to use a procedural device to do so. A state law in Arizona gave tax credits to individuals who paid tuition at parochial schools. A group of local taxpayers challenged the law, asserting that the credits amounted to government financial support of religion, in violation of the First Amendment. The specific issue in *Arizona Christian School Tuition Organization v. Winn* was whether the taxpayers had standing even to challenge the law. This was another challenge to a conservative bête noire: Chief Justice Warren's famous 1968 opinion in *Flast v. Cohen,* which held that taxpayers had the right to challenge actions that they believed amounted to government support of religion, in violation of the First Amendment.

Arizona Christian was the right's latest chance to cut back on *Flast*. In the oral argument, Anthony Kennedy sounded like a Tea Party protester: "I must say, I have some difficulty that any money that the government doesn't take from me is still the government's money." The result in the case was predictable—a 5–4 ruling that the taxpayers lacked standing to bring the suit. There were still only four liberals, but now two of them were new to the Court—and that, inevitably, changed the interpersonal dynamics for all nine justices.

Except when deciding cases, the Supreme Court operated somewhat like a university faculty. As dean, the chief justice established committees to allow the other justices to participate in the administrative business of the Court. The most coveted of these assignments was the building committee, because the justices took understandable pride in the beauty and durability of Cass Gilbert's marble masterpiece. On that committee, O'Connor and Souter fought for years to keep garish fire exit signs out of the corridors. Kennedy also dueled with the architect of the Capitol over the egregious congressional visitor center, which wrecked the vista between the Court and the Capitol. Thomas, a computer buff, enjoyed his tenure on the technology committee.

There was no doubt about the least desirable assignment. One justice always had to serve on the cafeteria committee, which dealt with the windowless and forlorn diner-style restaurant located in the Court's basement. By tradition, this assignment went to the junior justice. Because Breyer spent eleven years with the least seniority, he put in the most time on cafeteria matters. In his characteristically earnest way, Breyer spearheaded the introduction of wrap sandwiches, which he remembered fondly from the courthouse cafeteria in Boston. He mediated conflicts in matters of social class; Supreme Court police officers wanted meatloaf and mashed potatoes, while the law clerks demanded tofu. To address the persistent deficits generated by the enterprise, Breyer tried, with mixed success, to arrange for tour groups to be deposited within tempting distance of the cafeteria.

Kagan, now the newest justice, took another approach. Just as she brought a food-and-fun philosophy to Harvard Law School, she tried a similar experiment at the Supreme Court: she engineered the acquisition of a frozen yogurt machine in the cafeteria. It was perhaps testimony to the dour nature of life at the Supreme Court that such a modest enhancement was so celebrated. Even Roberts took to saluting Kagan's frosty coup in his speeches.

Kagan, who sometimes referred to herself as the Frozen Yogurt Justice, made her presence felt in more jurisprudentially significant ways as well, in large part thanks to her relationship with Ginsburg. It was perhaps predetermined that Ginsburg would adopt Kagan as a protégée.

Both were secular Jews from New York City who spent much of their lives as law professors. Ginsburg's daughter, Jane, who was five years older than Kagan, was also a law professor at Columbia. And Kagan, unlike Jane, was ebullient and outgoing, like Marty Ginsburg, whose death roughly coincided with Kagan's arrival. Ruth Ginsburg made Kagan her frequent date for the opera. For her part, Kagan kept her word to the senators and volunteered to go shooting with Scalia. To her surprise, she liked the guns (as well as Scalia), returned for more, and quickly graduated from clay pigeons to actual birds. The opera soon paled in comparison.

Now that Ginsburg had replaced Stevens as the senior justice on the liberal side, she had the responsibility for assigning the main dissenting opinions when the Court split in its predictable fashion. She gave *Arizona Christian* to Kagan, and here the Court saw for the first time what kind of justice Kagan would be in the way that mattered most—her writing. Kagan's voice was straightforward and colloquial, almost chatty. In her dissent, she assailed the supposed distinction the Court drew between a state giving tax credits (permissible) and direct subsidies (impermissible) to religious schools. "Suppose a State desires to reward Jews—by, say, $500 per year—for their religious devotion," Kagan wrote. "Should the nature of taxpayers' concern vary if the State allows Jews to claim the aid on their tax returns, in lieu of receiving an annual stipend? Or assume a State wishes to subsidize the ownership of crucifixes. It could purchase the religious symbols in bulk and distribute them to all takers. Or it could mail a reimbursement check to any individual who buys her own and submits a receipt for the purchase. Or it could authorize that person to claim a tax credit equal to the price she paid. Now, really—do taxpayers have less reason to complain if the State selects the last of these three options? The Court today says they do, but that is wrong." Later, she wrote: "I count 14 separate cases (involving 20 appellate and district courts) that adjudicated taxpayer challenges to tax expenditures alleged to violate the Establishment Clause. I suspect I have missed a few."

It was entertaining reading, but as a dissenting opinion that was all it was. In the Court's current configuration, Kagan could look forward to writing a lot more of them.

Alito, on the other hand, quickly established himself as an influential player in the conservative majority. On the big issues—civil rights, *Citizens United*, gun control—Alito was a reliable vote for the Roberts team, although there were differences, too, in his approach. Scalia and Thomas had a libertarian streak, especially in First Amendment cases, but Alito hewed to the more authoritarian tradition on the American right. In this way, Alito resembled Rehnquist more than Roberts.

While Scalia and Thomas seemed obsessed with the eighteenth-century world of the framers and Roberts channeled the corporate priorities of the Republican establishment, Alito had a different focus: the 1960s counterculture. When he came to Washington in 2006, Alito had a nearly invisible public profile, but he reinvented himself there as a culture warrior. Alito made speeches before groups like the Intercollegiate Studies Institute, a student leadership organization dedicated to "teaching future leaders the timeless principles that make America free and prosperous—the core ideas behind the free market, the American Founding, and Western civilization that are rarely taught in the classroom." Likewise, Alito spoke at a fund-raiser for the *American Spectator* magazine, a right-wing outlet best known for its attacks on Anita Hill and investigations of Bill Clinton's sex life.

In his speech, Alito joked that the *Spectator* was the "very center of the vast right-wing conspiracy," but that was actually a pretty apt description. Alito divided the country into two worlds—that of the conservatives' hero Ronald Reagan and that of liberals and their law schools. (The justice also repeatedly mocked Vice President Biden for an act of plagiarism he had committed many years earlier.) Alito juxtaposed the first "be-in" in San Francisco with the inauguration of Ronald Reagan as governor. "On October 26, 1967, John McCain's plane was shot down over North Vietnam," Alito said. "On November 30, Eugene McCarthy announced that he would seek the Democratic presidential nomination, promising to restore hope and bring about change," he continued—to much knowing laughter at the allusion to Barack Obama's 2008 slogan. (Like the other justices, Alito was not bound by formal ethical rules. But if he had still been a lower-court judge, his speech to raise money for the *Spectator* would have been inappropriate. In any case, Alito's behavior was more dubious than anything Thomas did, even though Thomas received a great deal more attention and criticism.)

Alito's aversion to anything-goes libertarianism was especially evident in his approach to cases involving free speech. Over the years, debates about vulgar or unpopular speech provided the grist for some of the Court's most famous and controversial decisions. But under Roberts, the Court reached a consensus that the government had little or no power to regulate in this area. Two cases proved the point. In 2010, the justices struck down a federal law that prohibited the sale of "crush videos"—which show small animals, often woodland creatures, being killed with a woman's bare foot or stiletto heel. The Court said Congress could ban the torture itself, but a limit on *depictions* of such behavior amounted to a violation of free speech. In a similar vein, the Court in 2011 overturned a multimillion-dollar judgment against members of the Westboro Baptist Church in Topeka, a fringe religious group with fanatically antigay views, for protesting at the funeral of a marine killed in Iraq. Because the protest took place on public land, well out of sight or hearing of funeral attendees, the Court said the damage award violated free speech rights.

Both decisions were 8–1, with only Alito in dissent. In the "crush" case, Alito, who owns a springer spaniel named Zeus, lingered over the horrific details of the videos. For example: "A kitten, secured to the ground, watches and shrieks in pain as a woman thrusts her high-heeled shoe into its body, slams her heel into the kitten's eye socket and mouth loudly fracturing its skull, and stomps repeatedly on the animal's head." Alito concluded that "the harm caused by the underlying criminal acts greatly outweighs any trifling value that the depictions might be thought to possess."

Alito was, if anything, even more outraged by his colleagues' decision in the case involving the funeral, *Snyder v. Phelps.* (The antics of the Westboro Baptist Church were familiar to viewers of cable news. Notwithstanding their name, the defendants were not "Baptist," or even a "church," but rather a single family led by a charismatic lunatic named Fred Phelps. His daughter Margie, a lawyer, argued the family's case in the Supreme Court and did a creditable job.) "Petitioner Albert Snyder is not a public figure," Alito wrote in his dissent. "He is simply a parent whose son, Marine Lance Corporal Matthew Snyder, was killed in Iraq. Mr. Snyder wanted what is surely the right of any parent who experiences such an incalculable loss: to bury his son in peace. But respondents, members of the Westboro Baptist Church, deprived him of that elementary right. They first issued a press release and thus turned Matthew's funeral into a tumultuous media event [and then] launched a malevolent verbal attack on Matthew and his family at a time of acute emotional vulnerability." He went on, "In order to have a society in which public issues can be openly and vigorously debated, it is not necessary to allow the brutalization of innocent victims like petitioner."

Roberts, for the majority, had the last word in the case, and he made his point eloquently, as usual: "Speech is powerful. It can stir people to action, move them to tears of both joy and sorrow, and—as it did here—inflict great pain. On the facts before us, we cannot react to that pain by punishing the speaker. As a Nation we have chosen a different course—to protect even hurtful speech on public issues to ensure that we do not stifle public debate. That choice requires that we shield Westboro from tort liability for its picketing in this case." (The chief justice used his family back in Indiana as a kind of reality check. Roberts's brother-in-law made a point of telling him that he agreed with Alito.)

The decision in *Snyder v. Phelps*, which came down on March 2, 2011, showed Roberts at his best. The oral argument in *Arizona Free Enterprise Club v. Bennett*, which took place later that month, featured the chief justice at his worst.

The case represented the Court's first return to the subject of campaign finance since *Citizens United* the previous year. The public had yet to see the full implications of the decision. Most of the campaign finance reports from the 2010 election had not yet been filed or digested. What became clear in the course of the oral argument on March 28, 2011, was that the conservative justices knew what they had achieved in *Citizens United*—and they wanted to push their position forward.

The case concerned the constitutionality of the Arizona Citizens Clean Elections Act, which had been passed by the voters in 1998, to address the state's appalling history of political corruption. This fairly modest reform established a system of optional public funding of campaigns for certain state offices. A candidate who chose to accept public funding would receive extra money from the state if his or her privately funded opponent exceeded a certain set spending limit. The basic idea was simple: to keep elections competitive if a privately funded candidate was vastly outspending a publicly funded one. The question in the case was whether the First Amendment permitted the government subsidies.

Kagan dominated the questioning of William Maurer, the lawyer who was challenging the law. Her point was straightforward—that no one's right to free speech was being violated by this law. "There's no restriction at all here; it's more speech all the way around?" she said.

"I would disagree with that, respectfully, Your Honor," Maurer answered. "There is a restriction here. Every time an independent expenditure group or a privately financed candidate speaks above a certain amount, the government creates real penalties for them to have engaged in unfettered political expression."

"Well, doesn't the government actually just give a selective subsidy?" Kagan continued. "It's not a penalty, it's just saying, in order to run an effective public financing system, when you speak, we're going to give a subsidy over a certain amount. So the trigger does not trigger a penalty; it triggers a subsidy."

Roberts said nothing during Maurer's argument, but when Bradley Phillips, the lawyer for Arizona, rose to defend the law, the chief justice tore into him. He raised several hypotheticals (mostly far-fetched) about multicandidate races and how the law might penalize the privately funded candidates. He then zeroed in on a distinction that had been drawn in *Citizens United* and other cases—one that reflected just what a mess the Court's campaign finance decisions had created.

Since the days of Theodore Roosevelt, the idea behind keeping corporations out of politics was to level the playing field. Without these limits, corporations would have too much political power. In a 1990 case called *Austin v. Michigan Chamber of Commerce*, the Court made the sensible observation that limits on campaign contributions by corporations served to curb the "corrosive and distorting effects of immense aggregations of wealth that are accumulated with the help of the corporate form and that have little or no correlation to the public's support for the corporation's political ideas." But *Austin* was one of the cases overturned by *Citizens United*, and Kennedy's opinion went on to say that Congress *never* could try to level the playing field with regard to campaign finance; that was now a forbidden rationale. Rather, the only permissible purpose for campaign laws was to fight corruption, which the Court defined in a very narrow way. Congress could outlaw only quid pro quo bribery, nothing more.

Against this confusing, and largely senseless, background, Roberts sprung a trap at the oral argument.

"Counsel, do you agree that under our precedents, leveling the playing field for candidates is not a legitimate State purpose?" Roberts asked William Jay, the lawyer in the solicitor general's office who was defending the Arizona law for the Obama administration.

"We do, Mr. Chief Justice," Jay said. "That, of course, is not what's at work here."

Then Roberts pounced. "Well, I checked the Citizens Clean Elections Commission website this morning," he said, "and it says that this act was passed to, quote, 'level the playing field' when it comes to running for office. Why isn't that clear evidence that it's unconstitutional?"

It was a nimble piece of lawyering by the chief justice—a touché moment. But to a layperson, it was an absurdity. The state of Arizona was caught trying to level the playing field—in other words, to do what most people would think was the right thing.

Jay did his best to recover. "Well, Mr. Chief Justice, whatever the Citizens Clean Elections Commission says on its website, I think isn't dispositive of what the voters of Arizona had in mind when they passed this initiative," he said. "The Court has recognized since *Buckley v. Valeo* that public financing serves a valid anticorruption purpose, and it does so because it eliminates the influence of private contributions on the candidates who take public financing." Jay was attempting to speak the chief's language, albeit in a clearly losing cause.

It was a moment that showed just how much the Court missed Sandra Day O'Connor. It was not just that she was an Arizonan who understood why her state had tried, in this small way, to clean up its politics. But O'Connor had actually run for political office (as no one on the Roberts Court had). She understood the danger of giving individuals and companies unlimited freedom to spend. But Roberts was on a mission— to deregulate American politics. And the chief had the votes.

No one knew this better than Stephen Breyer. He was seventy-two years old at this moment, not old for a Supreme Court justice, but not young, either. The days of his great collaboration with O'Connor were six years in the past. He had built his professional life around the idea that government could be a force for good in America. In particular, he had written a book, *Active Liberty*, that said limits on campaign contributions were the best way to preserve democratic values. And now he saw that the Court was dismantling those limits, sooner rather than later. Breyer gave in to his frustration.

"And what about—it's a general question. Answer this if you wish. Don't if you don't want to, and the same goes for your opponent," Breyer stammered, near the end of the argument in the Arizona case. "But as

I hear this argument, what's going through my mind is we are deeply into the details of a very complex bill. McCain-Feingold is hundreds of pages, and we cannot possibly test each provision which is related to the others on such a test of whether it equalizes or incentivizes or some other thing, because the answer is normally we don't know." Breyer could see that Roberts and the others were subjecting all campaign finance laws to such exacting scrutiny that none of them could ever survive.

Breyer went on. "And it is better to say it's all illegal than to subject these things to death by a thousand cuts, because we don't know what will happen when we start tinkering with one provision rather than another. That thought went through my mind as I've heard this discussion. Comment or not upon it as you wish."

Nervous laughter filled the courtroom. The justices often made speeches in the form of questions, but this was a speech in the form of a speech. No one knew what to say. As the day's events showed, Kagan was still in there fighting, but Breyer had thrown in the towel. *Just give up on all campaign finance limits. Return American politics to the law of the jungle.*

By the customary vote of 5–4, the Court declared the Arizona law a violation of the First Amendment. The opinions appeared to be a window to the next quarter century at the Supreme Court: Roberts for the majority, Kagan (again assigned by Ginsburg) in the lead dissent. Like *Citizens United*, *Arizona Free Enterprise* showed the conservative agenda for change. Roberts was a modern Republican, not an old-fashioned one (like Harlan, Stewart, Powell, or O'Connor) who believed in judicial restraint. Instead, Roberts was engaging in a consummate act of judicial activism, overruling the will of Arizona's voters to serve a newly invented legal theory. And, most obviously, the chief justice was doing the bidding of the contemporary Republican Party, which hated campaign finance reform, while Kagan was speaking for the Democrats, who embraced it.

" 'Leveling the playing field' can sound like a good thing," the chief justice wrote for the majority. "But in a democracy, campaigning for office is not a game. It is a critically important form of speech. The First Amendment embodies our choice as a Nation that, when it comes to such speech, the guiding principle is freedom—the 'unfettered interchange of ideas'—not whatever the State may view as fair."

Like the president who appointed her, Kagan sought to limit the power of the Court and to defer to the democratically elected branches of government. This case, like so many others, revealed how the parties had switched places at the Supreme Court since the 1960s. Then, it had been the Democrats who were the activists, striking down laws that were not to their liking. Now it was the Republicans. "This case arose because Arizonans wanted their government to work on behalf of all the State's people," Kagan wrote in her dissent. "On the heels of a political scandal involving the near-routine purchase of legislators' votes, Arizonans passed a law designed to sever political candidates' dependence on large contributors. The system discriminated against no ideas and prevented no speech. Indeed, by increasing electoral competition and enabling a wide range of candidates to express their views, the system furthered First Amendment values. Less corruption, more speech. Robust campaigns leading to the election of representatives not beholden to the few, but accountable to the many. The people of Arizona might have expected a decent respect for those objectives. Today, they do not get it. . . . Truly, democracy is not a game."

PART

FIVE

"YOU SHOULD DO IT"

Barack Obama bet his presidency on health care reform. He sacrificed every other legislative priority—including climate change, energy, and immigration—to drag the Affordable Care Act across the finish line. The president's political adversaries, knowing the stakes, threw everything they had into defeating him. The outcome in Congress was in doubt until the final votes were cast in the House and Senate.

By the time the ACA passed, it was clear that conservatives were going to challenge the bill in court. For two decades, the constitutionality of the individual mandate had never been questioned. But in just a few months, its illegality under the commerce clause became an article of faith within the Republican Party. Opponents of the law lined up to be first to challenge it in federal court. The legal fight over health care reform became a defining symbol of the role reversal that had taken place between liberals and conservatives over the past several decades. Liberals, once the apostles of judicial activism, embraced judicial restraint and deference to the democratically elected branches of government; conservatives, who had railed for so long against judges who, in George W. Bush's famous phrase, "legislate from the bench," set out to persuade judges to do just that. Even before the first lawsuit was filed against the ACA, everyone knew the Supreme Court would have the last word. When the case did come before the justices, nothing—no legal argument, no political maneuver, no public appeal—had as much to do with the ultimate fate of the legislation as a single four-word e-mail.

Even before Congress voted on the final form of the legislation, lawyers in the Obama administration began organizing a defense. In the typical way of bureaucracies, a group of deputies organized an initial meeting, which senior officials would then decide if they wanted to attend. On January 8, 2010, at 10:54 a.m., an aide to Thomas Perrelli, the associate attorney general, e-mailed Neal Katyal, the deputy solicitor general, about scheduling a meeting for "a group to get thinking about how to defend against inevitable challenges to the health care proposals that are pending."

Three minutes later, Katyal e-mailed back this enthusiastic reply: "Absolutely right on. Let's crush them. I'll speak with Elena and designate someone."

At the same time, Katyal forwarded the original invitation to Elena Kagan, the solicitor general, asking if she wanted to be included in the group. "I am happy to do this if you are ok with it," Katyal wrote to her.

Katyal was doing his job, asking his boss if she wanted to attend a strategy session on a major legal issue facing the Justice Department. It was, at one level, a routine communication about who should attend a meeting, and Kagan responded with four unelaborated words. At 11:01 a.m., she wrote Katyal: "You should do it." The exchange was like thousands that take place in offices every day. (As it turned out, the January meeting never took place. Once Scott Brown, a Republican, won a special election later that month for the Massachusetts Senate seat formerly held by Edward M. Kennedy, it looked like there would be no health care bill at all—so there was no need to figure out how to defend it.)

But the bill came back to life, and in March Obama and the Democrats finally won passage. The denouement came when the House approved a revised measure on Sunday, March 21, by a vote of 219–212. That same day, Perrelli e-mailed invitations to Katyal and others to convene, at long last, the health care litigation planning group. At 6:19 that evening, Katyal forwarded the invitation to Kagan and wrote, "I think you should go, no? I will, but feel like this is litigation of singular importance." A minute later, Kagan e-mailed Katyal back, asking him for his phone number.

When Kagan and Katyal spoke that evening, she said she had decided to stay away from the health care litigation—which was why, two months earlier, she had written to him, "You should do it." Kagan didn't want to be involved or even informed about work on this issue. Little more was said between them, but the reason for Kagan's decision was clear. She had been a finalist for the Souter seat the previous year. Stevens was dropping hints that he was going to leave in a matter of weeks. Kagan had a very real chance of being nominated for the Court, and the health care case was likely to come before the justices, sooner rather than later. She wanted to preserve her opportunity to take part. If she became a justice, Kagan did not want to have to recuse herself, so she was not going to participate at all in planning the health care litigation.

Later, when the challenge to the health care law did wind up in the Supreme Court, some liberals argued that Thomas should recuse himself from the case because of his wife's political activities. In short order, conservatives began asserting in response that Kagan should recuse herself because she must have participated in planning the defense of the law when she was solicitor general. It was a plausible argument. After all, Katyal himself had noted that the case was of "singular importance," and the solicitor general served, in effect, as the chief legal strategist for the Justice Department. As his e-mails showed, Katyal believed that Kagan should help to defend the law.

In light of all that followed, then, Kagan's e-mail—"You should do it"—ranks among the most consequential of such messages in American history. It was contemporaneous proof that the future justice had not participated in planning the defense of the law. Katyal's recollections of their exchanges backed her up. If Kagan had gone to even a single meeting where the legal defense of the health care law was discussed—even if she just sat there and didn't say a word—she would have been required to recuse herself from participating in the case as a Supreme Court justice. (Justices are not bound by the same formal ethics rules as other federal judges, but attendance at such a meeting would have created a very clear case for recusal.) As would later become clear, the loss of Kagan's vote would have meant the loss of the case for her side. Without her, at least the individual mandate of the Affordable Care Act would have been invalidated. The e-mail trail kept Kagan in the case.

That still left the question of how the Justice Department should defend the law. Even in the initial stages, the issue split the Obama lawyers into two camps. The internal differences were largely generational.

The principal constitutional justification for the health care legislation was the commerce clause of Article I, which authorizes Congress to "regulate Commerce . . . among the several States." After 1937, when the Court adopted Franklin Roosevelt's conception of the Constitution, the justices gave nearly unlimited scope to Congress's power under the commerce clause. In the famous case of *Wickard v. Filburn*, from 1942, the Court upheld congressional power to regulate how much wheat a farmer could grow—even if he didn't sell the wheat at all but rather used it to feed his own livestock. "If we were to be brutally frank," Justice Robert H. Jackson, the author of *Wickard*, wrote in a letter to a friend shortly after the decision, "I suspect what we would say is that in any case where Congress thinks there is an effect on interstate commerce, the Court will accept that judgment."

That clause became almost a blank check for Congress. By the days of the Warren Court in the 1960s, the justices routinely ignored the commerce clause as a meaningful limit on the power of Congress. As the Court held in 1964, upholding the Civil Rights Act, the test was simply whether the activity sought to be regulated is "commerce which concerns more States than one and has a real and substantial relation to the national interest." For decades, every act of Congress passed that test.

This wasn't just an abstract legal issue. The commerce clause was freighted with political significance. Among liberals, a broadly defined commerce clause was the indispensable constitutional provision for activist government. This sentiment was especially strong at the Justice Department, including among those lawyers who took initial charge of defending the health care law. They had grown up with the commerce clause as a settled issue, and they regarded any threat to its interpretation as a challenge to their entire worldview.

Neal Katyal didn't see it exactly the same way.

As the health care litigation began, Katyal had just turned forty years old, which may have been the most important thing about him with reference to the case. The son of immigrant parents from India, raised in Chicago, mother a physician, father an engineer, Katyal was the legal world's version of a prodigy. A champion debater at Dartmouth, he went on to a standout career at Yale Law School, which brought him a clerkship with Stephen Breyer. He served in the Clinton administration and then became a tenured professor at Georgetown University Law Center. He was blessed, occasionally cursed, with abundant self-confidence. And his legal career took place entirely during the new era of conservative hegemony at the Supreme Court.

Katyal himself was a Democrat, and a proud member of the Obama administration, who was determined to help protect the president's legacy. But he wanted to do so in a way that reflected the courts as they were—full of conservatives—not as he wished they would be. And that brought him into conflict with his colleagues at the Justice Department.

As much as liberals embraced a broad conception of the commerce clause, conservatives disdained it—and they had won a couple of important recent victories. In 1995, Rehnquist cobbled together a five-justice majority to strike down a federal law on commerce clause grounds for the first time in decades. In *United States v. Lopez*, the Court said Congress could not make it a federal crime to possess a firearm near a school. Five years later, in *United States v. Morrison*, the same five justices said that victims of gender-based violence could not file federal lawsuits against their attackers. In both cases, the majority said that the conduct Congress sought to regulate was too remote from actual interstate commerce to be constitutional. Both *Lopez* and *Morrison* were, in their way, originalist decisions—that is, the conservative majority was guided by what it said was the intent of the framers in crafting the commerce clause.

To defend the health care law, Katyal endorsed several heresies against the liberal orthodoxy. He embraced the holdings in *Lopez* and *Morrison*, even though many in the Justice Department still regarded them as nefarious departures from a true reading of the commerce clause. Even more controversially, Katyal was a kind of originalist himself. He thought conservatives had no right to sole claim on the framers of the Constitution as their political forebears. He thought liberals could claim the mantle of the framers, too—and he wanted to do so in the health care case.

Even for lawyers, these abstractions can mean very little, but for Katyal they translated into clear challenges in the defense of the ACA. Specifically, Katyal came to believe that the administration would win its case only if it could answer two simple questions: Are there any limits on what Congress can do under the commerce clause? And if the health care law is constitutional, does that also mean that Congress could mandate that every American eat broccoli as well?

Some two dozen lawsuits challenging the Affordable Care Act were filed in 2010. A few were clearly frivolous, but several were well financed and artfully argued. On the day Obama signed the bill, Bill McCollum, the attorney general of Florida, brought a case in federal court on behalf of his state and eventually twenty-five other states. Choosing his forum with care, McCollum filed the lawsuit in Pensacola, which had some of the most conservative judges in the country. There, Roger Vinson, a 1983 Reagan appointee, declared the entire law unconstitutional. According to the government's theory, Vinson wrote, "Congress could require that people buy and consume broccoli at regular intervals, not only because the required purchases will positively impact interstate commerce, but also because people who eat healthier tend to be healthier and are thus more productive and put less of a strain on the health care system." Around the country, several other judges upheld the law, some judges invalidated parts of it, and the appeals to the circuit courts began. (Almost without exception, district judges appointed by Democratic presidents upheld the law and those appointed by Republicans struck it down.)

When Kagan was nominated to the Supreme Court, in May 2010, Katyal became acting solicitor general, and he took responsibility for arguing all of the appeals of the health care cases in the circuit courts. Drafting the briefs was a contentious process within the Justice Department. Traditional liberals wanted to concede little on limits of the commerce clause; Katyal felt they needed to acknowledge the changed world that included *Lopez* and *Morrison*. On June 1, 2011, Katyal defended the law in the Sixth Circuit, based in Cincinnati. The exchanges were typical of the questions he received in every court.

"I hear your arguments about the power of Congress under the commerce clause and I'm having difficulty seeing how there is any limit to the power as you're defining it," said Judge James L. Graham, a district judge sitting by designation on the appeals court. "And I'm starting with the premise that just about everything that human beings do, about every human function I can think of, has some economic consequences." It was the key question: What was the limit of the commerce clause?

To Katyal, the answer was embedded in both *Lopez* and *Morrison*. Those cases related to noneconomic activities at the core of state functions: neither one regulated any actual economic activity. As Katyal told the judge, "What *Lopez* and *Morrison* say, is you've got to be economic in nature, and that it can't be the aggregation of a whole bunch of uneconomic activities. Zero plus zero plus zero is always going to equal zero. Here's what *we're* saying: we're saying in this [health care] market, what Congress is regulating is not the failure to buy something but the failure to secure financing for something that everyone is going to buy." Every American was going to buy health care at one time or another; the law simply regulated those transactions, before and after they took place.

Katyal also took on the "broccoli question." Opponents of the law said if the Congress was allowed to force people to buy insurance, legislators could make people buy General Motors cars, or cell phones, or broccoli—anything at all.

Health care was different, Katyal replied. "Congress made a specific finding, that people without insurance are causing everyone's premiums to rise to the tune of $1,000 per family, you and me, because hospitals have to take these people," he said. "And that makes this market different than many of the examples that we were talking about. The real question is, Can Congress regulate, in a market in which it knows that everyone is participating, that is, the health care market?"

"That's a generality," Judge Jeffrey Sutton, a conservative former Scalia clerk, said, "that's true of food, transportation, shelter markets."

"That's one aspect, but what sets up the cost shifting is not just that everyone needs it but that providers can't opt out of it," Katyal said. "So the food and transportation markets—I can't show up at the broccoli store without money and say, 'Give me broccoli.' " It was a compelling— and winning—argument. Sutton, the pedigreed conservative, wrote the opinion upholding the law.

Still, the political splits in the judiciary ultimately showed through in their various decisions on the health care law. Like the Sixth Circuit, the D.C. Circuit upheld the law, and the Fourth Circuit dismissed the case on procedural grounds. But once a three-judge panel of the Eleventh Circuit ruled that the individual mandate was unconstitutional, it was inevitable that the Supreme Court would hear the case. (The justices almost always grant certiorari in cases where a circuit court has declared a federal law unconstitutional.)

As acting solicitor general, Katyal had made one last important decision about how to handle the health care case. The issue was timing. The government can almost always contrive ways to delay appeals, and there were ways to keep the case away from the Supreme Court, at least until after the 2012 election. But Katyal canvassed his peers at the Department of Health and Human Services and other federal agencies and found that they were spending tens of millions of dollars a month preparing to implement the ACA. It was simply irresponsible to let the legal uncertainty around the law linger. The agencies needed a definitive answer about whether the law was valid or not. So Katyal, after consulting the White House, decided to press ahead. On November 14, 2011, the justices agreed to review the Eleventh Circuit decision, consolidated all of the remaining appeals, and put the case down for argument in the spring.

But Katyal wouldn't be there to argue it.

Kagan was nominated to the Supreme Court in May 2010 and confirmed in August. During those months and several more that followed, Obama did not nominate a successor. Katyal wanted the job, but it eventually became clear that he wasn't going to get it.

Katyal was still best known for his lonely and ultimately successful crusade on behalf of Salim Hamdan, the Guantánamo detainee, in the Supreme Court. Just as the solicitor general post became available, Liz Cheney, the daughter of the former vice president, attacked Katyal for being part of what she called the "Al Qaeda Seven," Justice Department lawyers who had, during the Bush years, done pro bono work challenging legal aspects of the war on terror. Of course, the profession has a long and distinguished history of encouraging the representation of unpopular clients—and several Republican lawyers, like Ted Olson, rebuked Cheney for impugning the lawyers who upheld this tradition—but Cheney's attacks made Katyal controversial.

In any event, Obama had a safer choice for solicitor general. Don Verrilli came to Washington to do good and stayed to do well. After compiling a distinguished academic record at Yale College and Columbia Law School, he clerked for two liberal legends, J. Skelly Wright, on the D.C. Circuit, and William Brennan, on the Supreme Court. Verrilli then went to work at the law firm of Jenner & Block, always meaning to do public service some day. Unlike most other corporate lawyers, Verrilli maintained a serious commitment to pro bono work throughout his career—he even argued five death penalty cases before the Supreme Court—but he found himself well into middle age without ever having done what he came to Washington to do. When Obama was elected, he vowed that he would go to work at the Justice Department even if it meant sweeping the hallways.

That turned out to be unnecessary. Verrilli worked first as associate deputy attorney general and then moved to the White House to work as a deputy to his friend Bob Bauer, the White House counsel. Verrilli had argued a dozen cases in the Supreme Court. His background in corporate law made him easy to confirm in the Senate. Unlike Katyal, Verrilli was without enemies. Finally, after dithering about his choice for solicitor general for eight full months, Obama nominated Verrilli on January 26, 2011. He was confirmed five months later. Obama had his lawyer for the health care case.

BROCCOLI

For all the grandeur of the Supreme Court's façade, the courtroom itself has a kind of intimacy. The lawyer's lectern is less than ten feet in front of the chief justice; the press seats begin about the same distance from Sotomayor, the justice to Roberts's extreme right; the justices' guests sit about as close to Kagan, who is on the opposite side. When the courtroom is completely full (which it rarely is), there are only about five hundred people inside and their collective presence gives the room an unmistakable barometric instability. The place buzzes. The justices notice.

In major cases, the justices are like themselves, only more so. The tension, the adrenaline, the stakes—all serve to exaggerate the quirks of their personalities. Court convened on Monday, March 26, 2012, for the first of three days of arguments in the health care case—the most important any of the justices had heard. Health insurance for thirty million people, to say nothing of the political future of the President of the United States, was riding on the outcome. Five justices remained from the Court that decided *Bush v. Gore*, but by the time that case was argued, on Monday, December 11, 2000, the Court had already voted to issue a stay to stop the recounts in Florida. The result of the argument that followed was largely a foregone conclusion. Not so in health care. According to Court protocol, the justices do not discuss cases with one another before they are argued. So no one—including the justices—knew how this one was going to come out.

First, though, there was an overture. Roberts had divided the argument by subject, and the first one was the most obscure. When the initial cases against the ACA were filed, the government argued that the suits were barred by a little-known 1867 law called the Anti-Injunction Act. In short, the law bars lawsuits challenging the legality of taxes before the taxes are actually due. In those first cases, the government asserted that the fee that individuals had to pay for failing to comply with the individual mandate—that is, for refusing to buy health insurance—was a tax. The lawsuits, the government contended, could therefore not proceed until the taxes were actually imposed, in 2015. But Katyal, when he was controlling the case as acting solicitor general, switched the government's position. He said for purposes of the Anti-Injunction Act, the law was not a tax but rather a penalty, and thus the Court could now hear the challenge to its constitutionality. Verrilli, the new solicitor general, stuck with that position, which in turn created a new complication.

At the Court on Monday, Verrilli was claiming that the ACA was not a tax but a penalty. But on Tuesday, when the Court would weigh the constitutionality of the individual mandate itself, Verrilli would argue that the law *was* a tax. Like Katyal, Verrilli had devoted most of his energy (and most of the space in his briefs) to the claim that the ACA was a legal exercise of Congress's power under the commerce clause. But he also asserted that the law was separately justified under a different provision of Article I: "The Congress shall have Power To lay and collect Taxes."

Typically, it was Alito, the most skillful questioner, who exposed the apparent contradiction in the government's position. "Today you are arguing that the penalty is not a tax," Alito told Verrilli on Monday. "Tomorrow you are going to be back and you will be arguing that the penalty is a tax. Has the Court ever held that something that is a tax for purposes of the taxing power under the Constitution is not a tax under the Anti-Injunction Act?"

Not exactly, Verrilli said, but he still had a response. "Tomorrow the question is whether Congress has the authority under the taxing power to enact it and the form of words doesn't have a dispositive effect on that analysis," he said. "Today we are construing statutory text where the precise choice of words does have a dispositive effect on the analysis."

Not for the last time in the case, the dispute seemed like a matter of semantics. A tax or a penalty? A tax for one purpose but not for another? A tax at an early stage of the litigation but not at a later one? Each argument made a kind of sense (at least to a lawyer), but there was something dispiriting about the fact that the fate of such an important piece of legislation turned on such ephemeral concepts. In a brief exchange on Monday, little noticed at the time, Roberts tried to pierce some of the artificiality.

"The whole point of the suit is to prevent the collection of penalties," he told Gregory Katsas, one of the lawyers challenging the law.

"Of taxes, Mr. Chief Justice," Katsas said.

"Well, prevent the collection of taxes. But the idea that the mandate is something separate from whether you want to call it a penalty or tax just doesn't seem to make much sense. It's a command. A mandate is a command. Now, if there is nothing behind the command, it's sort of, well, what happens if you don't follow the mandate? And if the answer is nothing, it seems very artificial to separate the punishment from the crime," Roberts said, adding a little later, "Why would you have a requirement that is completely toothless? You know, buy insurance or else. Or else what? Or else nothing?" The chief justice was suggesting that a tax and a penalty were effectively the same thing.

Still, in the course of the argument on Monday, the justices seemed more or less aligned, appearing to believe that the Anti-Injunction Act did not prevent them from reaching the merits of the case. They would decide whether the ACA was constitutional—and the key argument would take place the following morning.

"Mr. Chief Justice, and may it please the Court," Verrilli began, "the Affordable Care Act addresses a fundamental and enduring problem in our health care system and our economy. Insurance has become the predominant means of paying for health care in this country." He paused and said again, "Insurance has become the predominant means of paying for health care in this country. For most Americans, for more than 80 percent of Americans, the insurance system does provide effective access. Excuse me." Verrilli paused to take a drink of water, which went down the wrong pipe. Briefly, he lost his train of thought. And just then the assault began.[*]

Scalia: "Why aren't those problems that the federal government can address directly?"

Kennedy: "Can you create commerce in order to regulate it?"

Scalia: "If I'm in any market at all, my failure to purchase something in that market subjects me to regulation?"

---

[*] Immediately after the argument, no one was more critical of Verrilli's performance, or more wrong about its impact on the justices, than I was.

Verrilli reeled. Several times, he tried to make the point that the health care market was unique, because, as he said, "virtually everybody is either in that market or will be in that market, and the distinguishing feature of that is that people cannot generally control when they enter that market or what they need when they enter that market."

Roberts: "Well, the same, it seems to me, would be true, say, for the market in emergency services: police, fire, ambulance, roadside assistance, whatever. You don't know when you're going to need it; you're not sure that you will. But the same is true for health care. You don't know if you're going to need a heart transplant or if you ever will. So, there's a market there. To some extent, we all participate in it.

"So," Roberts went on, "can the government require you to buy a cell phone because that would facilitate responding when you need emergency services? You can just dial 911 no matter where you are?"

The argument was less than ten minutes old and Verrilli had already been hit with a torrent of hostility from the Court's conservatives. In the weeks leading up to the argument, the conventional wisdom had been that the Court would probably uphold the ACA as a valid exercise of Congress's power under the commerce clause. After all, such respected conservatives as Sutton, on the Sixth Circuit, and Laurence Silberman, on the D.C. Circuit, had just done so. But it was quickly obvious how wrong that consensus had been. The onslaught even shocked the four liberal justices, who were themselves frozen in silence.

Alito joined in next. "Do you think there is a market for burial services?" he asked.

"Yes, Justice Alito, I think there is," Verrilli answered.

"All right," Alito went on. "Suppose that you and I walked around downtown Washington at lunch hour and we found a couple of healthy young people and we stopped them and we said: 'You know what you're doing? You are financing your burial services right now because eventually you're going to die, and somebody is going to have to pay for it, and if you don't have burial insurance and you haven't saved money for it, you're going to shift the cost to somebody else.' Isn't that a very artificial way of talking about what somebody is doing?"

"No—" Verrilli began, but Alito cut him off. "And if that's true, why isn't it equally artificial to say that somebody who is doing absolutely nothing about health care is financing health care services?"

As usual in Supreme Court, the answers mattered less than the questions. In a flash, the four speaking conservatives had signaled one another that they were united in the commerce clause argument against the individual mandate. (Thomas observed his customary silence, but his long-established position on the clause made him a sure vote to overturn the law.)

Kennedy then asked an extraordinary question, one that reflected his judge-centered, almost messianic, approach to the law. "Could you help me with this," he said to Verrilli. "Assume for the moment that [the individual mandate] is unprecedented, this is a step beyond what our cases have allowed, the affirmative duty to act to go into commerce. If that is so, do you not have a heavy burden of justification?"

Kennedy had seventy-five years of constitutional law precisely backwards. During that time, the justices had repeatedly acknowledged that laws passed by Congress were presumed to be constitutional, especially in the economic sphere. It was supposed to be a rare thing indeed for unelected judges to overturn the will of the democratically elected branches of government. But here Kennedy was saying that the legislature had a "heavy burden" of proving that its health care law was constitutional. According to decades of settled law, it was the Court, including Kennedy, that had the heavy burden of justification for interfering in the political process. But Kennedy did not think that way. More than any other justice, he had the confidence, or arrogance, to trump the other branches of government. Sometimes, as when he struck down laws that discriminated against gay people, Kennedy's thirst for power pleased the left; more often, as with *Citizens United*, Kennedy pleased the right. "Judicial modesty," in Roberts's famous phrase, was never for Anthony Kennedy.

As usual, though, it was Scalia who called the most attention to himself during the argument. Two weeks earlier, he had turned seventy-six, and as with many other people, age had coarsened his rough edges. His belligerence had taken on a nastier edge, and his frame of reference became ever more political, less judicial. Even more than Kennedy, Scalia had a palpable contempt for Congress; he didn't even pretend that the Court owed some deference to the people's representatives. At one point, Scalia said, "If we struck down nothing in this legislation but the—what's it called, the 'Cornhusker Kickback'—OK, we find that to violate the constitutional proscription of venality, OK?" Scalia said, and the audience laughed. Scalia went on: "When we strike that down, it's clear that Congress would not have passed it without that. It was the means of getting the last necessary vote in the Senate. And you are telling us that the whole statute would fall because the Cornhusker Kickback is bad."

The level of distortion in this riff by Scalia was extraordinary. In late 2009, congressional leaders did sweeten the bill with several provisions designed to appeal to Nebraska's Ben Nelson; these became known as the Cornhusker Kickback. But after the changes generated bad publicity, congressional leaders removed it completely from the bill. There was no Cornhusker Kickback in the final version of the legislation, so the premise of Scalia's question was false. There is also no such thing as a "constitutional proscription of venality"; that was just another cheap shot at Congress. Scalia was merely reciting conservative talking points, instead of sticking to the facts of the case.

Scalia raised another issue that had a rich history in the right-wing popular culture. "Everybody has to buy food sooner or later," he said, "so you define the market as food, therefore, everybody is in the market; therefore, you can make people buy broccoli." In op-ed pieces, blog posts, Internet videos, even Judge Vinson's opinion in Florida, the broccoli example was cited as the reductio ad absurdum of the Obama proposal. (Katyal had answered a broccoli question in his argument in the Sixth Circuit.) Given its provenance in the conservative political world, it was not surprising that Scalia was the justice who raised broccoli in front of his colleagues.

Verrilli stumbled in response: "No, that's quite different. That's quite different. The food market, while it shares that trait that everybody's in it, it is not a market in which your participation is often unpredictable and often involuntary. It is not a market in which you often don't know before you go in what you need, and it is not a market in which, if you go in and seek to obtain a product or service, you will get it even if you can't pay for it." (Verrilli failed to note, as Katyal had observed, that Congress had made a specific finding that everyone's health care premiums rose because of the cost of treating uninsured people; there was no finding, nor could there be one, that food costs rose because some people refused to eat broccoli.)

At this point, finally, the liberals on the Court broke their stunned silence and came to the defense of Verrilli and the health care law. Ginsburg was plainly irritated at Verrilli's halting performance and tried to take over the defense of the law. At seventy-nine, she had limited patience, inside and outside the courtroom. (Ginsburg was known for exiling law clerks who disappointed her, even while she still nominally employed them.) If Verrilli couldn't make his case, she would make it for him.

"Mr. Verrilli, I thought that your main point is that, unlike food or any other market, when you made the choice not to buy insurance, even though you have every intent in the world to self-insure, to save for it, when disaster strikes, you may not have the money," Ginsburg said. "And the tangible result of it is, we were told there was one brief that Maryland hospital care bills seven percent more because of these uncompensated costs, that families pay a thousand dollars more than they would if there were no uncompensated costs. I thought what was unique about this is it's not my choice whether I want to buy a product to keep me healthy, but the cost that I am forcing on other people if I don't buy the product." Verrilli humbly assented.

Kennedy then brought the issue back to the critical question in the case: "Well, then your question is whether or not there are any limits on the commerce clause. Can you identify for us some limits on the commerce clause?"

It was here that the differences between Katyal's and Verrilli's arguments were most stark. Katyal had grown up in a world dominated by conservatives, and he tailored his appeal to them. He acknowledged that there were real limits on the power of Congress under the commerce clause. He told the appeals courts that Congress could not regulate quintessential state functions that were local and noneconomic in nature. A criminal law forbidding guns near schools, like the law in *Lopez*, was outside Congress's power under the commerce clause. Under the commerce clause, Katyal said, Congress could address national economic problems, like health insurance, but not local problems, like guns near schools.

But Verrilli had little to offer the justices as a meaningful limit on the commerce clause. As Kennedy told him, "If Congress says that the interstate commerce is affected, isn't, according to your view, that the end of the analysis?" Verrilli said no, but the real answer seemed to be yes. He was presenting a New Deal–era version of the commerce clause like the one Robert Jackson had described to a friend in 1942: "In any case where Congress thinks there is an effect on interstate commerce, the Court will accept that judgment." But not, clearly, the Roberts Court in 2012.

Scalia was partisan, Kennedy imperious, Alito incisive, Ginsburg demanding (and frustrated). When Paul Clement, who served as solicitor general under George W. Bush, rose to challenge the law, Stephen Breyer took him on.

Breyer was not a linear thinker (like Ginsburg, for instance), and he sometimes found himself caught up in his own curlicues of erudition. But no one knew this area of the law better than Breyer. He tried, in his professorial way, to show what a radical step the Court was considering. Chief Justice John Marshall upheld the creation of a national bank in the famous 1819 case of *McCulloch v. Maryland*; in *Wickard*, the Court said the commerce clause allowed the regulation of wheat growing for private consumption; in *Gonzales v. Raich*, the Court, in 2005, said the commerce clause allowed the prohibition on the use of homegrown marijuana.

"I think if we look back into history, we see sometimes Congress can create commerce out of nothing," Breyer said. "That's the national bank, which was created out of nothing to create other commerce out of nothing. I look back into history, and I see it seems pretty clear that if there are substantial effects on interstate commerce, Congress can act.

"And I look at the person who's growing marijuana in her house, or I look at the farmer who is growing wheat for home consumption. This seems to have more substantial effects. Is this commerce? Well, it seems to me more commerce than marijuana. I mean, is it, in fact, a regulation? Well, why not? If creating a bank is, why isn't this?"

Breyer was rambling, as was his wont, but he was making a serious point. The conservatives were pushing the idea that the government could never force anyone to take affirmative steps, or to create anything. But Breyer was pointing out that the Court had upheld many regulations and laws that had far less effect on interstate commerce than the ACA.

"And then you say, ah, but one thing here out of all those things is different, and that is you're making somebody do something," Breyer went on. "I say, hey, can't Congress make people drive faster than 45 miles an hour on a road? Didn't they make that man growing his own wheat go into the market and buy other wheat for his cows? Didn't they make Mrs. Raich, if she married somebody who had marijuana in her basement, wouldn't she have to go and get rid of it? Affirmative action? I mean, where does this distinction come from? It sounds like sometimes you can, and sometimes you can't." Breyer had dedicated his life to the idea that was at the core of the ACA: that government could help solve problems for people. The idea that the Constitution prohibited such attempts was anathema to him.

Suppose "a disease is sweeping the United States, and 40 million people are susceptible, of whom 10 million will die; can't the Federal Government say all 40 million get inoculation?" he went on, before finally getting to his point. "So here, we have a group of 40 million, and 57 percent of those people visit emergency care or other care, which we are paying for. And 22 percent of those pay more than $100,000 for that. And Congress says they are in the midst of this big thing. We just want to rationalize this system they are already in.

"So, there, you got the whole argument, and I would like you to tell me—"

And here, in light of the length of Breyer's question, Scalia could not avoid a wisecrack at his colleague's expense. "Answer those questions in inverse order," Scalia said.

"Well, no, it's one question," Breyer said, miffed at the interruption. "It's looking back at that history. The thing I can see is that you say to some people, go buy. Why does that make a difference in terms of the commerce clause?"

Sotomayor tried to help. Unlike Breyer's, Sotomayor's concerns tended toward the earthbound and practical. Sometimes, during oral arguments, she would go on tangents involving detailed questions about the facts of cases that would leave her colleagues stupefied, sinking into their chairs. This time, though, she had a simple line of inquiry. States require individuals to buy automobile insurance. "Do you think that if some states decided not to impose an insurance requirement," Sotomayor asked Clement, "that the federal government would be without power to legislate and require every individual to buy car insurance?"

The heart of the argument against the individual mandate was that it was an extreme departure from previous actions of the federal government. But states routinely required effectively the same thing that the federal government was asking here—for individuals to buy insurance. Was that so outrageous? Clement hedged in his reply, and in any event, the issue drew no traction from the Court's conservatives. Nothing did. They were locked in. Except, it turned out, for one of them.

By Wednesday, the justices were punchy. They dedicated one hour of oral argument to most cases. For certain important cases, they gave somewhat more. The second *Citizens United* argument took an hour and a half. But the six hours over three days for health care was the most they had devoted to any case in forty-five years. (Oddly, the Court had allotted eight hours in 1967 to an obscure and long-forgotten case about natural gas rates in western Texas and southeastern New Mexico.)

The Wednesday morning argument concerned the issue of severability. If the Court found the individual mandate unconstitutional, how much of the law would be invalidated—all of it or just part? The liberals could tell that the previous day's contest had gone badly for their side, so they argued, with some desperation, that the Court should invalidate only part of the law at most. As Ginsburg put it, "Mr. Clement, there are so many things in this Act that are unquestionably okay. I think you would concede that reauthorizing what is the Indian Healthcare Improvement Act, changes to the Black Lung benefits, why make Congress redo those? . . . So why should we say, it's a choice between a wrecking operation, which is what you are requesting, or a salvage job. And the more conservative approach would be salvage rather than throwing out everything."

Breyer made an almost poignant pitch for his favorite kind of solution: a "workable" compromise. Since parts of the law were clearly controversial and parts were not, could not the lawyers make those distinctions themselves?

Breyer said to Edwin Kneedler, the deputy solicitor general, who was representing the government in this part of the case: "Do you think that it's possible for you and Mr. Clement, on exploring this, to get together and agree on"—the audience started laughing—"I mean, on a list of things that are, in both your opinions, peripheral. Then you would focus on those areas where one of you thinks it's peripheral and one of you thinks it's not peripheral. And at that point, it might turn out to be far fewer than we are currently imagining . . . " Kneedler politely demurred, as if the suggestion came from a harmless eccentric.

Once more, Kennedy displayed a breathtaking sense of his own power. Kneedler asserted, with good reason, that the principle of judicial restraint would suggest that the Court should strike down as little of the law as possible. In other words, the Court should eliminate the unconstitutional parts of the law (if any) and leave the rest. Kennedy objected to this notion.

"When you say 'judicial restraint,' you are echoing the earlier premise that it increases the judicial power if the judiciary strikes down other provisions of the Act," Kennedy said. "I suggest to you it might be quite the opposite. We would be exercising the judicial power if one provision was stricken and the others remained to impose a risk on insurance companies that Congress had never intended. By reason of this Court, we would have a new regime that Congress did not provide for, did not consider. That, it seems to me, can be argued at least to be a more extreme exercise of judicial power than to strike the whole."

"I—I think not, Justice," Kneedler stammered, incredulous. Only Anthony Kennedy could assert that eliminating more rather than less of plainly constitutional statutes represented "judicial restraint." (It is notable too that Kennedy expressed particular concern for the effect of the law on insurance companies, not the millions of individuals who would receive insurance coverage.)

Scalia, by the end of the day, only wanted to get laughs. When Kneedler made the reasonable suggestion that the Court would have to separate the constitutional parts of the law from the unconstitutional, Scalia shot back, "Mr. Kneedler, what happened to the Eighth Amendment? You really want us to go through these 2,700 pages?" In other words, making them read so much would be "cruel and unusual punishment." Scalia went on, "And do you really expect the Court to do that? Or do you expect us to give this function to our law clerks?" More laughter. "Is this not totally unrealistic? That we're going to go through this enormous bill item by item and decide each one?"

At one point, Scalia grew so raucous that the chief justice had to shut down his comedy routine, saying, "That's enough frivolity for a while."

As the six long hours came to a close, with a discussion of whether the expansion of Medicaid imposed unconstitutional duties on the states, the differences between Roberts and Scalia appeared to be more than just stylistic. Scalia had taken every opportunity to announce his hostility to the law—and his belief that the whole law, not just the individual mandate, had to be invalidated. Kennedy and Alito were nearly as contemptuous of Congress's, and President Obama's, work. To be sure, Roberts did not sound like his four liberal colleagues—who were clearly boosters of the law—nor did the chief justice publicly commit himself to the law's demise.

At 2:24 p.m. on Wednesday, March 28, Roberts said, "The case is submitted."

THE "EFFECTIVE" ARGUMENT

On Friday, March 30, Roberts gathered his eight colleagues around the table in his conference room to vote on the health care case.

The Supreme Court was actually considering consolidated appeals from several health care decisions by the circuit courts. The lead case was known as *National Federation of Independent Business v. Sebelius*, which was the Eleventh Circuit decision striking down the individual mandate. In accord with the Court's custom, the chief justice introduced the case, defined the issues, and opened the discussion. According to the same informal rules, no justice spoke twice before everyone had a chance to speak once. Then, in order of seniority, Roberts called on each justice to vote.

Scalia: affirm.
Kennedy: affirm.
Thomas: affirm.
Ginsburg: reverse.
Breyer: reverse.
Alito: affirm.
Sotomayor: reverse.
Kagan: reverse.
Four to four.

Chief Justice Roberts would decide the outcome of the case.

In the conference room, Roberts sometimes looked wistfully at Charles Evans Hughes's massive desk, which anchored one wall. Hughes would occasionally preside from the desk, while his colleagues sat like suppliants at the conference table. Roberts had no comparable sway. He couldn't even control the conference table itself, much less the decisions made there, without dissent. When Roberts had the temerity, as part of the Court renovation project, to rotate the conference table by ninety degrees, Stevens launched an extended attack on the decorating decision in his memoir, *Five Chiefs*. "Some might consider the change trivial," Stevens wrote, but he then devoted several pages to disparaging the alteration. Stevens said the new location of the table left insufficient room for the justices' carts containing their research material; it was too far from the telephone; there was less space for coffee and baked goods; it made it harder for the justices to autograph group photographs at the same time; the acoustics were worse.

Roberts's vote in the health care case would trump even *Citizens United* as a symbol of his tenure. *Citizens United* defined the public image of the Roberts Court in the way that *Bush v. Gore*, another decision steeped in partisan politics, symbolized the Rehnquist Court. In terms of public perception, the health care case represented the third installment of this legal trilogy—the next occasion when the Court would wade into the political thicket. Unlike *Bush v. Gore* and *Citizens United*, the newer case did not deal directly with the business of elections but instead represented something almost as inflammatory: the Republican-dominated Court's verdict on the central achievement of a Democratic president.

Roberts told his colleagues that, as he had indicated at oral argument, he thought Congress had exceeded its powers under the commerce clause in creating the individual mandate. This position was in accord with Scalia, Kennedy, Thomas, and Alito. It was less clear to his colleagues how the chief felt about the other questions in the case. Most importantly, what did the commerce clause ruling mean for the future of the health care law as a whole? Would just the individual mandate be struck down? Or the whole law? And what of the law's imposition on the states to expand Medicaid coverage? Was that permissible? Discussions at conference are conducted at a fairly general level. The details are worked out in the opinions. Roberts assigned himself *National Federation of Independent Business v. Sebelius*. His colleagues would see a draft in about a month, which was normal for a major case.

Roberts and the other justices couldn't simply devote themselves to resolving the health care case. They had to keep up with the rest of their calendar, too. On April 25, the last day of oral arguments for the term, the justices heard a challenge to Arizona's immigration law, which included several measures to limit illegal immigration and punish undocumented people who were already in the state. The measure, known as SB 1070, had received a great deal of criticism for its possible effect on the lives of Hispanics in the state, but the Obama administration challenged the law on narrower grounds—that the state infringed on responsibilities that belonged exclusively to the federal government.

After the Arizona case was argued, Roberts joined Kennedy, Ginsburg, Breyer, and Sotomayor in a compromise verdict. (Kagan did not participate.) The justices found that three provisions of the law, including one that banned undocumented immigrants from seeking work, were preempted by federal law. But the five justices also upheld the most controversial part of SB 1070—the so-called "show me your papers" provision, which expanded the ability of state law enforcement officers to inquire about individuals' immigration status.

Scalia disagreed—vehemently. His passions had shifted in recent years from the scholarly to the political. Increasingly, his preoccupations, with topics like illegal immigration, mirrored those of Fox News. (Barack Obama himself was another Scalia fixation.) All justices have a political ideology as well as a legal philosophy—that's a big reason presidents choose them in the first place—but Scalia was letting the two merge in an ever more public way. Implicitly, if not explicitly, Scalia expected his colleagues, including the chief justice, to share his obsessions.

At the same time, Scalia was making it clear that he thought Roberts's opinion in the health care case should strike down the entire law, not just the individual mandate. Based on the oral argument, this result was obviously a possibility, but the implications of such a resolution weighed on Roberts. The law had dozens of provisions, many of them uncontroversial, many also critical to continued operations of both the federal government and all fifty states. (Pursuant to the law, for example, many millions of federal dollars had already been transferred to the states to pay for the existing Medicaid system; that whole system would have been thrown into chaos if the law had been completely struck down.)

Roberts was a conservative and a lifelong partisan Republican. The chief justice had no particular affection for Obama. Roberts had dual goals for his tenure as chief justice—to push his own ideological agenda but also to preserve the Court's place as a respected final arbiter of the nation's disputes. Scalia's vision of the justices as gladiators against the president unnerved Roberts. A complete nullification of the health care law on the eve of a presidential election would put the Court at the center of the campaign, especially if the majority in the case consisted only of the five Republican appointees. Democrats, and perhaps Obama himself, would crusade against the Court, eroding its moral if not its legal authority. As chief justice, Roberts felt obligated to protect the institutional interests of the Court, not just his own philosophical agenda.

Gradually, then with more urgency, Roberts began looking for a way out.

Don Verrilli had given it to him. Verrilli always liked the taxing power argument. No one doubted that Congress had the constitutional power to levy taxes, even if any individual decision to do so could be politically fraught. When the first cases against the health care law had been filed, in 2010, lawyers in the White House had been squeamish about using the taxing power argument. Obama had promised that the ACA would not represent a tax increase and, more generally, politicians never want to be associated with taxes. But as judges began to take the commerce clause challenge more seriously, the politicos deferred to the lawyers and allowed them to use the taxing power argument.

Verrilli was determined to raise the issue during oral argument. Toward the end of his defense of the individual mandate, Verrilli tried to pivot to the subject off a question from Roberts, saying, "Mr. Chief Justice, let me answer that, and then if I may, I'd like to move to the tax power argument."

Scalia cut him off with another wisecrack, which drew laughter. Roberts, Scalia, and Alito jumped in with questions, until finally Sotomayor came to Verrilli's rescue, saying, "General, could you turn to the tax clause?"

"Yes," Verrilli said.

Soon enough, though, Scalia spoke up and tried to embarrass Obama.

"The president said it wasn't a tax, didn't he?" Scalia asked Verrilli. "Is it a tax or not a tax? The president didn't think it was."

Verrilli was ready for this: "The president said it wasn't a tax *increase* because it ought to be understood as an incentive to get people to have insurance. I don't think it's fair to infer from that anything about whether that is an exercise of the tax power or not."

Then came an exchange that passed quickly but turned out to be of considerable significance. "Why didn't Congress call it a tax, then?" Roberts asked.

"Well—" Verrilli began.

"You're telling me they thought of it as a tax, they defended it on the tax power. Why didn't they say it was a tax?"

Verrilli answered: "They might have thought, Your Honor, that calling it a penalty as they did would make it more *effective* in accomplishing its objectives. But it is in the Internal Revenue Code, it is collected by the IRS on April 15th. I don't think this is a situation in which you can say—"

The word "effective" amused the chief justice. "Well, that's the reason," Roberts said with a big smile. "They thought it might be more 'effective' if they called it a penalty." Verrilli meant "effective" in the sense that the fee would compel people to buy insurance. But Roberts, a Washington veteran, knew the real reason Obama and the Democrats in Congress didn't use the word "tax"—because it was more politically "effective" to avoid it.

In any event, the tax argument stayed with the chief justice.

In April and May, it started to become apparent to the other justices that Roberts was going "wobbly" in his determination to overturn the law. Votes are never final until the decisions are announced in open court. Votes at conference are by definition tentative. It is well within the bounds of acceptable behavior for justices to change their minds once opinions begin circulating. Still, that rarely happens. But now, it appeared it was happening with Roberts—in the most important case of his tenure as chief justice.

What happened next was unprecedented in recent Supreme Court history. For pending cases, the Court had a nearly perfect record for avoiding leaks. But conservatives on the Court—especially law clerks—were so outraged that Roberts might betray them that they started to talk.

The chatter became so pervasive that, in short order, prominent conservatives decided to challenge Roberts to stick to his guns in the health care case. On May 22, an editorial in the *Wall Street Journal*, referring to recent remarks by Senator Patrick Leahy, said, "You can tell the Supreme Court is getting closer to its historic ObamaCare ruling because the left is making one last attempt to intimidate the Justices. The latest effort includes taunting Chief Justice John Roberts that if the Court overturns any of the law, he'll forever be defined as a partisan 'activist.'" That same day, Kathleen Parker, a conservative columnist in the *Washington Post*, wrote, "Novelist John Grisham could hardly spin a more provocative fiction: The president and his surrogates mount an aggressive campaign to intimidate the chief justice of the United States, implying ruin and ridicule should he fail to vote in a pivotal case according to the ruling political party's wishes. If only it were fiction."

George Will, the dean of conservative columnists, had heard from a law student who had heard from a law clerk that Roberts was vacillating in the case. On May 25, Will wrote that various progressives were "waging an embarrassingly obvious campaign, hoping [Roberts] will buckle beneath the pressure of their disapproval and declare Obamacare constitutional." Will concluded, "Such clumsy attempts to bend the chief justice are apt to reveal his spine of steel."

The following week, the rumors broke into the open, if a panel discussion at a Princeton reunion counts as the open. There, on June 2, Ramesh Ponnuru '95, a senior editor at *National Review*, said:

> My own sort of educated guess, based on people I talk to at the Supreme Court, is that—Well, as I'm sure people know, there's an initial vote the same week, on the Friday of the oral arguments. And my understanding is that there was a 5–4 vote to strike down the mandate and maybe *some* related provisions but not the entire act. Since then, interestingly, there seem to have been some second thoughts. Not on the part of Justice Kennedy, but on the part of Chief Justice Roberts, who seems to be going a little bit wobbly. So right now, I would say, [the outcome of the case] is a little bit up in the air.

Barton Gellman, a writer for *Time* who was present, tweeted about Ponnuru's remarks. (Ryan Lizza, the Washington correspondent of *The New Yorker*, retweeted Gellman's tweet, as did others.) It may have been just gossip, but it turned out to be remarkably accurate gossip. The story was getting out.

The four conservatives had overplayed their hand with the chief justice. By demanding that Roberts kill off the entire health care law, they prompted him to look for some kind of middle ground. The liberals, in contrast, welcomed any overture from the chief justice. Like the four conservatives, Roberts regarded the expansion of Medicaid as a violation of states' rights. Even though both Breyer and Kagan had vociferously defended the Medicaid expansion during oral argument, they agreed to join Roberts in striking that portion down—giving the chief valuable political cover on the issue. Roberts now had seven votes on the Medicaid issue.

In early June, Roberts circulated an opinion that declared that Congress had violated the commerce clause by imposing the individual mandate but that upheld the mandate as an exercise of the taxing power. The chief justice worked hard to try to bring Kennedy to his side. He turned one of Kennedy's questions in oral argument into part of his opinion, practically verbatim. Kennedy had told Verrilli: "Here the government is saying that the federal government has a duty to tell the individual citizen that it must act . . . and that changes the relationship of the federal government to the individual in a very fundamental way." Roberts wrote: "Accepting the government's theory would give Congress the same license to regulate what we do not do, fundamentally changing the relation between the citizen and the federal government." Neither man budged.

One clue about the resolution of the health care case appeared in plain view—and still everyone missed it. On June 15, Ginsburg spoke to the national convention of the American Constitution Society, the liberal counterpart to the Federalist Society. For the most part, she limited herself to an anodyne review of the cases decided by the Court so far, but she also warned that there were sharp disagreements ahead. In sum, Ginsburg said, the year "has been more than usually *taxing*."

Scalia was enraged at the chief. On Monday, June 25, when the Arizona immigration case was announced, Scalia's dissenting opinion marked his transition from conservative intellectual to right-wing crank. Speaking from the bench, he ranged over contemporary controversies, whether or not they had any relevance to the Arizona case. He noted, for example, that Obama had recently used an executive order to accomplish some of the goals of the DREAM Act and exempt certain young people from deportation. (This decision came well after the Arizona case was argued and was legally irrelevant to the issue at hand.) "The president said at a news conference that the new program is 'the right thing to do' in light of Congress's failure to pass the administration's proposed revision of the Immigration Act," Scalia said. "Perhaps it is, though Arizona may not think so. But to say, as the Court does, that Arizona contradicts federal law by enforcing applications of the Immigration Act that the president declines to enforce boggles the mind." Scalia did not explain how declining to deport these individuals boggled his mind.

"The issue is a stark one," he went on. "Are the sovereign states at the mercy of the federal executive's refusal to enforce the nation's immigration laws? A good way of answering that question is to ask: Would the states conceivably have entered into the union if the Constitution itself contained the Court's holding?" If this had been the original view of the framers of the Constitution, "the delegates to the Grand Convention would have rushed to the exits from Independence Hall." In other words, according to Scalia, if Arizona had known what was coming from his colleagues in 2012, the state never would have joined the Union. No other state would have either. The Arizona ruling, in Scalia's telling, would have destroyed the country even before it was born.

Scalia was indeed unhappy with the immigration decision, but the splenetic excess of his Arizona opinion owed far more to his failure (as yet unknown to the public) in the health care case.

The last few weeks of a Supreme Court term are always tense and confusing. Only the most controversial cases remain. Drafts of opinions fly between chambers. Memos comment on the opinions, and some propose alternatives, which in turn lead to more correspondence. The goal among the justices is always the same: to receive memos from colleagues that say, in the peculiar diction of the Court, "Please join me." That's how justices sign on to one another's opinions.

The manic intensity of June 2012 surpassed any year in recent memory. The outcome in *National Federation of Independent Business v. Sebelius* remained in doubt long after cases were usually settled. Roberts wrote a draft opinion. Ginsburg wrote a draft dissent. As Roberts hedged, Scalia, Kennedy, Thomas, and Alito adopted some of the chief's arguments as their own—in part as a possible dissent, in part as a lure to Roberts to make a new majority. (Dissenting opinions are invariably written by a single justice; other justices may then sign on. It's rare, if not unprecedented, for four justices to affix their names as coauthors to a dissent.) With all the changes, the cross-references among the various opinions became confused. The Scalia & Co. opinion referred to the Ginsburg opinion as "the dissent," when Ginsburg wound up *not* dissenting, except on the matter of the Medicaid provision. At one point, of course, it did look like the Ginsburg opinion would be "the dissent." Likewise, the Scalia & Co. opinion for the most part does not even address Roberts's opinion for the Court, which is unusual in a dissent.

Still, by the last week in June, the ragged passage had reached an end. By a vote of 5–4, the Court would uphold the heart of the Affordable Care Act. All that was left was to tell the world.

At ten o'clock on Thursday, June 28, the justices appeared as they always do. The three red curtains parted, pulled open by unseen hands, and the nine materialized simultaneously in groups of three: Roberts, Scalia, and Kennedy in the center; Sotomayor, Breyer, and Thomas on one side; Ginsburg, Alito, and Kagan on the other. On this day, they looked as they had never appeared before: haggard, exhausted, spent. Sotomayor was bent with fatigue; Alito needed a haircut; Kagan seemed thin and drawn. (This was partly intentional; she had lost thirty pounds in a year.) Scalia appeared as he had seven years earlier, when he stood by William Rehnquist's casket: bereft, heartbroken, and angry, too.

Even those tortured visages could not prepare anyone for the sound of John Roberts's voice. The brisk midwestern confidence was gone, replaced by a mournful near whisper. This was an unpleasant duty for him. It took a few minutes to find out why. He began with the commerce clause, and his conclusions were those telegraphed by the oral argument. The individual mandate, Roberts wrote, "does not regulate existing commercial activity. It instead compels individuals to *become* active in commerce by purchasing a product, on the ground that their failure to do so affects interstate commerce. Construing the Commerce Clause to permit Congress to regulate individuals precisely *because* they are doing nothing would open a new and potentially vast domain to congressional authority. Every day individuals do not do an infinite number of things." He went on, "To an economist, perhaps, there is no difference between activity and inactivity; both have measurable economic effects on commerce. But the distinction between doing something and doing nothing would not have been lost on the Framers, who were 'practical statesmen,' not metaphysical philosophers." The mandate, and the law, appeared at that moment as good as dead.

"That is not the end of the matter," the chief justice went on. "Because the Commerce Clause does not support the individual mandate, it is necessary to turn to the Government's second argument: that the mandate may be upheld as within Congress's enumerated power to 'lay and collect Taxes.' " Slowly, as members of the audience looked at one another in astonishment, it became clear that Roberts was endorsing the view that the mandate was a tax. "The Affordable Care Act's requirement that certain individuals pay a financial penalty for not obtaining health insurance may reasonably be characterized as a tax," he wrote. "Because the Constitution permits such a tax, it is not our role to forbid it, or to pass upon its wisdom or fairness."

There was no grand peroration at the conclusion of Roberts's remarks—more like an apology. "But the Court does not express any opinion on the wisdom of the Affordable Care Act," Roberts said. "Under the Constitution, that judgment is reserved to the people."

As the senior justice in the minority, Scalia had the right to read the dissenting opinion from the bench. But he was either too tired, too angry, or too overwrought to take on that duty, and he passed it off to Kennedy. "In our view," he said simply, "the act before us is invalid in its entirety."

Ginsburg went last. The statement she read in court marked a notable contrast to the words in her printed opinion. She had written at a time when it looked like the Court might strike down the individual mandate, or even the full statute. The opinion is caustic, almost bitter. But by the time the Court's decision was announced, Ginsburg realized, of course, that she had won. Her criticism of Roberts was, accordingly, mild.

More than any other justice, Ginsburg seemed obsessed with what she called "the broccoli horrible," and she made sure to take on that argument. "Although an individual might buy a car or a crown of broccoli one day, there is no certainty she will ever do so," Ginsburg wrote. "And if she eventually wants a car or has a craving for broccoli, she will be obliged to pay at the counter before receiving the vehicle or nourishment. She will get no free ride or food, at the expense of another consumer forced to pay an inflated price." (The word "broccoli" appeared twelve times in the course of all the opinions.)

Ginsburg's statement in court included an observation that appeared nowhere in her written opinion but served as a fitting epitaph to this epic case. "In the end," she said, "the Affordable Care Act survives largely unscathed."

THE ROBERTS COURT

O n the day after the health care opinion was announced, Roberts went to a judicial conference in Pennsylvania. There he was asked about his plans for the summer. He said he was leaving shortly to teach a class for two weeks in Malta. "Malta, as you know, is an impregnable island fortress," Roberts said. "It seemed like a good idea."

Conservatives turned on Roberts swiftly, and with a vengeance. A *Wall Street Journal* editorial written on the day of the decision described the chief justice's opinion as "grim," "shot through with confusion," "without real restraint," "a tragedy," and "damaging to the Court's institutional integrity." Ramesh Ponnuru, the *National Review* senior editor (and uniquely well-informed Princetonian), wrote that Roberts "acted less like a judge than like a politician, and a slippery one." Mitt Romney, who had earlier promised to make appointments to the Supreme Court in the mold of Roberts, changed his tune. "Well, I certainly wouldn't nominate someone who I knew was going to come out with a decision I violently disagreed with—or vehemently, rather, disagreed with," Romney told an interviewer. "And [Roberts] reached a conclusion, I think, that was not accurate and not an appropriate conclusion."

The outrage was understandable. A late and unexpected change of vote by a Republican appointee to the Supreme Court had again cost the conservative movement a cherished goal. The closest parallel was the *Casey* decision, in 1992, when O'Connor, Kennedy, and Souter (all Republican appointees) joined with Stevens and Harry Blackmun (also Republican appointees) to save the core of *Roe v. Wade* and thus to preserve abortion rights. In a way, Roberts's betrayal was more agonizing.

Unlike the members of the *Casey* trio, Roberts had never before sided with the liberals in a major contested case. And in the health care case, Roberts even embraced the conservatives' main argument, about the commerce clause. Victory was within reach!

But then, at the last moment, Roberts reached out for a subsidiary argument, about the taxing power—which had been only lightly briefed by the parties—to change the result in the case. And the chief justice's description of the individual mandate as a tax rather than a penalty might charitably be described as plausible at best. (To this point in the litigation, no other judge had upheld the ACA on that ground.) And in the same opinion, of course, while Roberts said the ACA *was* a tax for constitutional purposes, he also said that the law was *not* a tax for purposes of the Anti-Injunction Act. Some cynicism from conservatives, to say nothing of frustration, seemed reasonable.

In fact, for Roberts personally and the conservative cause generally, his vote and opinion in the health care case were acts of strategic genius. One cannot know for sure how future courts will interpret the decision in *National Federation of Independent Business*, but Roberts at a minimum laid down a marker on the scope of the commerce clause. As Ginsburg noted in her opinion, Roberts's "rigid reading of the Commerce Clause makes scant sense and is stunningly retrogressive," possibly even auguring a return to the pre-1937 days when the Court invalidated economic regulations with regularity. Roberts's opinion is potentially a significant long-term gain for the conservative movement.

In the short term, Roberts took the Supreme Court off the Democratic agenda for at least the foreseeable future. With the exception of Obama's complaint about *Citizens United* at the State of the Union in 2010, the president showed little interest in using opposition to the Court as a political weapon; the ruling in the health care case guaranteed that Obama would keep his distance for the duration of the 2012 campaign. In addition, Roberts bought enormous political space for himself for future rulings. In the Court's 2012–13 term, the justices will take nearly as many combustible issues as they did in the previous year. They will render a verdict on affirmative action in college admissions in a case from the University of Texas, raising the possibility that they will overturn O'Connor's signature achievement in the *Grutter* case of 2003. They will examine the future, if any, of Section 5 of the Voting Rights Act of 1965—which has long required mostly southern states to obtain Justice Department permission before making any changes in their electoral rules. Roberts is long on record as being deeply skeptical of any consideration of race by the government. The Court will probably also decide the fate of the Defense of Marriage Act, in the first major test of gay rights in the Roberts Court. Controversies related to *Citizens United* will also likely return in different forms. In these and other cases, Roberts can advance the conservative movement—and, after health care, he runs little risk of embroiling the Court in partisan politics.

Did Roberts, by his late switch in the health care case, poison his relations with his conservative allies on the Court? That is very unlikely. On the very night of the Court's decision, June 28, Thomas attended a dinner in Washington for local alumni of Yale Law School. (In December 2011, Thomas finally ended his long estrangement from his alma mater with a cheerful visit to New Haven.) In a question-and-answer session with attendees, Thomas paid a lengthy tribute to the way Roberts handled the health care case. Given the complexity and competing pressures, Thomas said, "he handled it just right." Several days later, Kennedy spoke to a gathering at the Aspen Institute, where he made a pointed defense of a justice's right to change his mind while a case was pending. He noted he had often done it himself. Scalia was furious, but what did Roberts have to fear from his senior colleague? After all, at this late date Scalia was not going to start moving to the left to punish the chief. Anyway, even by Supreme Court standards, Scalia was old—and Roberts was still young. Leaks before and after the decision were more likely the work of petulant law clerks rather than of their bosses. The justices knew where the power resided on the Supreme Court, and they understood that it seldom paid to hold grudges against colleagues.

Conservatives and liberals, on the Court and off, recognized the health care decision for what it was: an act of leadership by the chief justice. It's John Roberts's Court now.

"Good afternoon," President Obama said in the East Room of the White House. "Earlier today the Supreme Court upheld the constitutionality of the Affordable Care Act, the name of the health care reform we passed two years ago. In doing so, they've reaffirmed a fundamental principle: that here in America, in the wealthiest nation on earth, no illness or accident should lead to any family's financial ruin." He said nothing more about the decision, preferring instead to tout the benefits of the reform plan itself.

The Obama administration illustrated a fundamental difference between contemporary Republicans and Democrats. Starting with Ronald Reagan and proceeding through both sets of Bush years, Republicans demonstrated a profound commitment to their vision of the Constitution. There was a Republican judicial agenda for change: expand executive power, end racial preferences intended to assist African Americans, speed up executions, prohibit all forms of gun control, welcome religion into the public sphere, deregulate political campaigns, and, above all, reverse *Roe v. Wade* and allow states to ban abortion. There was a Republican judicial philosophy: originalism. Republican presidents talked publicly about this agenda. They made judicial appointments, including to the lower courts, a major priority. Republican legislators fought for their party's judicial nominees—and obstructed and harassed Democratic nominees to the courts, even uncontroversial ones.

Barack Obama was not only an outstanding law student and a practicing lawyer but also, as he often pointed out during his first campaign for president, a professor of constitutional law. In the White House, he enjoyed reminding his subordinates of his mastery of legal issues. (On greeting a delegation from his counsel's office, the president sometimes joked, "Oh, the lawyers! This is the *easy* part of my day.") But Obama rarely discussed the Constitution outside the Oval Office.

Obama made two sterling appointments to the Supreme Court, and he was justly proud of these accomplishments. But his interest in judicial nominations appeared almost to have begun with Sonia Sotomayor and ended with Elena Kagan. Obama's lassitude regarding the lower courts was astonishing. In the summer of 2012, when the Senate more or less shut down confirmations until the election, there were 77 vacancies on the federal bench out of a total of about 874 judges. At that point, Obama had failed even to submit nominations for 43 of the judgeships, and Republicans will prevent many of Obama's 34 nominees from coming up for votes. During Obama's presidency, Republicans engaged in an unprecedented level of obstruction toward Obama's judicial nominees; they filibustered and threatened filibusters against more judges than Democrats did in the Bush years. But Republicans could hardly be blamed for blocking judges that Obama failed to nominate in the first place. And since Obama almost never discussed the issue in public,

Republicans faced no political consequences for delaying or obstructing confirmations. In the early days of Obama's administration, it was plausible to blame this failure on staffers like Greg Craig or Cassandra Butts; by the end of his term, the only reason could be that the president himself chose not to invest his own time or effort in the issue.

For Obama, and Democrats generally, this failure to engage on legal issues extended to more than just judgeships. To the extent there is a contemporary liberal agenda, it consists roughly of a pallid embrace of the status quo: preserve *Roe* and affirmative action. (Support for the rights of gay people may turn out to be an exception to this pervasive timidity. Obama did direct his administration to argue that the Defense of Marriage Act violated the equal protection clause, and announced his support for same-sex marriage.) Both Bill Clinton and Obama also displayed a major commitment to diversity in filling judgeships, and their nominees included dramatically more women and minorities than those of Republican presidents. But it was a lot harder to say what these Democratic judges stood for.

Even after the health care case, it is easy to say what John Roberts stands for. He remains a skilled and powerful advocate for the full Republican agenda; he is still the candidate (in robes) of change. Roberts did refrain from embracing the unprecedented extremism of his conservative colleagues in the health care case; on that occasion, the chief justice acted like a true conservative and deferred, as judges have for seventy-five years, to the elected branches of government on issues relating to managing the economy. But it was folly to pretend that Roberts had discovered his inner moderate. He had not changed, except that he was more powerful than ever. The only thing that is certain about January 20, 2013, is that John Roberts will be there to administer the oath of office.

There was some irony in the conservative embrace of originalism, in the insistence by Scalia and others that the Constitution is "dead" and unchanging. With their success, driven by people, ideas, and money, conservatives proved just how much the Constitution can change, and it did. Obama and his party were the ones who acted like the Constitution remained inert; they hoped the Constitution and the values underlying it would somehow take care of themselves. That has never happened, and it never will. Invariably, inevitably, the Constitution lives.

ACKNOWLEDGMENTS

My thanks to my friends at Doubleday, starting with my editor, Bill Thomas. Phyllis Grann also lavished attention on this book and improved it a great deal. Thank you as well to Coralie Hunter, Todd Doughty, Roslyn Schloss, and Bette Alexander. For our sixth book together, my agent, Esther Newberg, has steered me the right way. My thanks as well to John Q. Barrett, of the St. John's University School of Law, and Samuel Issacharoff, of the New York University School of Law, for their helpful comments on the manuscript. For fact-checking and research assistance, I am grateful to Lila Byock, Alex Bernstein, and Avi Zenilman. Thank you as well to Silvia Berinstein. Ellen and Adam Toobin were away at college when I wrote this book, but their inspiration to me is ever present.

I remain privileged to work at *The New Yorker*, where David Remnick has been a generous boss and a loyal friend. I am fortunate to work with Dorothy Wickenden, John Bennet, and Amy Davidson.

Amy McIntosh is my wife and true love. She's a good editor, too.

NOTES

This book is based principally on my interviews with the justices and more than forty of their law clerks. The interviews were on a not-for-attribution basis—that is, I could use the information provided but without quoting directly or identifying the source.

In addition to the works cited in the text and below, I have benefited from the day-to-day coverage of the Supreme Court press corps, especially that of Adam Liptak, Lyle Denniston, Dahlia Lithwick, Tony Mauro, David Savage, Nina Totenberg, Pete Williams, and my CNN colleague Bill Mears. My thanks also to the Public Information Office of the Court, its excellent website, www.supremecourt.gov, and Kathy Arberg, Patricia McCabe Estrada, and Scott Markley.

The Court's opinions are widely available online. I generally relied on Cornell University's www.law.cornell.edu/supct/. For transcripts and recordings of the Court's oral arguments, www.oyez.org, created by Professor Jerry Goldman of the Chicago-Kent College of Law, is indispensable. I am also a regular reader of www.scotusblog.com, the blog of record about the Court, and http://howappealing.law.com.

PROLOGUE: THE OATHS

1 only a single provision: I am grateful to Professor Akhil Reed Amar, of Yale Law School, for introducing me to the history of the oath. In particular, I relied on his book *America's Constitution*, pp. 177–78.

3 whether he did: For an evocative account of Washington's inauguration, see Ron Chernow, *Washington: A Life*, ch. 46.

3 wrote to the chief justice about it: *Time*, March 25, 1929, http://www.time .com/time/magazine/article/0,9171,846311,00.html#ixzz1WAMUAeom.

16 standing athwart history yelling "Stop!": William F. Buckley Jr., "Publisher's Statement," *National Review*, Nov. 19, 1955, p. 5.

CHAPTER 1: THE POLITICIAN'S PATH

23 friends and colleagues found Obama more analytical than confrontational: David Remnick, *The Bridge*, pp. 163–67.

26 "Do you even *want* popcorn?": Remnick, *The Bridge*, p. 189.

27 "for a lot of the changes that have been made": Remnick, *The Bridge*, pp. 207–08.

32 compromise on racial profiling by the police: Remnick, *The Bridge*, pp. 350–51.

CHAPTER 2: "ON BEHALF OF THE STRONG IN OPPOSITION TO THE WEAK"

36 a justice who might overturn Roe v. Wade: David Remnick, *The Bridge*, p. 434.

40 "Whoever had the 15- to 20-minute slot won that money": Roger Parloff, "On History's Stage: Chief Justice John G. Roberts Jr.," *Fortune*, Jan. 3, 2011, http://management.fortune.cnn.com/2011/01/03/on-historys-stage-chief-justice -john-roberts-jr/.

41 Roberts was the leading figure in his generation: See http://www .scotusblog.com/2006/03/the-expansion-of-the-supreme-court-bar/.

CHAPTER 3: THE ERA OF GOOD FEELINGS

49 "in the event that you do lead the defense team at the military tribunals, to offer my help": Jonathan Mahler, *The Challenge*, ch. 4.

55 "two implants on each side and a total of three pints of fluid": Dan P. Lee, "Paw Paw & Lady Love," *New York*, June 5, 2011, http://nymag.com/news/ features/anna-nicole-smith-2011-6/.

CHAPTER 4: THE LEGACY OF APPENDIX E

58 the quorum for the official prayers: Abigail Pogrebin, *Stars of David*, p. 19.

60 "That makes no sense": Speech by Ruth Bader Ginsburg, Tenth Circuit Conference, Aug. 27, 2010, http://www.c-spanvideo.org/program/295217-1.

65 "the right most valued by civilized men": *Olmstead v. United States,* 277 U.S. 438 (1928) (Brandeis, J., dissenting).

65 "not legal reasoning but fiat": Robert Bork, *The Tempting of America*, p. 114.

65 "her ability to stand in relation to man, society, and the state as an independent, self-sustaining, equal citizen": Ruth Ginsburg, "Some

Thoughts on Autonomy and Equality in Relation to Roe v. Wade," 63 *North Carolina Law Review* 375 (1985).

65 **"the tall doctor and the little woman who needs him"**: http://www
.nytimes.com/2009/07/12/magazine/12ginsburg-t.html?_r=2&pagewanted=all.

69 **"dissenting judge believes the court to have been betrayed"**: Charles Evans Hughes, *The Supreme Court of the United States* (1936), p. 68, quoted in Ruth Bader Ginsburg, "The Role of Dissenting Opinions," 95 *Minnesota Law Review* 1 (2010), http://www.minnesotalawreview.org/wp-content/uploads/2011/07/Ginsburg_MLR.pdf.

69 **"The Constitution, as we have known it, is gone"**: John Q. Barrett, "Commending Opinion Announcements by Supreme Court Justices," http://www.stjohns.edu/media/3/55c14b0772794f148fec48e3c14851a7.pdf. See also James F. Simon, *FDR and Chief Justice Hughes*, p. 256.

69 **each read dissents from the bench exactly once**: I am grateful to William Blake, of the University of Texas, for sharing his research with me. See William D. Blake and Hans J. Hacker, "The Brooding Spirit of the Law: Supreme Court Justices Reading Dissents from the Bench," *Justice System Journal* 31(1): 1–25 (2010).

CHAPTER 5: THE BALLAD OF LILLY LEDBETTER

72 **"public law litigation"**: Abram Chayes, "The Role of the Judge in Public Law Litigation," 89 *Harvard Law Review* 1281 (1976).

CHAPTER 6: THE WAR AGAINST PRECEDENT

82 **was able to assemble a majority in only a quarter of them**: These statistics are drawn from the annual compilations by scotusblog.com.

CHAPTER 7: THE HUNTER

100 **took his rifle, a .22 carbine, with him on the subway**: Joan Biskupic, *American Original*, pp. 21–22.

100 **after a string of bank robberies**: The Miller story is laid out in entertaining detail in Brian L. Frye, "The Peculiar Story of *United States v. Miller*," *NYU Journal of Law & Liberty* 3(1): 48–82 (2008).

101 **the colonists formed militias**: Adam Winkler, *Gunfight*, pp. 103–04.

103 **the 1976 platform opposed it**: Reva B. Siegel, "Dead or Alive: Originalism as Popular Constitutionalism in Heller," 122 *Harvard Law Review* 191 (2008).

103 **advocated for the individual rights view in conferences and seminars**: Winkler, *Gunfight*, pp. 67, 97.

103 "for protection of himself, his family, and his freedoms": Quoted in
      Siegel, "Dead or Alive."

103 later joined the Reagan Justice Department: Ibid.

CHAPTER 8: LAWYERS, GUNS, AND MONEY

107 Reagan-era Justice Department official with close ties to the
      conservative movement: Adam Winkler, *Gunfight*, p. 57.

108 drug dealers broke her car windows and drove into her back fence:
      Brian Doherty, *Gun Control on Trial*, p. 29.

113 Stevens who hewed more closely to the actual debates of the framers:
      Post by Jack Rakove, http://balkin.blogspot.com/2008/06/thoughts-on-heller
      -from-real-historian.html.

113 as did the state legislators who ratified their work: The most often cited
      critique of originalism remains Paul Brest, "The Misconceived Quest for
      Original Understanding," 60 *Boston University Law Review* 204 (1980).

113 they never indicated that they understood their *intentions* should bind
      future generations: H. Jefferson Powell, "The Original Understanding of
      Original Intent," 98 *Harvard Law Review* 885, 903 (1984).

113 and then find their twenty-first-century analogue: Winkler, *Gunfight*,
      pp. 283–86. See also Nelson Lund, "The Second Amendment, Heller, and
      Originalist Jurisprudence," 56 *UCLA Law Review* 1343 (2009).

CHAPTER 9: THE UNREQUITED BIPARTISANSHIP OF
BARACK OBAMA

116 had voted against his confirmation three years earlier: Tony Mauro, The
      Blog of *Legal Times*, Jan. 14, 2009. http://legaltimes.typepad.com/blt/2009/01/
      a-chat-around-the-fireplace-for-obama-biden-and-the-supreme-court.html.

CHAPTER 10: WISE LATINA

130 "adapt it to their own needs and uses": Diane P. Wood, "Our 18th Century
      Constitution in the 21st Century World," http://www.scotusblog.com/wp
      -content/uploads/2009/05/80_nyulr_1079_5-13-09_1224.rtf.

130 was the case of *National Organization for Women v. Scheidler*, in 2001:
      For a clear discussion of that case, see Emily Bazelon's discussion in *Slate*, http://
      www.slate.com/articles/news_and_politics/jurisprudence/2010/04/defining
      _radical_down.html.

132 suddenly of a heart attack at the age of forty-two: Antonia Felix, *Sonia
      Sotomayor: The True American Dream*, pp. 12–14.

132 "mark that I wasn't able to succeed at those institutions": Quoted in Felix, *Sonia Sotomayor*, p. 39.

133 she toured Israel with a group of Latino activists: Lauren Collins, "Number Nine," *New Yorker*, Jan. 11, 2010, p. 48.

134 including the son of her dentist: Collins, "Number Nine," p. 48.

CHAPTER 11: MONEY TALKS

146 "make constitutional law on his own": Jack Beatty, *Age of Betrayal: The Triumph of Money in America, 1865–1900*, p. 176. Beatty points out that Davis's credibility was suspect because Karl Marx (!) complained that Davis had misquoted him in a report. On *Santa Clara*, see also Morton J. Horwitz, *The Transformation of American Law, 1870–1960*, pp. 66–71.

147 "'the government is best which governs least'": Horwitz, *The Transformation of American Law*, p. 33.

148 "then he did not stay bought": Frick made the comment to the journalist Oswald Garrison Villard, who recounted it in his book *Fighting Years*, p. 181.

149 required extensive disclosure of campaign contributions and expenditures: Samuel Issacharoff, Pamela S. Karlan, and Richard H. Pildes, *The Law of Democracy*, p. 334.

149 Warren Burger, Potter Stewart, Lewis Powell, and William Rehnquist: Seth Stern and Stephen Wermiel, *Justice Brennan: Liberal Champion*, p. 442.

150 Congress had tried to set up a tightly controlled system for financing campaigns: Frank J. Sorauf, *Inside Campaign Finance: Myths and Realities*, pp. 238–39.

CHAPTER 12: SAMUEL ALITO'S QUESTION

159 named Bossie his "chief researcher" and the pair narrowed their focus to the personal and financial affairs of Bill and Hillary Clinton: Joe Conason and Gene Lyons, *The Hunting of the President: The Ten-Year Campaign to Destroy Bill and Hillary Clinton*, pp. 72–75.

159 various Washington journalists who printed or broadcast his accusations: Sidney Blumenthal, *The Clinton Wars*, pp. 76–77.

159 he had doctored certain transcripts to eliminate exculpatory information about Hillary Clinton: Howard Kurtz, "Some Reporters Heard Unedited Tapes," *Washington Post*, May 11, 1998. See also Blumenthal, *The Clinton Wars*, pp. 443–44.

160 "conspiring against my husband since the day he announced for

president": Jeffrey Toobin, *A Vast Conspiracy: The Real Story of the Sex Scandal That Nearly Brought Down a President*, pp. 254–56.

CHAPTER 13: THE ROOKIE

174 **social studies to fifth and sixth graders:** For the reflection of one former Gloria Kagan student, see Blake Eskin, "The Ghost of Mrs. Kagan," http://www.newyorker.com/online/blogs/newsdesk/2010/05/the-ghost-of-mrs-kagan.html.

CHAPTER 14: THE NINETY-PAGE SWAN SONG OF JOHN PAUL STEVENS

186 **embezzled funds from the insurance company to prop up the hotel:** Bill Barnhart and Gene Schlickman, *John Paul Stevens: An Independent Life*, p. 31.

186 **one of the boys was forced to open a safe in the first-floor library:** Barnhart and Schlickman, *John Paul Stevens*, pp. 32–33.

CHAPTER 15: "WITH ALL DUE DEFERENCE TO SEPARATION OF POWERS"

195 **spotty at best in recent years:** Pete Williams of NBC News compiled the statistics: http://firstread.msnbc.msn.com/_news/2011/01/25/5914956-will-chief -justice-roberts-be-in-attendance-after-all. See also Adam Liptak, "For Justices, State of the Union Can Be a Trial," *New York Times,* Jan. 23, 2012, http://www .nytimes.com/2012/01/24/us/state-of-the-union-can-be-a-trial-for-supreme-court -justices.html.

198 **"juvenile spectacle":** Adam Liptak, "Six Justices to Attend State of the Union," Jan. 25, 2011, *New York Times,* http://www.nytimes.com/2011/01/26/us/ politics/26justices.html?_r=3.

CHAPTER 16: THE RETIRED JUSTICES DISSENT

212 **"and have them all over":** http://www.abajournal.com/news/article/oconnor_ lawyers_judges_need_to_wake_up_to_judicial_funding_threat_prep_for_/.

213 **call meant that he had died:** http://www.lvrj.com/news/robocall-mishap -shows-nevadans-dont-want-any-questions-at-1-a-m—105738278.html?ref=278.

215 **"So forget it. It's over!":** Jeffrey Rosen, "Why I Miss Sandra Day O'Connor," July 1, 2011, http://www.tnr.com/article/politics/91146/sandra-day-o-connor -supreme-court-alito.

216 **"It's not always positive":** Joan Biskupic, "O'Connor Says Rulings Being

'Dismantled,' " Jan. 5, 2010, http://www.usatoday.com/news/washington/
judicial/2009-10-05-sandra-day-oconnor_N.htm.

CHAPTER 17: SOFTBALL POLITICS

228 laying out the absurdities of contemporary confirmation hearings: Elena
Kagan, "Confirmation Messes, Old and New," 62 *University of Chicago Law
Review* 919 (1995), http://lawreview.uchicago.edu/archive/Front%20Page/Kagan/
ConfirmationMessesOldAndNew.pdf.

229 "I know it when I see it": *Jacobellis v. Ohio,* 378 U.S. 164, 197 (1964) (Stewart,
J., concurring).

CHAPTER 18: THE TEA PARTY AND
THE JUSTICE'S WIFE

231 "their belief in citizen activism": Theda Skocpol and Vanessa
Williamson, *The Tea Party and the Remaking of Republican Conservatism*,
p. 53.

231 "minimize the risk of another monarchy": Glenn Beck, *The Original
Argument*, p. xxv.

232 "in academia claim it to mean": Mark R. Levin, *Liberty and Tyranny: A
Conservative Manifesto*, pp. 57, 60.

233 family prominent in Republican politics: Jane Mayer and Jill Abramson,
Strange Justice: The Selling of Clarence Thomas, pp. 144–45.

235 "And you pay a penalty if you don't": Quoted in Paul Starr, *Remedy and
Reaction*, p. 87.

235 unless there was a mandate: Starr, *Remedy and Reaction*, pp. 87–88.

236 the conservative Heritage Foundation: The plan was created by Stuart
Butler and Edmund Haislmaier. See http://online.wsj.com/article/SB1000142405
2970204618704576641190920152366.html.

236 repeated his support for the idea as recently as 2005: Josh Hicks, "Newt
Gingrich's Changing Stance on Health-Care Mandates," Dec. 12, 2011,
http://www.washingtonpost.com/blogs/fact-checker/post/newt-gingrichs
-changing-stance-on-health-care-mandates-fact-checker-biography/2011/12/
09/gIQAVl0lkO_blog.html.

237 "Constitutional Implications of an 'Individual Mandate' in Health Care
Reform": See http://www.fed-soc.org/publications/detail/constitutional
-implications-of-an-individual-mandate-in-health-care-reform.

237 translating the Urbanowicz-Smith article into more colloquial
language: David B. Rivkin Jr. and Lee A. Casey, "Constitutionality of Health
Insurance Mandate Questioned," *Washington Post*, Aug. 22, 2009, http://www

.washingtonpost.com/wp-dyn/content/article/2009/08/21/AR2009082103033
.html.

CHAPTER 19: THE THOMAS COURT

240 **Crow who made the $500,000 contribution to Liberty Central:** Kenneth P. Vogel, Marin Cogan, and John Bresnahan, "Justice Thomas's Wife Virginia Thomas Now a Lobbyist," *Politico*, Feb. 4, 2011, http://www.politico.com/news/stories/0211/48812.html; Mike McIntire, "Friendship of Justice and Magnate Puts Focus on Ethics," *New York Times*, June 18, 2011, http://www.nytimes.com/2011/06/19/us/politics/19thomas.html?pagewanted=all.

240 **who are leading benefactors of the Tea Party movement:** Eric Lichtblau, "Common Cause Asks Court about Thomas Speech," *New York Times*, Feb. 14, 2011, http://www.nytimes.com/2011/02/15/us/politics/15thomas.html. The circumstances of the appearances by Thomas and Scalia at the Koch brothers' event are not clear. In his financial disclosure statement, Thomas listed reimbursement for a Federalist Society event at the time and place of the Koch event.

241 **"price to pay today for standing in defense of your Constitution":** The audiotape of this speech was first disclosed by *Politico*. Kenneth P. Vogel, "Defiant Clarence Thomas Fires Back," *Politico*, Feb. 27, 2011, http://www.politico.com/news/stories/0211/50277.html.

247 **"He does not believe in stare decisis, period":** Ken Foskett, *Judging Thomas: The Life and Times of Clarence Thomas*, pp. 281–82.

249 **"the perversion of the Constitution took off during the presidency of Franklin Delano Roosevelt":** Kate Zernike, *Boiling Mad: Inside Tea Party America*, p. 70.

CHAPTER 20: "DEMOCRACY IS NOT A GAME"

254 **his speech to raise money for the *Spectator* would have been inappropriate:** On Alito's speeches for the *Spectator*, see Lee Fang, "Exclusive: Supreme Court Justice Sam Alito Dismisses His Profligate Right-Wing Fundraising as 'Not Important,'" Nov. 10, 2010, http://thinkprogress.org/politics/2010/11/10/129395/sam-alito-republican-fundraiser/. See also http://lawprofessors.typepad.com/conlaw/2010/11/alito-and-ethics.html.

CHAPTER 21: "YOU SHOULD DO IT"

266 **"the Court will accept that judgment":** John Q. Barrett, "*Wickard v. Filburn* (1942)," http://www.stjohns.edu/media/3/638cd994e8484fd3bdb841f31b11952f.pdf?d=201.

271 **sweeping the hallways:** Nina Totenberg, profile of Donald Verrilli, NPR, http://www.npr.org/2012/03/22/148947199/the-man-behind-the-defense-of -obamas-health-law.

CHAPTER 22: BROCCOLI

277 **"you can make people buy broccoli":** For a history of the broccoli example in the health care case, see James B. Stewart, "How Broccoli Landed on Supreme Court Menu," *New York Times*, June 14, 2012, http://www.nytimes .com/2012/06/14/business/how-broccoli-became-a-symbol-in-the-health-care -debate.html?pagewanted=all.

CHAPTER 23: THE "EFFECTIVE" ARGUMENT

284 **"Some might consider the change trivial":** Stevens, *Five Chiefs*, p. 212.

284 **he thought Congress had exceeded its powers under the commerce clause in creating the individual mandate:** In addition to my own reporting, I relied on the following sources in my account of the Court's deliberations: Jan Crawford, "Roberts Switched Views to Uphold Health Care Law," July 1, 2012, http://www.cbsnews.com/8301-3460_162–57464549/roberts-switched -views-to-uphold-health-care-law/?tag=contentMain;contentBody; Paul Campos, "Roberts Wrote Both Obamacare Opinions," *Salon*, July 3, 2012, http://www .salon.com/2012/07/03/roberts_wrote_both_obamacare_opinions/. See also http://www.volokh.com/2012/07/03/so-now-we-have-supreme-court-leaks -disagreeing-with-supreme-court-leaks/; http://www.volokh.com/2012/07/03/ more-on-the-supreme-court-leak/.

288 **"a little bit up in the air":** Quoted at http://www.volokh.com/2012/07/03/ more-on-the-supreme-court-leak/.

289 **"changing the relation between the citizen and the federal government":** Jan Crawford first made this connection. See http://www .cbsnews.com/8301-3460_162-57464549/roberts-switched-views-to-uphold -health-care-law/?tag=contentMain;contentBody.

BIBLIOGRAPHY

Abraham, Henry J. *Justices, Presidents, and Senators.* Rev. ed. New York: Rowman & Littlefield, 1999.

Amar, Akhil Reed. *America's Constitution: A Biography.* New York: Random House, 2005.

Atkinson, David N. *Leaving the Bench: Supreme Court Justices at the End.* Lawrence: University Press of Kansas, 1999.

Barnhart, Bill, and Gene Schlickman. *John Paul Stevens: An Independent Life.* Chicago: Northern Illinois University Press, 2010.

Beatty, Jack. *Age of Betrayal: The Triumph of Money in America, 1865–1900.* New York: Vintage, 2008.

Beck, Glenn. *The Original Argument: The Federalists' Case for the Constitution, Adapted for the 21st Century.* New York: Threshold Editions, 2011.

Biskupic, Joan. *American Original: The Life and Constitution of Supreme Court Justice Antonin Scalia.* New York: Farrar, Straus and Giroux, 2009.

———. *Sandra Day O'Connor: How the First Woman on the Supreme Court Became Its Most Influential Justice.* New York: Ecco Books, 2005.

Blumenthal, Sidney. *The Clinton Wars.* New York: Farrar, Straus and Giroux, 2003.

Bork, Robert. *The Tempting of America: The Political Seduction of Law.* New York: Free Press, 1990.

Brady, Diane. *Fraternity.* New York: Spiegel & Grau, 2012.

Breyer, Stephen. *Active Liberty: Interpreting Our Democratic Constitution.* New York: Knopf, 2005.

———. *Making Our Democracy Work: A Judge's View.* New York: Knopf, 2010.

Calabresi, Steven G., ed. *Originalism: A Quarter-Century of Debate.* Washington, D.C.: Regnery, 2007.

Chernow, Ron. *Washington: A Life.* New York: Penguin, 2010.

Conason, Joe, and Gene Lyons. *The Hunting of the President: The Ten-Year Campaign to Destroy Bill and Hillary Clinton.* New York: St. Martin's Press, 2000.

Doherty, Brian. *Gun Control on Trial.* Washington: Cato Institute, 2009.

Feldman, Noah. *Scorpions: The Battles and Triumphs of FDR's Great Supreme Court Justices.* New York: Twelve, 2010.

Felix, Antonia. *Sonia Sotomayor: The True American Dream.* New York: Berkley, 2010.

Foskett, Ken. *Judging Thomas: The Life and Times of Clarence Thomas.* New York: Harper Perennial, 2005.

Greenburg, Jan Crawford. *Supreme Conflict.* New York: Penguin, 2007.

Horwitz, Morton J. *The Transformation of American Law, 1870–1960.* New York: Oxford University Press, 1992.

Issacharoff, Samuel, Pamela S. Karlan, and Richard H. Pildes. *The Law of Democracy.* 3rd ed. New York: Foundation Press, 2007.

Klarman, Michael J. *From Jim Crow to Civil Rights: The Supreme Court and the Struggle for Racial Equality.* New York: Oxford University Press, 2004.

Kramer, Larry D. *The People Themselves: Popular Constitutionalism and Judicial Review.* New York: Oxford University Press, 2004.

Levin, Mark R. *Liberty and Tyranny: A Conservative Manifesto.* New York: Threshold Editions, 2009.

Mahler, Jonathan. *The Challenge: How a Maverick Navy Officer and a Young Law Professor Risked Their Careers to Defend the Constitution—and Won.* New York: Picador, 2009.

Manaster, Kenneth A. *Illinois Justice: The Scandal of 1969 and the Rise of John Paul Stevens.* Chicago: University of Chicago Press, 2001.

Margulies, Joseph. *Guantanamo and the Abuse of Presidential Power.* New York: Simon & Schuster, 2006.

Maroon, Suzy, and Fred J. Maroon. *The Supreme Court of the United States.* New York: Thomasson-Grant & Lickle, 1996.

Mayer, Jane, and Jill Abramson. *Strange Justice: The Selling of Clarence Thomas.* Boston: Houghton Mifflin, 1994.

Obama, Barack. *The Audacity of Hope.* New York: Three Rivers Press, 2006.

O'Brien, David M. *Storm Center: The Supreme Court in American Politics.* 6th ed. New York: Norton, 2003.

Peppers, Todd C. *Courtiers of the Marble Palace: The Rise and Influence of the Supreme Court Law Clerk.* Stanford: Stanford University Press, 2006.

Pogrebin, Abigail. *Stars of David: Prominent Jews Talk about Being Jewish.* New York: Broadway, 2005.

Posner, Richard A. *Not a Suicide Pact: The Constitution in a Time of National Emergency.* New York: Oxford University Press, 2006.

Rehnquist, William H. *The Supreme Court: How It Was, How It Is.* New York: Morrow, 1987.

Remnick, David. *The Bridge: The Life and Rise of Barack Obama.* New York: Knopf, 2010.

Rosen, Jeffrey. *The Most Democratic Branch: How the Courts Serve America.* New York: Oxford University Press, 2006.

————. *The Supreme Court.* New York: Times Books, 2007.

Savage, David G. *Turning Right: The Making of the Rehnquist Supreme Court.* New York: Wiley, 1993.

Scalia, Antonin. *A Matter of Interpretation: Federal Courts and the Law.* Princeton: Princeton University Press, 1997.

Schwartz, Bernard. *A History of the Supreme Court.* New York: Oxford University Press, 1993.

Shesol, Jeff. *Supreme Power: Franklin Roosevelt vs. the Supreme Court.* New York: Norton, 2010.

Simon, James F. *The Center Holds: The Power Struggle inside the Rehnquist Court.* New York: Simon & Schuster, 1995.

————. *FDR and Chief Justice Hughes: The President, the Supreme Court, and the Epic Battle over the New Deal.* New York: Simon & Schuster, 2012.

Skocpol, Theda, and Vanessa Williamson. *The Tea Party and the Remaking of Republican Conservatism.* New York: Oxford University Press, 2012.

Slaughter, Anne-Marie. *A New World Order.* Princeton, N.J.: Princeton University Press, 2004.

Sorauf, Frank J. *Inside Campaign Finance: Myths and Realities.* New Haven, Conn.: Yale University Press, 1994.

Starr, Kenneth W. *First Among Equals: The Supreme Court in American Life.* New York: Warner Books, 2002.

Starr, Paul. *Remedy and Reaction.* New Haven, Conn.: Yale University Press, 2011.

Stern, Seth, and Stephen Wermiel. *Justice Brennan: Liberal Champion.* New York: Houghton Mifflin Harcourt, 2010.

Stevens, John Paul. *Five Chiefs: A Supreme Court Memoir.* New York: Little, Brown, 2011.

Stohr, Greg. *A Black and White Case: How Affirmative Action Survived Its Greatest Legal Challenge.* Princeton, N.J.: Bloomberg Press, 2004.

Stone, Geoffrey R. *Perilous Times: Free Speech in Wartime.* New York: Norton, 2004.

Sunstein, Cass R. *One Case at a Time: Judicial Minimalism on the Supreme Court.* Cambridge, Mass.: Harvard University Press, 1999.

————. *Radicals in Robes: Why Extreme Right-Wing Courts Are Wrong for America.* New York: Basic Books, 2005.

Teles, Steven M. *The Rise of the Conservative Legal Movement.* Princeton, N.J.: Princeton University Press, 2008.

Thomas, Clarence. *My Grandfather's Son: A Memoir.* New York: Harper, 2007.

Toobin, Jeffrey. *A Vast Conspiracy: The Real Story of the Sex Scandal That Nearly Brought Down a President.* New York: Touchstone, 1999.

Tribe, Laurence H. *God Save This Honorable Court: How the Choice of Supreme Court Justices Shapes Our History.* New York: Random House, 1985.

Tushnet, Mark. *A Court Divided: The Rehnquist Court and the Future of Constitutional Law.* New York: Norton, 2005.

Villard, Oswald Garrison. *Fighting Years.* New York: Harcourt, Brace, 1939.

Ward, Artemus, and David L. Weiden. *Sorcerers' Apprentices: 100 Years of Law Clerks at the United States Supreme Court.* New York: New York University Press, 2006.

Winkler, Adam. *Gunfight: The Battle over the Right to Bear Arms in America.* New York: Norton, 2011.

Woodward, Bob, and Scott Armstrong. *The Brethren: Inside the Supreme Court.* New York: Simon & Schuster, 1979.

Yarbrough, Tinsley E. *David Hackett Souter: Traditional Republican on the Rehnquist Court.* New York: Oxford University Press, 2005.

Zernike, Kate. *Boiling Mad: Inside Tea Party America.* New York: Times Books, 2010.

PHOTO CREDITS

Grateful acknowledgment is given to the following for permission to reprint the photos in this book:

Page 1, inset.	Master Sgt. Cecilio Ricardo, U.S. Air Force
Page 1, top.	Win McNamee/Getty Images
Page 1, bottom	Pete Souza/The White House/Getty Images
Page 3, top.	Photo by Pete Souza
Page 3, bottom.	Ron Edmonds/AP
Page 4, top left.	Jewel Samad/AFP/Getty Images
Page 4, top right.	Jose Luis Magana/AP
Page 4, bottom.	Official Whitehouse Photo by Pete Souza
Page 5, top.	Evan Vucci/AP
Page 5, middle.	Official White House Photo by Pete Souza
Page 5, bottom.	Alex Wong/Getty Images
Page 6, top left.	Courtesy of the University of Chicago Law School
Page 6, top right.	Steve Petteway, Collection of the Supreme Court of the United States
Page 6, bottom.	Steve Petteway, Collection of the Supreme Court of the United States
Page 7, top.	Official White House Photo by Pete Souza
Page 7, middle.	Jeff Malet Photography/Newscom
Page 7, bottom.	Charles Dharapak/AP
Page 8, top.	Melissa Golden/Redux
Page 8, bottom.	Chip Somodevilla/Getty Images

INDEX

ALSO BY JEFFREY TOOBIN

"Compelling. . . . Driven by the author's assured narrative voice, *The Nine* is as informative as it is fascinating, as insightful as it is readable."
—Michiko Kakutani, *The New York Times*

THE NINE
Inside the Secret World of the Supreme Court

In *The Nine*, acclaimed journalist Jeffrey Toobin takes us into the chambers of the most important—and secret—legal body in our country, the Supreme Court, revealing the complex dynamic among the nine people who decide the law of the land. An institution at a moment of transition, the Court now stands at a crucial point, with major changes in store on such issues as abortion, civil rights, and church-state relations. Based on exclusive interviews with the justices and with a keen sense of the Court's history and the trajectory of its future, Jeffrey Toobin creates in *The Nine* a riveting story of one of the most important forces in American life today.

Current Affairs

ANCHOR BOOKS
Available wherever books are sold.
www.vintagebooks.com